HOUSING PROBLEMS AND
HOUSING POLICY

LONGMAN SOCIAL POLICY IN BRITAIN SERIES

Series Editor:
Jo Campling

Published Titles:
Health Policy and the NHS: Towards 2000, 2E
Judith Allsop

Foundations of the Welfare State
Pat Thane

Elderly People in Modern Society 3E
Anthea Tinker

The Personal Social Services
Robert Adams

Crime and Criminal Justice Policy
Tim Newburn

Forthcoming Titles:
Responding to Poverty
Saul Becker

Disabled People
Brian Oliver

Foundations of the Welfare State 2E
Pat Thane

LONGMAN SOCIAL POLICY IN BRITAIN SERIES

Housing Problems and Housing Policy

Brian Lund

LONGMAN
London and New York

Addison Wesley Longman Limited,
Edinburgh Gate,
Harlow, Essex CM20 2JE, England
and Associated Companies throughout the world.

*Published in the United States of America
by Longman Publishing, New York*

First published 1996

ISBN 0 582 23883 8 PPR

British Library Cataloguing-in-Publication Data

A catalogue record for this book is
available from the British Library

Library of Congress Cataloging-in-Publication Data
Lund, Brian, 1945–
    Housing problems and housing policy / Brian Lund.
        p. cm. — (Longman social policy in Britain series)
    Includes bibliographical references and index.
    ISBN 0-582-23883-8
        1. Housing policy—Great Britain—History.   2. Great Britain—Social
conditions.   3. Great Britain—Economic conditions. 4. Homelessness—Government
policy—Great Britain. I. Title. II. Series.
HD7333.A3L96 1996
363.5′ 0941—dc20   95–26704 CIP

Set by 5 in 10/11pt Times
Produced through Longman Malaysia, GPS

CONTENTS

LIST OF TABLES

ACKNOWLEDGEMENTS

We are grateful to the following for permission to reproduce copyright material:

ADC/AMA and HMSO for a Table from *Hansard*, Jan. 1994, Col 900–901, ADC/AMA Housing Finance Survey, 1944–95, 1995–96; Catholic Housing Aid Society for a Table from *All in One Place: the British Housing Story 1973–1993* by J. Newton (CHAS, 1994); Commission for Racial Equality for an extract from *Race and Council Housing in Hackney: Report of a Formal Investigation* (1971); The Controller of Her Majesty's Stationery Office for a Table from *General Household Survey*, 1992, a Table from *Hansard*, Written Answers, October 1993 HMSO, a Table from *Housing and Construction Statistics 1983–1993*, 1994 DoE, extracts from *The Local Government and Housing Act 1989: Area Renewal, Unfitness and Enforcement Action, Circular 6/90*, March 1990 DoE, *The PEP Guide to Local Housing Management* by A. Power, 1987 DoE, *Homelessness, Code of Guidance for Local Authorities* 3/E, 1991 DoE, *Housing and Community Care, September 1992* Joint Circular from the DoE and DoH, *Access to Local Authority and Housing Association Tenancies, A Consultation Paper*, January 1994 DoE, a Table from *Social Trends*, 1995, all Crown Copyright; Institute of Public Policy Research (IPPR) for an extract from *Housing and Social Justice* (1993) by Robina Goodlad and Kenneth Gibb; International Thomson Publishing Services for an extract from *The Last Refuge* by Peter Townsend (Routledge 1964); International Thomson Publishing Services/University of Chicago Press for an extract from *The Constitution of Liberty* by F.A. Hayek (Routledge 1960); Joseph Rowntree Foundation and the author, S. Wilcox for Tables from *Housing Finance Review 1994/5*; New Statesman and Society for an extract from the article 'In the Work-house' by Mary Cecil in *The New Statesman*, 12.1.62; Shelter, The National Campaign for Homeless People, for an extract from *Slum Clearance* (1973); Weidenfeld & Nicholson (Orion Publishing Group) for an extract from *The Rise of the Welfare State* by M. Bruce (1973).

We have been unable to trace the copyright holders in Tables 3.7 and 4.2 and would appreciate any information that would enable us to do so.

INTRODUCTION

Talking once with a miner I asked him when the housing shortage first became acute in his district: he answered 'When we were told about it'.

(Orwell, 1937)

The response of the miner to George Orwell's question illustrates the approach to housing problems taken in this book. Housing problems are socially constructed. In simple terms this means that the identification of housing conditions as social problems is the outcome of social processes involving ideologies, 'discourses' (ways of thinking about issues developed by professional elites), the media and the use of political and economic power. Housing problems are not objective phenomena capable of identification and solution by rational analysis alone; the values involved in the designation of certain conditions as problems, and the ideology underlying proposed solutions, must be addressed.

The 'modernist' approaches to the study of social problems that dominated thinking on social policy for over a century interpreted housing problems as 'pathological' conditions which prevented society from functioning in a harmonious manner. The model of harmony used as the benchmark by which 'undesirable' conditions were assessed was different in each approach but they all contained a vision or 'metanarrative' of how a harmonious, functioning society must and should operate. Social problems were defined, causation attributed and solutions proposed according to the tenets of each ideology. Chapter 1 sets out the ideologies that have influenced both academic studies of housing problems and the housing policies adopted by politicians. Three dominant ideologies are identified: *laissez-faire* economics, social reformism and Marxist political economy.

Comparative studies can illuminate British housing policy and an extensive literature on housing issues in other countries now exists. However, the specific historical context in which housing problems have been identified and solutions adopted remains the fundamental factor influencing the pattern of housing provision in a particular country; nations build up their housing stock over time and history is reflected in contemporary residential patterns, forms of tenure, systems of subsidy and political attitudes. Chapters 2 and 3 examine the politics of housing policy in Britain from the middle of the nineteenth century onwards; they attempt to demonstrate how changes in the political system have influenced the perception of housing problems. Their key themes are the initial involvement of the state in housing matters through concern about the impact of poor housing on the 'public good'; the reluctance of the Conservative Party and a significant element of the Liberal Party to allow the state to provide subsidised homes; the ways that fear of the radical potential of the working class pushed the state into providing homes; the influence on the form of state housing of those who claimed to speak on behalf of working people; and the retreat from state involvement in the housing that started in the late 1970s. Chapter 4 outlines the principal agencies involved in the formation and implementation of housing policy and gives an indication of the financial context in which they operate.

Homelessness, a problem that has received extensive media, academic and political attention in the 1980s and 1990s is discussed in Chapter 5 in the context of ideological approaches to the construction of housing problems. In Chapter 6 the relatively neglected problems of unfit and overcrowded dwellings are addressed. Chapter 7 explores the construction of the question of 'problem' estates using managerial, architectural and structural perspectives to illuminate the issue. Structural inequalities in access to housing, and the wealth accumulating from property ownership, are analysed in Chapter 8 using gender, 'race' and class as organising concepts. Chapter 9 examines the relationship between housing and community care, pointing out that if community care is to become more than a slogan then the accommodation requirements of people with specific needs have to be addressed.

Housing policy in the 1980s and the first half of the 1990s has been dominated by the attempt to roll back the state, allowing the 'neutral judge' of the market a dominant role in the supply and distribution of housing. Chapter 10 considers the impact of this approach and, in an attempt to stimulate discussion, a different direction for housing policy is outlined.

References

Orwell, G. (1937) *The Road to Wigan Pier*, Gollancz, London.

PART ONE

The Political and Administrative Context

CHAPTER 1

Ideology and housing

An ideology is a 'value or belief system that is accepted as fact or truth by some group' (Sargent 1978: 3). It provides 'a comprehensive and systematic perspective whereby human society can be understood together with a framework of principles to guide future action' (Jones 1991: 99).

Any taxonomy of ideologies is open to dissent and there are several classifications available for use in structuring a discussion of housing policy (see Barr 1993, George and Wilding 1994, Williams 1989, Clarke, Cochrane and Smart 1987, Pierson 1991). Three 'grand narratives' or ideologies are highlighted in this chapter: social reformism, *laissez-faire* economics and Marxist political economy. This classification is justified on the grounds that the chosen ideologies have dominated thinking on the housing issue in Britain during the twentieth century and, despite the claims of feminism, anti-racism, environmentalism, neo-conservativism and 'one-nation' Toryism (George and Wilding 1994) they continue to hold leading positions in academic and political debate.

Social reformism

Social reformism is an inelegant and sweeping term but it serves to connect strands of thought that have combined, fragmented and coalesced at various times during the nineteenth and twentieth centuries. Two dominant elements in the development of social reformism can be identified – Fabian socialism and social liberalism. These merged during the Second World War and formed the basis of a consensus on social policy that was to last until the late 1970s.

Fabian socialism

Willetts (1992: 22) – with some justification – has declared that 'the Fabians achieved the greatest shift in ideas on public policy since Adam Smith destroyed mercantilism and put free markets at the centre of the political consensus'. The Fabian Society was formed in 1884 and named after the Roman General Quintus Fabius Maximus, known as 'Cuncta-tor' (the delayer) because he deployed tactics of delay and attrition to defeat his enemies. The illustrious members of the society were not noted for the compatibility of their ideas, and therefore the views of

Sidney Webb (1859–1947) and Beatrice Webb (1858–1943) – the most influential of the Fabians – will be used to illustrate the essential features of the approach during its formative years.

In contrast to Karl Marx (1818–1883), who thought that workers were so exploited by capitalism that its immediate removal, by violent means if necessary, could be justified, the Webbs believed that capitalism could be reformed in stages. Rational argument, based on the facts of a situation established by 'scientific' social enquiry, was to be the principal driving force of social change. Armed with the facts, 'unassuming experts' employed by the state would eradicate social problems by the application of rational administrative principles. Given time such a process would lead to the creation of a socialist society in which the needs of the individual and the community would be seen as one.

Marx regarded the exploitation of workers by capitalists as total: capitalists took *all* the surplus created by the working class. The Webbs held a less extreme view arguing that, at least in the early stages of capitalism, capitalists had a useful and perhaps necessary part to play in the evolution of society because of their skills of initiation and management. According to them, although the exercise of such skills did not entitle capitalists to all the profit arising from the difference between the exchange value of a product (its price when sold on the market) and the amount paid to workers for its production, the workers were not quite so exploited as Marx had asserted. The Webbs (1913) maintained that the unjust profit of the capitalist class was created by the special features of certain types of capital that produced a dividend above the profit arising from the general capital in use. Capitalists were not entitled to these 'rents' (as the Fabians called them), so they could be appropriated by the state and used to promote the 'common good'. A major source of unjust profits according to the theory of rents was the appropriation of the extra value of land suitable for development, a value that clearly had not been created by the efforts of the capitalist class. If this value could be retained in the hands of the community by means of taxation or by the state acting as developer then, in time, a substantial surplus would be available for the provision of community facilities. The identification of the unjust appropriation of 'special' value by capitalists gave the Fabians a legitimate source of revenue for state expenditure to meet housing needs.

State welfare and national efficiency: The belief of the Fabians in the gradual but inevitable social change to be achieved by rational argument rested on their notion that socialism was itself *the* rational social system and, in the long run, the interests of the individual and the state were identical. A contented, educated, and efficiently organised labour force, living in healthy homes, was good for the working class and good for everyone with citizenship of a nation-state. Fabians believed that welfare was not only about the redistribution of existing resources; it was also about efficient production, because national efficiency depended on the quality of human capital. Thus when the blueprints for the 'model dwellings' to be built for the working class were prepared they included features designed to produce worker contentment and health. As one member of the Fabian Society stated:

.... and there can be no doubt that our present knowledge of the importance of sunlight to health makes it needful to add to the first condition a second, that every house shall be open to a sufficiency of sunshine ... let no house be built with a sunless living room: and this condition must cease to be regarded merely as desirable when it can be conveniently arranged: it must be insisted on as an absolute essential ...

(Unwin 1902: 3)

Social liberalism

'Old' liberalism was the sum of the political ideas surrounding classical economics: the belief that a *laissez-faire* economic system would produce maximum gains for both the individual and society. The 'new' or 'social' liberalism that sprang to prominence in the second half of the nineteenth century was more collectivist than its namesake. It parted company from the 'old liberalism' in its definition of freedom. T. H. Green (1836–1882), an Oxford professor and leading advocate of the social liberal approach, stated that when discussing liberty 'we mean not merely freedom to do what we like irrespective of what it is that we like ... When we speak of freedom as something to be highly prized, we mean the positive power or capacity of doing or enjoying something worth doing or enjoying' (Green, 1893: iii, 371). Thus liberty was recognised by social liberalism as meaning not the absence of restraint on individual action but as behaviour in accordance with our will to do what is *right*. This recognition that true freedom comes when we respond to our considered will opened the door to forms of state intervention designed to liberate the rational will of every citizen. What really concerned the adherents of social liberalism were the revelations by social researchers on the appalling housing conditions experienced by many working-class people. Squalor, the 'new' liberals argued, prevented the considered will of such people from emerging; potential citizens were being brutalised by their environment. Thus state action aimed at the eradication of slums could be justified insofar as it was necessary to liberate the rational will of each citizen. Nonetheless the state was limited in what it could achieve and hence in what it should aim to achieve. According to Green (1889: 332) 'no one can convey a good character to another. Every one must make his character for himself. All that one man can do to make another better is to remove obstacles, and supply conditions favourable to the formation of good character.'

Although Green supplied the basic philosophy of social liberalism, the ideology was subject to a variety of interpretations. Some saw no need to involve the state in the creation of the conditions necessary for men and women to act according to their considered wills; voluntary charitable effort was all that was required and state action was likely to produce the opposite of the desired outcome. Octavia Hill – sometimes regarded as the founder of the profession of housing management – was a leading exponent of this view. She believed that slums were the product of two influences: greedy, uneducated and uninterested landlords out to make a quick profit from poor quality dwellings, and the behaviour of unsupervised tenants. 'The people's homes are bad', she said 'partly because they are badly built and arranged; they are tenfold worse because the tenant's habits and lives are what they are' (Hill 1883). Her philosophy of housing management was to combine the administration of sound but basic property with the reformation of the character of her tenants through the personal influence of a housing worker and the incentive of better accommodation. She was against subsidies to tenants because she thought that state support would produce a 'pauper mentality' but she did not believe in extracting the maximum profit from the need for housing.

Other commentators working within the social liberalism paradigm thought that the development of working-class self-help movements – of building societies, cooperatives, trade unions and friendly societies – was the mechanism to promote social change and create good character. Working people would develop their autonomy through participatory movements; what was required from the state was not the provision of a service but the removal of unfair restraints on equality of opportunity such as the system of land ownership. The link between equality and liberty was developed in the inter-war period, under the influence of such writers as J. A. Hobson, D. G. Richie and L. T. Hobhouse. As the egalitarian aspects of social liberalism were emphasised its latent statist tendencies emerged and it began to assume some of the characteristics of Fabian socialism.

During the Second World War Fabian socialism became the dominant element of social reformism and its hegemony continued until the early 1970s. Three questions will be asked of the ideology in order to provide an account of how it has been applied to the housing issue. How does it explain the development of housing policy? What does it regard as the major outcomes of state intervention? What is the nature of the ideal form of housing system implicit in the ideology?

Explanations of the development of housing policy

The Fabian tradition has explained the development of state involvement in housing as a consequence of the interaction between three forces: the process of industrialisation and urbanisation; the need of society for mechanisms to promote social integration; and the democratisation of politics.

The industrialisation and associated urbanisation of the eighteenth and nineteenth centuries form the background to the explanatory framework. The movement of people from rural areas to the developing towns and cities created two new problems for society: congestion, with its associated welfare problems, and the loss of a sense of community. The Fabians believed that both these problems needed to be overcome by collective action so that all elements of society could function in harmony. The state was the natural instrument for eliminating the problems of capitalist industrialisation because it could use the illegitimate rewards of capitalists – the rent of 'special' value – to finance improved conditions. In addition, by including everyone in the gains of progress a new sense of community around the nation-state could be created. Everyone would have citizenship rights. The fact that – regardless of the party in power – the British state did assume such a role and that similar tendencies were evident in other countries was confirmation to Fabian socialists that the process was organic and inevitable.

Despite its basic determinism, the Fabian tradition has recognised the importance of the democratisation of politics in the development of social provision. However the tradition has placed emphasis on *representative* rather than *participatory* democracy. Fabians believed that the role of the electorate was to choose between rival elites who would then be given the authority to run the country in such a way as to maximise the common good. The notion that the recipients of welfare should have an ongoing role in the delivery of social welfare services was alien to the Fabian approach and hence tenant involvement in the management of council housing did not reach the academic or political agenda.

The consequences of state intervention

Fabians expected the outcome of state intervention in housing to be beneficial to all. it would increase the quality of human capital, improve the status and welfare of the working class and foster social harmony. As the outcomes of state welfare became manifest in the 1960s and 1970s, a tension developed between the ideal and the reality. Homelessness and unsatisfactory housing conditions persisted, council tenants seemed to be treated as second-class citizens, state intervention in housing appeared to make little impact on the distribution of real income, and some of the 'mass' housing schemes constructed in the late 1950s and 1960s were seen to have produced more problems than they had solved.

Social reformers continued to search for the 'facts' about social problems and found that new power structures had been created, such as 'urban managers' who, through their allocation and gatekeeper roles, carried some of the responsibility for the continuation of social problems (Pahl 1970). The Fabian perspective began to fragment as it was exposed to the reality of its own creation. Absorbing elements of the Marxist approach, 'radical social administration' (as labelled by Williams 1989) insisted that what had gone wrong in the application of Fabianism was a failure to take control of the economic system. As a result of this error the economic system retained excessive influence on the nature of the new social welfare institutions which had became mechanisms of control rather than liberation. According to the 'radical social administration' perspective, economic planning had to accompany social planning and the state must become much more interventionalist in the economic sphere. In contrast 'welfare pluralists' became concerned about the power of the new 'urban managers' who had acquired substantial influence in the allocation of scarce resources. 'Welfare pluralists' began to embrace the ideas of 'associative democracy' (Hirst, 1994) and to call for housing to be run by self-governing voluntary organisations with the local and central state adopting a strategic role in promoting greater equality (Clapham, 1989). Others wished to retain the welfare state as a provider of services but demanded greater participation and citizen empowerment within the existing state apparatus.

Characteristics of an ideal form of housing provision

The fragmentation of social reformism in the 1980s has meant that it is not possible to provide a single account of how the perspective now expects an ideal system of housing to function. There are several visions but any account located within the perspective would include the following elements:

- extensive state involvement in housing (although not necessarily by direct provision), because housing is a special (merit) good with profound implications for any individual's plan of life and because the market cannot guarantee that appropriate standards of housing are accessible to all;
- producer subsidies to stimulate the supply of housing, together with consumer subsidies to ensure that all citizens can afford the standard of housing necessary to fulfil their human capabilities and to ensure that inequalities in housing are not so great as to endanger social solidarity;
- the planning of housing provision to balance the preservation of the environment with the objectives stated above.

Document 1 (page 201) gives an indication of this perspective.

Laissez-faire economics

This approach to the study of housing policy is sometimes called neoclassical economics because it is a revival of the classical economic theories of the eighteenth century. Free exchange, according to Adam Smith in his 1776 treatise on *An Inquiry into the Nature and Causes of the Wealth of Nations* (Smith 1977) allowed labour to be divided and specialised so that individuals could concentrate on the production of those goods that they were most suited to create. The invisible hand of the market would coordinate all these productive activities. If the state confined itself to doing what only the state can do – the maintenance of law and order, policing of contracts and the 'erecting and maintaining certain public works and certain public institutions, which it can never be in the interest of any individual or small group of individuals, to erect and maintain' (Smith, 1977) – then the pursuit of self-interest would eventually promote the welfare of all. This *laissez-faire* economic doctrine dominated housing policy for most of the nineteenth century. State involvement in the housing market was restricted to its 'public good' dimension: the removal of 'nuisances' to public health and public order through the clearance of slums.

During the twentieth century the influence of *laissez-faire* ideology declined and the state assumed a larger role in shaping, directing and replacing the housing market through the policies of subsidised local authority housing, rent control and the creation of a favourable tax regime for home ownership. Although the spirit of economic liberalism was by no means extinguished, it was on the defensive until its political revival in the 1970s. Friedrich Von Hayek was the most important figure in the promotion of the free market at a time when Britain was least receptive to the idea. He took Adam Smith's notion of the market as 'a system of natural liberty', added lessons drawn from the experience of state intervention, and produced a set of ideas for the renewed application of market principles to social and economic life (Hayek 1944, 1960, 1973, 1976, 1979). Hayek disseminated his ideas through the Mont Pèlerin Society formed in 1947 (Cockett, 1994). Ten years later the Institute of Economic Affairs was established to convert Hayek's beliefs into policy proposals (Graham and Clarke, 1986) and by the middle 1970s a developed philosophical critique of the unjustified activities of the state and a rationale for a return to market principles as the only legitimate basis for social allocations was available.

Explanations of the development of housing policy

The impact of Britain's democratic system was regarded in the 1940s, 1950s and the 1960s as a legitimate justification for the existence of state welfare. Thus, for instance, T. H. Marshall in a respected article, 'Citizenship and Social Class' (first published in 1949), argued that the social rights created in the twentieth century were the outcome of the civil rights obtained in the eighteenth century (freedom of speech, freedom of religion) and the political rights granted in the nineteenth century (the right to vote and the right to stand for election). Hayek and his acolytes specifically exclude the operations of the democratic system as a legitimate justification for state welfare. They believe that the political system as it has operated in Britain in the twentieth century has produced undesirable consequences. In order to understand this somewhat extraordinary view it is necessary to appreciate Hayek's definition of what he regards as the most important condition of humankind: liberty. Hayek (1960) defines liberty as 'a state in which man is not subject to coercion by the arbitrary will of another or others' – a person is free when there is no human agent with the power to direct his or her activities along a particular path. Hayek insists that his definition of liberty is the real and original definition – it is that which has always differentiated a free person from a slave. He takes great care to distinguish his definition of freedom from other 'false' definitions. One such false definition is political liberty: 'the participation of men in their choice of government, in the process of legislation, and in the control of administration' (Hayek 1960: 13). It is false because it allows only an occasional choice of ruler and, during the periods between the moments of choice at elections, the individual may be subject to arbitrary political decisions.

Public choice theory: Hayek's rejection of the legitimacy of democracy has resulted in others who share his basic outlook scrutinising existing democratic institutions and finding them to be deficient. Dunleavy (1991) has called this group the 'new right public choice theorists'. Such theorists divide the democratic process into three elements: the voting system, the activities of interest groups and the behaviour of state officials organised into bureaucracies. All the actors in the political process are thought of in terms of the basic premise of neoclassical economics: they are rational maximisers of their self-interest. As one of the leading members of the group has stated: 'the theory is "economic" in the sense that, like traditional economic theory, the building blocks are individuals, not corporate entities, not societies, not communities, not states' (Buchanan, 1978). Politicians, far from being statesmen and women with a view of the common good to promote, are seen as interested in securing election to pursue power, prestige and material advantage. In order to secure such advantages they must win more votes than their rivals and will adopt a number of strategies to gain these votes. These strategies can be illustrated by examples from housing policy.

Public choice theorists assert that once local authorities started to house a substantial proportion of the electorate, politicians regarded tenants as a specific voting interest to be encouraged to vote for a particular party by a policy of low rents. As a result rents were kept down to such low levels that insufficient resources were available for maintenance and hence the short-term interests of the politicians took precedence over the public good of having a well maintained housing stock for use by future generations (Ricketts, 1986).

The need to attract the median voter (the additional voter necessary to secure a majority) also helps to explain why political processes do not result in either the promotion of individual liberty or the public interest. Politicians will direct their concern not to the rich or the poor, who are likely to have clear economic interests in voting for a particular party, but to the 'floating' voter with no such attachment. Any scheme to help the poor must therefore include the 'middle earner' with the consequence that 'universal' social policy measures, such as tax relief on mortgage interest, will be promoted. Paying for such universal coverage involves taking resources from those who have secured their affluence by legitimate entrepreneurial activity (thereby undermining their liberty to hold what they create and destroying the motive for wealth creation), and/or securing the resources by sacrificing the future through borrowing or neglect of investment. Rent control from the 1920s to the 1950s, when the majority of households rented their accommodation from private landlords, serves as an example of this. It is alleged that state regulation kept rents at well below the market level with the result that landlords withdrew from the business of providing rented accommodation with serious consequences for the future provision of affordable housing.

According to public choice theory, politicians, in seeking to gain and retain power, are prone to fall under the influence of interest groups. Interest groups exist to take a 'free ride' on their fellow citizens. They seek to persuade politicians to give special privileges to the domains of life in which they have a vested interest. Politicians may rely on interest groups to secure a 'winning coalition' at elections and, when in power, they may respond to the demands of interest groups to ensure cooperation in regulating a complex sphere of activity and to secure opportunities for future employment. Interest groups will engage in a variety of tactics to maximise their control over politicians and bureaucrats. One such strategy is 'log rolling', where a variety of interest groups may act together against unorganised groups to secure advantage for their domain of interest. Thus, for example, the construction industry, estate agents, land owners and the building societies may combine to demand government intervention in the form of subsidies to 'kick start' the housing market in a period of stagnant house prices. They will make their demands 'in the public interest' but there will be losers (such as new entrants to the housing market who would benefit from falling prices) if the government agrees to the demands.

The self-interest of bureaucrats is the third influence on the growth of welfare systems identified by new right public choice theorists. State officials are seen not as impartial arbitrators between conflicting interests but as maximisers of their own welfare. Bureaucratic self-interest consists of 'salary, perquisites of the office, public reputation, power, patronage, output of the bureau' (Niskanen 1973: 22–23) and all these can be obtained by maximising the agency's budget. Niskanen goes so far as to assert that since bureaucrats have a virtual monopoly on information about the costs of the bureau, and its 'sponsors' (the politicians who provide the cash) are fragmented between committees, then there will always be a degree of inefficiency in its delivery of services to the consumer. According to this line of reasoning any housing department of a local authority that has not been subject to market competition *must* be inefficient.

The consequences of state intervention

If the activities of the state produced desirable outcomes but did so inefficiently then there would be a problem, but neoclassical economic thinking adds the charge that, on balance, state intervention whether by regulation, finance or provision has made social problems worse. Hayek again presents the most polished exposition of the position and his analysis of the consequences of slum clearance will be presented at some length. He argues that:

The old buildings which at most stages of the growth of a city will exist at the centre, on land which is already in such great demand for other purposes that it is no longer profitable to build new dwellings on it, and which are no longer wanted by the better off, will often provide for those of low productivity an opportunity to benefit from what the city offers at the price of very congested living.

(Hayek 1960: 346–7)

Since the dwellers in the slums gain opportunities from their position in the city but at the cost of poor living conditions then:

If we want to abolish the slums we must choose between two alternatives. We must either prevent these people from taking advantage of what to them is part of their opportunity, by removing the cheap but squalid dwellings from where their earning opportunities lie, and effectively squeeze them out of the cities by insisting on certain minimum standards for all town dwellings; or we must provide them with better facilities at a price which does not cover costs and thus subsidise both their staying in the city and the movement of more people into the city of the same kind. . . . The solution of the problem would be either to let the economic deterrents act or to control directly the influx of population; those who believe in liberty will regard the former as the lesser evil.

(Hayek 1960: 348)

Underlying Hayek's account of slum clearance and subsidised public housing (see Document 2, page 203) is the distinction he makes between a 'spontaneous' order and a 'man-made' order. Markets are 'spontaneous' and capable of assimilating a wide range of dispersed information. In contrast the state which, when stripped of its mystique is simply the minds of men and women thinking together, cannot gather or comprehend all the information necessary for a truly rational decision. Unintended consequences, such as the influx of workers seeking cheap accommodation and opportunities into a subsidised area, constantly intrude.

Hayek's basic insights into the housing market have been developed by his followers. Black and Stafford (1988) maintain that state control of the rents charged by private landlords has reduced the supply of rented accommodation, impaired maintenance, given an indiscriminate subsidy to tenants, encouraged discrimination (some landlords have rationed by prejudice rather than price) and restricted labour mobility. Minford, Peel and Ashton (1987) have argued that subsidised local authority housing has had a detrimental impact on labour mobility and hence on levels of employment because of the artificial barriers it has created to the movement of workers in the search for employment. Gray's examination of public sector house building produced the conclusion that:

Rising construction costs, spurious commitments to perpetually increasing standards in pursuit of nebulous obligations to the future, and other symptoms of political management of a commercial service leave little doubt that government house building is inefficient both in comparison with the present achievement of the private sector and what might be achieved under alternative institutional arrangements.

(Gray 1968: 64)

The characteristics of an ideal form of housing provision

Neoclassical economics recognises that free markets may contain imperfections and unregulated markets may not be suitable to the production and distribution of all types of goods. A great deal of economic thinking in the twentieth century has been devoted to exploring the nature of these 'public' goods and the degree to which they may be suited to market forces. Powerful arguments have been advanced – mainly from social liberals – to justify the claim that housing has special characteristics that make it an inappropriate domain for the operation of market principles. *Laissez-faire* economics has refuted many of these points. The debate is summarised below. The case that housing is different from other commodities is stated first followed by the response of the market economists.

* *Housing is essential to life and therefore different from other consumer goods such as televisions, motor cars and books*

Food is also an essential of life, respond the neoclassical economists, and food has been marketed successfully. Moreover, although a minimum standard of housing is clearly a necessity of life, the vast majority of housing consumption is for personal satisfaction. Pennance (1969) quotes Alfred Marshall when he said that 'house room satisfies the imperative need for shelter from the weather; but that need plays very little part in the effective demand for house room ... relatively large and well-appointed house room is, even in the lowest ranks, at once a "necessity for efficiency" and the most convenient and obvious way of advancing a material claim to social distinction' (Pennance 1969: 23).

* *Housing is expensive relative to average earnings and thus markets operate inefficiently because intermediate financial institutions offering loans come between buyer and seller.*

This is not a problem because there can be a market in loans that can operate through variations in the interest rate.

* *Housing is immobile and therefore the stock of houses is geographically fixed whereas demand for houses in different locations can vary significantly and quickly.*

The fixed stock of houses will have different utilities for different individuals and thus markets are an excellent way of allocating houses in accordance with consumer preferences. High house prices in areas of high demand will result in people moving elsewhere to find cheaper accommodation.

* *Houses are expensive and have a long production span, thus the national housing stock will not be responsive to sudden changes in demand; housing supply is inelastic.*

The supply of houses *is* inelastic in the short term because houses take a long time to produce but, given time, supply and demand will balance. Empirical studies demonstrate this. Annez and Wheaton (1984) examined 20 countries at different stages of economic development and according to Nesslein (1988) found that 'in the long run supply of housing is close to perfectly price elastic'.

* *Low income groups will not be able to afford adequate housing.*

The truth of this statement depends on what is meant by 'adequate' and 'affordable' housing. Renting rather than purchase will reduce the cost of housing to the lowest income groups and, if it is necessary to provide subsidies, this can be done by concentrating help on the poor only to the extent necessary to enable them to obtain a minimum standard of accommodation. In a free market it is likely that consumers will spend a high percentage of their disposable incomes on new houses, thereby contributing to the housing stock and leaving properties into which the lowest income groups can 'filter'.

* *Housing has 'external' impacts in that poor housing conditions can lead to the creation and spread of disease and unrestricted house building destroys countryside and open space thus affecting the welfare of the whole of society.*

Contagious disease caused by poor housing is not a problem in twentieth century Britain and planning regulations could be relaxed without causing significant environmental problems.

Whereas not all the arguments presented above are acceptable to all economists who believe in the use of market forces, all the members of the school favour a restricted role for the state in regulating the housing market. Subsidy to the poor is the maximum extent of intervention that most are prepared to advocate.

Marxist political economy

Marxist political economy asserts that relationships between individuals and social institutions are determined by the mode of production used in a particular society. Capitalism is a form of production based on two classes; a capitalist class that owns the means of production and a proletariat or working class that is forced to work for the capitalist class in order to subsist because it does not own capital. This basic economic relationship is the real foundation of all other legal, political and ideological forms; it provides the structure on which all other superstructures are based. There is an underlying logic to capitalist development that can be identified through the application of Marxist theory.

Explanations of the development of housing policy

Recent academic interpretations of the work of Marx and Engels have identified two major models of the role of the state in capitalism: the instrumental model and the arbiter model (see Pierson 1991 for a subdivision of these models). The instrumental model was dominant in Marxist theory until the late 1970s. It finds a clear if limited expression in the later works of Marx where he attempted to explain the nature of the state as the product of a more fundamental reality – the dominant form of production. In the 1970s 'instrumental Marxism', following Marx's dictum that 'the state is but a committee for the management of the common affairs of the whole bourgeoisie', claimed that the state is the mechanism used by the ruling class to dominate society and ensure the continuation of the capitalist system. The capitalist class uses the state for a variety of purposes: to take the steam out of radical movements by means of temporary concessions at times of social unrest; to maintain profits in times of surplus production; to sustain capitalist ideology through the nature of the institutions supported by the state; to keep workers fit for capitalism; and to maintain the 'reserve army of labour' that capitalism has to have in order to be able to respond to its boom/bust cycle of production. Supporters of the instrumental model underpinned their thesis with a variety of evidence:

- Quotations from capitalist politicians where they admit their true motives in promoting state welfare. Disraeli's declaration that 'the palace is not safe whilst the cottage is poor' (1875) and Balfour's statement that 'social legislation . . . is not merely to be distinguished from Socialist legislation, but it is its direct opposite and most effective antidote' (1895) are favourite citations.
- The claim that state welfare does not redistribute income vertically between classes but within classes and across life spans. Thus it is argued that although a local authority house may be let at less than its current market value or cost of production at a particular point in time it will, over its entire useful life, produce a surplus for the capitalist class.
- The occupational groupings that support capitalism through the basic form of their method of operation are allowed to control a professional domain whereas occupational groups that adopt even a modest anti-capitalist stance will find themselves strictly controlled by the state. Thus medicine and law with their focus on the individual as the appropriate level of intervention have been granted more professional autonomy than community work and housing management, which have a more 'social' orientation.

- Welfare expands and contracts according to the degree of social unrest; subsidised local authority housing and rent control were introduced at a time when urban unrest had reached such a level that it became a threat to the capitalist system.

If these arguments are applied to housing then several lines of argument and investigation emerge:

- The real exploitation of the worker by the capitalist system takes place at the point of production when workers are paid less for their labour than the exchange (market) value of the house they have helped to create. In addition, since housing has special characteristics as a commodity – it is expensive to produce relative to the earnings of the worker – then special institutions are necessary to realise the value of the house (Short 1982). These institutions – building societies, banks, private landlords – spread the cost of housing production and the profits of the capitalist over the lifetime of the worker. They all demand a share of the surplus value created when houses are constructed and hence add to the exploitation of the working class.
- There are factions of housing capital with different short-term interests but the same long-term interest in ensuring the continuation of the capitalist system. Industrial capital wants to ensure that its workers can be housed at minimal cost to itself. Land capital wants to ensure that the value of land is as high as possible, whereas 'development' capital wants to secure access to cheap land so that development gain is maximised. Unrestricted competition between the various factions of capital may undermine the system so it is the business of the state to ensure that the activities of the factions of capital are complementary rather than contradictory. Thus the state uses its power to assist the development process in an attempt to ensure maximum profitability for all. The work of David Harvey (1978) offers the most developed example of this approach.
- Capitalism needs a contented, efficient labour force and a 'reserve army of labour' that can be injected into the economy when required and ejected when superfluous. It is the role of the state in its housing policy to provide such a flexible, efficient workforce – to 'reproduce labour power' – and thus the state will respond in a manner that reflects capitalist values. Home ownership – designed to convince working people that they have an investment stake in capitalism, to promote an ethic of 'possessive individualism' and to provide the 'psychic' benefits of security, independence and respectability will be encouraged (Cater and Jones 1989); housing forms which emphasise the role of males as breadwinners and females as carers will be promoted; standardised cheap housing forms will be used and only a minimum level of housing provision will be on offer.

● Housing has an exchange value to capitalists (its efficiency in generating profits) but a use value (in meeting human needs) to the working class, and therefore housing will be affected by its investment value as well as by the need for accommodation.

Document 3 (page 204) offers an extract from the work of Marx on which some of the ideas expressed above are based.

The arbiter model is grounded on the earlier works of Marx in which – whilst disputing the notion that the capitalist state can ever act in accordance with the 'common good' – he recognised that the state may obtain a degree of neutrality from capitalism and that it can act in the interests of the proletariat at certain moments in history. This model allows the organised working class some enduring influence in the historical construction of state housing policy and offers a degree of optimism about the outcome of future struggles within and against the state. By placing its emphasis on class power as the mechanism for viable change within the existing state apparatus, the arbiter model promises the possible erosion of capitalism by the ceaseless pressure from the working class arising from its everyday experience as producers and recipients of welfare. It also allows Marxists to provide a more convincing account of the evolution of housing policy with genuine improvements being made in working class housing provision at times when the labour movement was strong as, for example, between 1945 and 1951. However, although the attribution of relative autonomy to the state makes the Marxist account more plausible, it also reduces its distinctness when compared to other perspectives.

The consequences of state intervention

The writings of Engels reveal no doubts about the impact of state intervention on the housing condition of the people: it would not improve their circumstances for it was in the logic of capitalist development that the working class would become more impoverished as competition between capitalists forced wages down.

The breeding places of disease, the infamous holes and cellars in which the capitalist mode of production confines our workers night after night, are not abolished: they are merely shifted elsewhere! The same economic necessity that produced them in the first place produces them in the next place also! As long as the capitalist mode of production continues to exist it is folly to hope for an isolated settlement of the housing question affecting the lot of the workers. The solution lies in the abolition of the capitalist mode of production.

(Engels 1969 edn: 352–53)

The fact that such absolute impoverishment did not occur in the twentieth century prompted some contemporary Marxists to invoke the arbiter model. O'Connor (1973), Offe (1984) and Gough (1979), in their different ways, have argued that during the period after the Second World

War capitalism had to appease an increasingly powerful labour movement. Such 'social expenses' (the costs of keeping the working class attached to capitalism) were essential to the long-term survival of the system but they generated a crisis in production. The 'social expense' of elements in the Welfare State became a drain on investment and hence a threat to the continuance of capitalism. Gough (1979) predicted that a variety of tactics would be pursued to limit the cost of welfare: the privatisation of services, higher charges for state services and an attempt to weaken the working class. The events of the 1980s have confirmed Gough's prophesy although such trends were evident in the late 1970s. If this line of reasoning is applied to housing then it can be argued that the growing power of the labour movement in the twentieth century has forced capitalism to provide accommodation for the working class – mainly in the form of local authority housing – of a standard and at a price that has undermined the capitalist accumulation process as represented by private landlordism. Thus, when the impact of the system of local authority housing became clear in the late 1970s, it was necessary for the state to undermine its operations and to restore private landlordism as a generator of profits for capitalism.

Characteristics of an ideal form of housing provision

Marx abandoned systematic thinking about the nature of society under communism at an early stage of his intellectual development arguing that since 'it is not the consciousness of men that determines their being, but on the contrary, their social being that determines their consciousness' (Preface to the *Critique of Political Economy* 1859) then new forms of organisation would emerge only from the new economic relationships created by the ending of capitalism. This 'it will be all right on the night' approach to exploring the nature of communism has been maintained by most of his academic followers. Marx predicted that after the removal of capitalism there would be a transitional stage based on the domination of the state by the working class but eventually the state would 'wither away' and communism would emerge. Academic followers of Marx have insisted that the housing policies of the Eastern bloc countries were based on 'state socialism' rather than communism, but they have produced few guidelines on how housing policies under communism should operate.

New times

The dominance of Thatcherism in the 1980s and the collapse of state socialism in the Eastern bloc culminated in a reappraisal of Marxist theory that was expressed most cogently in a series of articles first published in *Marxism Today* (Hall and Jacques 1989). It was declared that capitalism was shifting into a new phase; a move from 'Fordist' to 'post-Fordist' or from 'organised' to 'disorganised' capital. This new stage is marked by the 'globalisation' of economic relationships which have weakened the coherence and unity of particular societies and the organisation of production into smaller enterprises aimed at 'niche' rather than mass markets. The technological developments that have produced these economic changes have also generated a more fragmented and variegated society requiring a response from the Left that recognises this new diversity. Leadbeater (1991) advocates 'an appeal to the culture of individual citizenship' rather than the individual consumerism of neoclassical economics. He recommends the use of regulated markets in public service provision, the right to cash compensation for poor service delivery, the development of networks of providers, the correction of unjustifiable inequalities through universal rights to child care and the introduction of minimum wage legislation.

It appears that an influential element of the Marxist Left has abandoned class politics based on divisions arising from the process of production in favour of the politics of consumption. The emphasis is now placed on the radical potential of social movements organised around specific issues such as the environment and the 'personal identities' linked to race and gender. It is expected that this form of politics will lead to the use of regulated markets and a diversity of suppliers as methods of satisfying human needs – a similar programme to the social liberalism and welfare pluralist elements of the social reformist perspective.

Conclusion

Academics are not immune from ideology. Although academics strive to maintain impartiality in the gathering and presentation of information, this evidence is assembled within an overall framework that influences the choice of issues regarded as important and the conclusions reached on each matter reflect the values held about certain fundamental aspects of life: the liberties held by individuals, the proper role of the family and the correct boundaries of state action. Although subject to considerable cross-fertilisation and influenced by the introduction of new areas of concern such as the position of women and ethnic minorities, the three major 'grand narratives' identified in this chapter continue to provide the main academic frameworks for the consideration of housing issues and are reflected in political approaches to the housing issue.

References

Barr, N. (1993) *The Economics of the Welfare State*, Weidenfeld and Nicolson, London.
Black, J. and Stafford, D. (1988) *Housing Finance and Policy*, Routledge, London.

Buchanan, J. M. (ed.) (1978) *The Economics of Politics*, Institute of Economic Affairs, London.

Cater, J. and Jones, T. (1989) *Social Geography*, Edward Arnold, London.

Clarke, J., Cochrane, A. and Smart, C. (1987) *Ideologies of Welfare: from dreams to disillusion*, Hutchinson, London.

Clapham, D. (1989) *Goodbye Council Housing*, Unwin Paperbacks, London.

Cockett, R. (1994) *Thinking The Unthinkable*, HarperCollins, London.

Dunleavy, P. (1991) *Democracy, Bureaucracy and Public Choice*, Harvester Wheatsheaf, Hemel Hempstead.

Engels, F. (1969) 'The Housing Question', in Marx, K. and Engels, F. *Selected Works*, Vol. 2, Progress Publishers, Moscow.

George, V. and Wilding, P. (1994) *Welfare and Ideology*, Harvester Wheatsheaf, London.

Gough, I. (1979) *The Political Economy of the Welfare State*, Macmillan, London.

Graham, D. and Clarke, P. (1986) *The New Enlightenment*, Macmillan, London.

Gray, H. (1968) *The Cost of Council Housing*, Institute of Economic Affairs, London.

Green, T. H. (1893) 'On the Different Senses of "Freedom" as Applied to Will and the Moral Progress of Man', in Nettleship, R. L. (ed.) *The Works of T. H. Green*, Vol. 2, Longman, London.

Green, T. H. (1889) *The Prolegomena to Ethics*, 4th edn, edited by Bradley, A.C., Clarendon Press, London.

Hall, D. and Jacques, M. (eds) (1989) *New Times, the changing face of politics in the 1990s*, Lawrence and Wishart, London.

Harvey, D. (1978) 'Labor, Capital and Class Struggle around the Built Environment in Advanced Capitalist Societies', in Cox, K. (ed.) *Urbanisation and Conflict in Market Societies*, Methuen, London.

Hayek, F. A. (1944) *The Road to Serfdom*, Routledge, London.

Hayek, F. A. (1960) *The Constitution of Liberty*, Routledge, London.

Hayek, F. A. (1973) *Law, Legislation and Liberty*, Vol. 1, Routledge and Kegan Paul, London.

Hayek, F. A. (1976) *Law, Legislation and Liberty*, Vol. 2, Routledge and Kegan Paul, London.

Hayek, F. A. (1979) *Law, Legislation and Liberty*, Vol. 3, Routledge and Kegan Paul, London.

Hill, O. (1883) *Homes of the London Poor*, 2nd edn, Macmillan, London.

Hirst, P. (1994) *Associative Democracy*, Polity Press, Cambridge.

Jones, B. (1991) 'Understanding Ideology', *Talking Politics*, 3 (3), pp. 98–103.

Leadbeater, C. (1991) 'Manifesto For Public Policy', *Marxism Today*, May.

Marshall, T. H. (1949) 'Citizenship and Social Class', reprinted in Marshall, T.H. (1964) *Sociology at the Crossroads*, Doubleday, New York.

Minford, P., Peel, M. and Ashton, P. (1987) *The Housing Morass*, Institute of Economic Affairs, London.

Nesslein, T. (1988) 'Housing: the market versus the welfare model state revisited', *Urban Studies*, 25, pp. 95–108.

Niskanen, W. A. (1973) *Bureaucracy: servant or master*, Institute of Economic Affairs, London.

O'Connor, J. (1973) *The Fiscal Crisis of the State*, St Martin's Press, New York.

Offe, C. (1984) *Contradictions of the Welfare State*, Polity Press, Cambridge.

Pahl, R. E. (1970) *Patterns of Urban Life*, Longman, London.

Pennance, F. G. (1969) *Housing Market Analysis and Policy*, Hobart Paper No. 48, Institute of Economic Affairs, London.

Pierson, C. (1991) *Beyond The Welfare State*, Polity Press, Cambridge.

Ricketts, M. (1986) 'The Politics Of Housing Unmasked', *Economic Affairs*, October/November.

Sargent, L. S. (1978) *Contemporary Political Ideologies*, Dorsey Press, Illinois.

Short, J. (1982) *Housing in Britain*, Methuen, London.

Smith, A. (1977) *An Inquiry into the Nature and Causes of the Wealth Of Nations*, Everyman Edition, Longman, London. (First published in 1776.)

Unwin, R. (1902) *Cottage Plans and Common Sense*, Fabian Tract 109, Fabian Society, London.

Webb, S. and Webb, B. (1913) 'An Inference From the Law of Rent', *New Statesman*, 10 May.

Willetts, D. (1992) *Modern Conservatism*, Penguin Books, London.

Williams, F. (1989) *Social Policy: A Critical Introduction*, Polity Press, Cambridge.

CHAPTER 2

The politics of housing policy: 1832–1939

The public health problem in the nineteenth century

William Cobbett, writing in the 1820s, described the rural cottages of Wiltshire as 'little better than pig-beds', a description confirmed by historians as applicable to many parts of rural England in the early nineteenth century (Gauldie 1974, Rule 1986). Most rural workers lived in overcrowded and insanitary dwellings (Burnett 1986) but these conditions were not a source of national concern. Housing was identified as a social problem only in the middle years of the nineteenth century; it was urbanisation and the associated *concentration* of the unfit dwellings that fashioned housing into a public issue.

Urban growth was rapid in the nineteenth century. Initially expansion developed through the short-distance moves (less than 30 miles) of young people, supplemented by the migration from Ireland and the highlands of Scotland but, because the migrants were of child-bearing age, those born in towns and cities provided the main source of population growth in the second part of the century. The provision of drainage, sewerage and houses could not keep pace with this billowing population and the result was a concentration of people in poor quality, insanitary and overcrowded accommodation. These 'slums', 'cess pits', 'rookeries' and 'fever nests' – to use the terminology of the times – were seen as a threat to morality, public order and public health.

The movement for public health

Before the enlargement of the franchise in 1867 the political system consisted of diffuse factions competing for the right to influence the policies of Her Majesty's Government. Neither of the major cliques – the Whigs (who merged with other groups after 1859 to form the Liberal Party) or the Tories (who were to become the backbone of the Conservative Party) – represented a clearly identifiable element of capitalism; political divisions tended to revolve around support or opposition to the policies of the leaders invited to form a government.

The 'public health problem' did not become a matter of sharp division between Conservatives and Liberals. It was more a battle between a new group of experts in the 'public good' who thought it necessary to centralise administration to secure a more wholesome nation against those who fought in the name of the right to local governance. Social investigators such as Dr Southwood Smith, Dr Lyon Playfair, Sir Edwin Chadwick and Dr James Kay assembled statistical evidence to demonstrate that the conditions in parts of the rapidly developing towns and cities were a threat to the national interest. Insanitary dwellings, so they claimed, yielded a number of undesirable consequences. They caused physical and moral degradation: 'the fever nests and seats of physical depravity are also seats of moral depravity' (Sanitary Institute of Great Britain, 1874, quoted in Wohl 1983). High death rates replaced young and unskilled labour for that which was skilful and productive, and added to the poor rate by the premature death of the main breadwinner (Chadwick 1842 in Flinn 1965). Conditions in the slums depressed the human spirit to such a degree that 'the temptation to drown care in intoxicating liquors . . . is seldom permanently resisted' (Chadwick 1842 in Flinn 1965) and slum areas provided the breeding grounds for disease that could affect all members of society. Although humanitarian concern for the inhabitants of the afflicted areas was expressed it took second place to concern about 'externality' (the impact on the general community caused by poor housing conditions).

Administrative reform

Specific social reform to promote individual welfare contradicted the dominant *laissez-faire* principle of the times, so measures taken to deal with the housing issue concentrated on regulatory activity directed towards ensuring that an infrastructure for the promotion of environmental health was in place, and that the established 'nuisance' of the slum was eliminated. It took many years of conflict between the central experts in public health and the representatives of the localities to deliver an infrastructure conducive to public health; local dignitaries fought on the issue of property rights, the notion of local governance and the need to keep the rates down.

Local government had evolved in a piecemeal manner and in the early nineteenth century it consisted of a potpourri of undemocratic institutions: vestries (parish councils), corporations, Justices of the Peace and some 'improvement commissions' established under local acts. Elected councils to replace the undemocratic corporations were established in some urban areas by the Municipal Corporations Act 1835 but the Act covered only 178 boroughs, did not transfer the functions of the improvement commissions established under local legislation, and used tight boundaries to define the administrative areas of the new corporations. Although the Poor Law Amendment Act 1834 led to the grouping of some 15,000 parishes into 700 Boards of Guardians it was not until the setting up of county and borough councils under the Local Government Act 1888 and the establishment of elected urban, rural and district councils in 1894 that a comprehensive system of local government was established. In the interim, *ad hoc* boards provided the administrative mechanism for reform, and private local acts supplied the main legislative powers.

The 1848 Public Health Act set up the Central Board of Health with powers to establish local boards to regulate offensive trades, remove nuisances, provide parks and public baths and manage sewers wherever the death rate in an area exceeded 23 per 1,000. The attempts of Edwin Chadwick, the Secretary to the Board, to use its powers to cajole the localities into action were firmly resisted on the grounds that he was interfering with the right to local governance. Such resistance led to the abolition of the Board in 1858 in a climate of opinion captured well in the quotation reproduced as Document 4 (page 205).

Bylaw houses

Despite the downfall of Chadwick and his board, gradual if slow progress was made towards improving public health through the analysis of the statistics on the dimensions of the problem produced by the General Register Office (set up in 1837); better understanding of the causes of ill-health; the panic of the middle-class during the periodic outbreaks of cholera (the disease spread into the areas of middle-class residences); and the dedicated work of local medical officers of health appointed by some of the localities under private legislation.

The persuasive powers of Sir John Simon, who became medical officer to the Privy Council Department (which inherited some of the functions of the Central Board of Health), achieved more than Chadwick's hectoring. The 1875 Public Health Act, which consolidated and integrated earlier legislation, was a major progressive step that was to have implications for future housing conditions as well as for public health. It set out in detail the duties of sanitary authorities to be established in every locality. The new authorities had to secure the provision of an adequate sewage disposal system, a water supply and a method of drainage. The Act also allowed local authorities to supervise street widths and building heights. Using the authority of the act the Local Government Board – established in 1871 – issued a *New Code of Model Bylaws* which, although not compulsory, were adopted by many local authorities. Under these bylaws, tens of thousands of the terraced dwellings were built, each with an indoor water supply and a walled yard containing a privy and perhaps a coalhouse, and laid out in such a way as to facilitate the removal of sewage and to provide ventilation to the homes. Sir John Simon who framed the 1875 Public Health Act described it as 'the end of a great argument'. So it was. Commenting on the application of the model bylaws to Preston, Morgan (1993: 59) asked 'Was Preston's housing revolutionised?' and came to the conclusion that 'the short answer is that most new housing was, and that it was good enough to have survived to the present day, still mostly in good condition.'

The establishment of standards for the erection of new dwellings was accompanied by an attempt to eradicate the existing nuisance of the slum, but the action paid scant attention to the impact of such nuisance removal on those who could not afford to pay for a higher standard of housing. Thus the living conditions of the displaced residents declined as they were forced to crowd other areas of poor housing.

The electoral reforms of 1867 and 1885 which gave about 60 per cent of men over the age of 21 the right to vote in national elections had an important impact on the nature of the established parliamentary parties. They now had to compete for the votes of the majority of adult males and had to establish an organisation capable of ensuring that their message was communicated to the electorate so that the maximum vote was obtained. Despite Disraeli's rhetoric about 'one nation Toryism' expressed in his novel *Sybil or The Two Nations*, the Conservative Party was lukewarm on social reform and sought popular appeal through the promotion of the Empire and its defence of the pleasures of the working people against erosion by the 'high-minded' Liberals. The principal appeal of the Liberal Party came from the staunch support that it gave to free trade, thereby bringing the benefit of cheap food to working people. The cause of social reform did not begin to play an important role in the Liberal Party programme until the last two decades of the nineteenth century, but its momentum was rapid and culminated in the celebrated 'Liberal reforms' of 1906–14.

State provision of housing 1851–1939

State housing played an insignificant role in the social programmes of the late nineteenth and early twentieth centuries. Lord Shaftesbury's Labouring Classes' Lodging Houses Act 1851 granted local authorities the power to erect 'separate houses or cottages for the working class whether containing one or several tenements' and in 1866 Treasury loans to local authorities became possible. This legislation was rarely used; few local authorities thought that building homes was an appropriate use of their capital resources and subsequent legislation made it clear that central government believed local government to be unsuitable for involvement in mainstream housing provision and management. The Artisans' and Labourers' Dwellings Improvement Act 1875, which allowed local authorities to demolish slum areas, stated that 'the local authority shall not themselves, without the express approval of the confirming authority, undertake the rebuilding of the houses or any part of the scheme'. If the local authority did gain consent to build, then the dwellings had to be sold within ten years. It was not until 1890, under the Housing of the Working Classes Act, that local authorities obtained a clear and firm power to erect dwellings outside clearance areas. This legislation, the outcome of the deliberations of the Royal Commission on the Housing of the Working Classes 1884–85, was not intended to promote local authorities as mass suppliers of cheap homes. It was designed to give a lead to private developers by demonstrating that 'model dwellings' could be produced with a reasonable profit for the investor. As Morton has commented:

There was no question at this point of any agency operating on other than restrained commercial terms. Authorities were expected to act like the Trusts and companies and seek a return not exceeding 5 per cent. A return was essential, as Octavia Hill pointed out at the time of the Commission, to ensure the continued funding that enabled the work to go on. It was also seen to be a vital operating principle if the market was then to be able to take up the example offered.

(Morton, 1991: 2)

Local authorities were unable to demonstrate that affordable and sanitary dwellings for the urban poor could be provided without public subsidy; by 1914 only about 20,000 local authority homes had been built.

The Housing and Town Planning Act, 1909

This act was motivated by an attempt to ensure that the expansion of suburbia did not produce the problems of existing urban areas (Hennock 1987) rather than by a desire to increase the supply of homes through direct state action. The Act made it mandatory for each local authority to establish a housing and public health committee, abolished the duty to sell homes built in redevelopment areas within ten years and allowed local authorities to make a town planning scheme 'as respects any land which is in the course of development or appears likely to be used for building purposes, with the general objective of securing proper sanitary conditions, amenity and convenience in connection with the laying out and the use of the land'. It also prohibited the building of back-to-back dwellings but with the loophole that the provision did not apply to street plans approved before 1909, thus allowing developers in Leeds to continue to build back-to-backs up to the late 1930s.

Who needs council housing?

A number of reasons can be suggested for the lack of specific state action on the housing issue in the last decades of the nineteenth century and the early years of the twentieth century. A polarised housing market seems to have existed: a slum market catering for the urban and rural poor and a mainstream market serving the rest of society. The mainstream market appears to have worked quite well, especially after the suburban railway system began to develop, and reduced fares for workmen were introduced under the Cheap Trains Act 1893. There is extensive evidence of unlet property following the boom periods of the house building cycle and as Daunton (1987: 15) points out, it would 'be perverse to talk about a failure of the private market in housing when the problems arose from an *oversupply* of accommodation'.

During the late nineteenth century neither the skilled workers in regular employment nor their leaders in the developing labour movement showed a strong inclination to change this system in favour of state housing. State provision of services was often regarded as a form of social control designed to impair the working-class self-help organisations (trade unions, cooperatives, friendly societies and building societies) that were beginning to become involved in the provision of houses in the late nineteenth century. If from time to time artisans experienced difficulty in paying their rent then their natural response was to demand higher wages or react to a specific grievance such as the ending of the practice of collecting rates with the rent without a corresponding reduction in the total payment demanded by the landlord (Cole and Furbey 1994). Most of the skilled working class would probably have agreed with the Liberal L. T. Hobhouse (1911: 53) when he argued that the function of the state was 'to secure conditions upon which its citizens are able to win by their own efforts all that is necessary to a full civic efficiency. It is not for the state to feed, house, or clothe them'.

It was the masses without regular employment or with low paid jobs who shouldered the burden of low quality dwellings and homelessness. All women and many men were excluded from the right to vote: the receipt of poor relief carried the penalty of disenfranchisement until 1918 and the urban poor were not sufficiently organised to make use of their limited political muscle. They lived in overcrowded and insanitary dwellings because they could afford nothing better; private landlordism could not meet their need for decent accommodation and make a profit, hence both overcrowding and unlet dwellings coexisted (Dennis 1989). The response of the urban poor to their housing conditions was to engage in hostilities with landlords using all available means – including 'moonlight flits' and collective resistance to evictions – to avoid paying rent (Englander 1983).

Until the early years of the twentieth century there were four responses to the problem of poor housing. A few employers established 'model villages' attached to their factories. Edward Akroyd built two such villages (Copley and Akroydon) near Halifax, Titus Salt erected Saltaire, William Lever founded Port Sunlight, George Cadbury built Bournville and Joseph Rowntree developed New Earswick. An attempt was made to use public money to eradicate slum areas and rely on philanthropic voluntary organisations – whose benevolent investors limited their return on capital to 5 per cent – to build new dwellings. Unfortunately the rents that had to be charged to guarantee a 5 per cent return meant that the new dwellings were beyond the income of the poorest people displaced from the slums. The charitable Peabody Trust, which charged the lowest rents in London, was offering accommodation at 5 shillings (25p) for three rooms and a scullery, when many people had wages of less than 10 shillings (50p) per week (Burke 1981). The claim was made that the 'levelling up' process would help the poorest to secure better accommodation. 'Levelling up' was a nineteenth century version of the 'trickle down' economics to be promoted by right-wing politicians in the 1980s. It was argued that if the more affluent sections of the working class secured new accommodation then they would vacate property for occupation by poorer people – a theory that did not work in practice because of the numerous new households entering the market. Octavia Hill adopted a different approach. Her abhorrence of any form of subsidy led her to set up an organisation that bought dilapidated properties, carried out urgent repairs and rented them to poor tenants who were able to pay the rent on a regular basis.

The main areas of state activity – the demolition of slums and the installation of the infrastructure for new building – seemed costly at the time, and it was from analysis of the cost problem that a policy emerged which was to be influential in the twentieth century. The Liberal Party argued that land owners – as distinct from the owners of the built environment – were undertaxed. The local tax on property (the rates), which was expected to finance infrastructure improvements, had to be paid by property owners who found that their profit margins were being squeezed. Land, whose value, according to the popular theory of Henry George (1879), was created by the community, needed to be taxed more heavily. Elements of this theory were embodied in legislation which gave local authorities the power to impose a levy of 20 per cent on sites where values had been increased by planning regulations.

The growth of council housing 1919–1939

Rent control

The first major departure from the principle that the state should not intervene in the housing market to promote individual welfare came with the imposition of rent control by the Increase of Rent and Mortgage Interest (War Restrictions) Act, 1915. Historians disagree about the precise reasons for the introduction of control (see Englander 1983, Daunton 1983, Holmans 1987). The simplest and most plausible interpretation is that the rationale of a free market in rents had disappeared in wartime when, because house building had stopped, there was no mechanism to adjust supply and demand. The movement of labour into the munitions factories produced the momentum for rents to increase and, faced with working-class unrest, it seemed reasonable and politically astute to control rents for the duration of the hostilities (see Document 5, page 206). Rent control was buttressed by security of tenure to prevent landlords from evicting sitting tenants to extract a higher rent and by the central state providing houses for munitions workers. Such intervention in the market was to lead to further measures because, without an increase in the supply of houses, the possibility of ending rent control after the war was remote.

The Housing and Town Planning etc. Act 1919 (the Addison Act)

This legislation, known as the Addison Act, introduced a new era in housing policy. It offered a central government subsidy to local authorities of the difference between the cost of providing homes at existing rents and the product of a penny rate. This 'open-ended' subsidy lasted only until 1921 but it established local authority housing provision as a credible means of overcoming the housing shortage.

Local authorities as providers? A case can be made that local authorities were the obvious, consensus choice to supply the homes necessary to the 'land fit for heroes to live in' promised by Lloyd George. Private landlordism had experienced a severe slump in the early twentieth century with housing construction in 1913 at 'less than half that of 1900' (Short 1982). The housing shortage was acute with 9.7 million families inhabiting 8.8 million dwellings. Local authorities had the necessary expertise for building houses in their professional officers, who had long experience of civil engineering. Their involvement as suppliers was supported by the activists in the labour movement through the Workmen's National Housing Council, although mainly to provide a check on exploitative rents and to provide a a model of good design (Damer 1980, Ravetz 1986). The principle of state provision was also supported by a few Conservatives who perhaps believed that private landlords were expendable in the class struggle in order to protect land owners from more radical reform (Daunton 1983). But if local authorities were such an obvious choice for producing houses why was their involvement as providers not included in the 1918 manifestos of the major political parties? The Coalition manifesto stated that one of the 'first tasks of the Government will be to deal on broad and comprehensive lines with the housing of the people'; Labour demanded a 'substantial and permanent improvement in the housing of the whole people ... at the State's expense' and the Liberals mentioned housing only in the context of establishment of some national minimum which 'makes life worth living' (Craig 1970).

Why were grants also offered to the private sector in 1919 and why were central subsidies to local authorities abandoned so readily between 1921 and 1923? There was no clear demand from the working class (as distinct from Labour Party activists) for municipal houses, and although Lloyd George's Land Campaign before the war had promised a house building programme for the farm worker organised through a Ministry of Lands and special commissioners (with local authorities specifically excluded from building) it made only one commitment to the urban worker: to place a statutory duty on local authorities to 'see that the population of their district are adequately housed' (Herbert Samuel, quoted in Swenarton 1981). Prior to 1914 the Liberals placed emphasis on 'public utility' societies (a form of cooperative) and had little confidence in local authorities as providers of housing (Skilleter 1993).

The influence of the Fabians: The important aspect of the debates surrounding the housing issue in the period preceding the Housing and Town Planning Act 1919 was the relative influence of those who favoured private enterprise and those who advocated a form of community provision. The partisans of community provision were not homogeneous in their views but they shared one idea: Henry George's notion that it was unjust for any individual to gain from the increase in the value of land caused by development. George argued that rent was a portion of the product of the earth paid to the landlord for the power of the soil. Any increase in rent above the value of the earth was the result of general economic growth to which the owner of the land was not entitled.

George visited London in 1882 and put forward his views to interested social reformers. His idea of community ownership of the development value of land was to be the foundation of different approaches to the housing issue in the years leading up to the passing of the 1919 Housing and Town Planning Act. Ebenezer Howard placed great stress on the local community ownership of development gain. In his book *Tomorrow: A Peaceful Path to Real Reform*, later published as *Garden Cities of Tomorrow* (1902), he argued that the benefits of living in the town and the country could be combined by citizens residing in a planned garden city surrounded by a rural 'green belt'. An essential element of Howard's scheme was the quasi-public ownership of the land. Although Howard never worked out the correct relationship between those who provided the initial capital for the garden city and its future residents he envisaged a substantial surplus arising from development gain. As the town grew, its land value would increase and this community gain could be used for the provision of community facilities for local residents and to stimulate cooperative housing ventures.

The Fabian socialists adopted George's notion of the community value of developed land but were sceptical about the feasibility of the garden city idea, maintaining that it was more productive to concentrate new building in existing built-up areas. Fabians played a significant role in construction of the 1919 Housing and Town Planning Act. Although some form of state intervention in the housing market was widely accepted as necessary as early as 1916, the form and extent of such intervention was still in question. Three Fabians, including Beatrice Webb, were appointed to the Reconstruction Committee set up by Asquith in March 1916 and another member of the society, Greenwood, acted as Secretary to the Committee. When the Ministry of Reconstruction was set up in 1917, Mrs Webb became a member of its Housing Advisory Panel. Orbach (1977: 43) notes that the Housing Advisory Panel was '. . . not entirely open in its approach, for it was generally assumed that the State would have to accept the burden of providing housing . . .'. Mrs Webb spoke out against subsidising private developers arguing that 'any proposal to make a government grant to speculative builders to enable them to build cottages for their own profit would arouse such a storm of public indignation and disapproval as to be quite impracticable' (quoted in Johnson 1968: 92).

Raymond Unwin, also a member of the Fabian Society and a keen supporter of garden cities, was another key figure in the promotion of local authority housing. He was Secretary to the Tudor Walters Committee established to make recommendations on the standard of working-class dwellings to be erected after the war. It reported in 1918 and associated municipal housing with planned estate layout (at a time when local authorities had few powers over private development), made the point that houses built to high standards of amenity would meet the needs of future generations (hence its recommendation that a bath in a separate bathroom should be a standard fixture), and argued that although subsidies may be necessary in the short term, 'ultimate economy in the provision of dwellings will depend on the relation between the average rental secured over a long period' and the initial cost of the dwelling. In all this it had a distinctively Fabian tone which can also be detected in the paternalism of some of its recommendations. Only 40 per cent of houses were to be provided with parlours on the grounds that they were under-utilised by the working class, and external ornament was ruled inappropriate because of expense and aesthetic considerations. Nevertheless, as Swenarton (1981: 108) has noted 'in the context of the contemporary debate on housing the Tudor Walters Report was a radical statement. On policy and administration, on standards of accommodation and on layout and design, the report was recognised as an endorsement of the views of the radicals.'

Thus it was the Fabians who advanced the positive case for local authority involvement in the provision of houses (Cherry 1993). They received valuable support from the advocates of garden cities who, although maintaining that the creation of 100 garden cities was the correct way to provide 'homes fit for heroes', endorsed the view that community provision rather than profit-motivated private enterprise was the way to proceed (Beevers 1988). Opposition to local authority provision came from the Treasury (Gilbert 1970) but was overcome by the need to provide work for the demobilised troops and the fear of social unrest. Lloyd George put the issue bluntly to the cabinet meeting that endorsed the measures contained in the 1919 Act, arguing that 'even at the cost of £100,000,000 what was that compared with the stability of the State' (quoted in Johnson 1968: 346).

Quality homes: The 1919 Housing and Town Planning Act granted 'open-ended' subsidies to local authorities for house building and made it mandatory for each authority to compile a plan to meet housing needs in its area. A housing manual was issued by the Local Government Board containing advice – based on the Tudor Walters Report – on the design of the new houses. In order to be eligible for subsidy houses had to be built at no more than 12 per acre and these houses could be either parlour (type A) or non-parlour (type B). Homes were to contain amenities such as an inside toilet, a garden, electricity and a bathroom. Such homes proved to be popular but, despite the subsidy, expensive to rent and most of the houses were occupied by skilled workers and sometimes by the middle class.

Well, it was different in those days, those houses housed a very different class of tenant. People who lived in those houses when they were first built were well-off, some very well-off indeed. My father, for example, was managing director of a furniture company and a chauffeur-driven car would pick him up every morning to take him to work. You see we were very comfortably placed. My father always paid for my education, first infants and then juniors and when I was eleven he paid for me to go to Holly Lodge and that was a school for real ladies in those days.

It was posh, our next-door neighbour used to have tea on the grass, the lawn she used to call it. Some of them even had cars, even in them days, and yes, a number used to have cleaning ladies to do for them.

(Interview with a former tenant in Liverpool quoted by McKenna 1991: 182)

The Labour Party and housing 1919–1939

Labour gradually replaced the Liberal Party as the main opposition to the Conservatives in the inter-war years and during this period the differences in the housing policies of the two major parties were set. The attitude of the Labour Party to housing policy reflected the dominance of Fabian socialist thinking. Leading Fabians were appointed to the policy panels of the party and a housing strategy was constructed consisting of the following elements:

- The belief that local authority housing, unlike 'speculative building', was a plannable instrument; hence under the Housing (Financial Provisions) Act – known as the Wheatley Act – passed by a minority Labour Government in 1924, building workers and manufacturers were given the assurance of continued work by means of a 15 year programme which would gradually raise the output of houses.
- State control of house building would promote good standards of design.
- Community gains would arise from the increased value of developed land.
- Housing built today should meet the standards that would be required for future generations and thus subsidies were necessary to enable workers to be able to afford the high quality homes. The Wheatley Act gave subsidies to local authorities on a more generous scale than was available under Conservative Party legislation.
- There was no reason why private landlords should benefit from the additional value of their property which had been derived from the skills of building workers and community decisions on land use.
- Special subsidies were necessary to encourage local authorities to tackle the problem of unfit dwellings (such subsidies were introduced in the Greenwood Act 1930), but the slum problem would not be finally overcome until congestion in the cities had been alleviated by the planned movement of people into the suburbs and to new towns.

The Conservative Party and housing 1919–39

The 1919 Act may have represented a victory for radical views on the housing question but there were those who did not share the enthusiasm for continued state involvement in the provision of homes. Stanley Baldwin described the Conservatives elected in 1919 as 'hard faced men who looked as if they had done well out of the war', and the party soon came to regard public housing as a temporary expedient necessary only until the housing shortage created by war conditions had been overcome. The Conservative Party was instrumental in ending exchequer assistance when Addison's Act ran into difficulties because the housing market was overheated by too many local authorities competing for the limited services of the construction industry. Two years later Chamberlain introduced a Housing Act which reintroduced subsidies to local government but, this time, local authorities were not allowed to build homes with parlours, private enterprise received assistance on equal terms to local government and, for a time, councils were able to build only when they had demonstrated that the private sector could not meet the need for new dwellings: a direct reversal of the policy of 1919 when the Housing (Additional Powers) Act provided a subsidy to private housebuilders only if sufficient materials and labour were available in a particular area to support both public and private sector building.

The Conservative Party spent most of the inter-war years attempting to back out of rent control and building council houses for general needs. Both tasks proved difficult; they had to be tackled gradually and with circumspection, for sharp rises in rents would have provoked unrest and unpopularity. Nonetheless some success was achieved. New building for rent was taken out of control in 1919 and by 1939 private rented houses for the middle class were decontrolled; artisan and lower middle-class houses became decontrolled on vacant possession and only working-class houses for rent remained immune from market forces. The general approach to rent control in the period was to classify dwellings according to their markets and to decontrol those sectors where it was thought that supply and demand were in balance. It was anticipated that eventually all controls could be ended.

... when natural forces have their free play, they can be left to their free play, but when you are restraining and confining them by laws, you have constantly to exercise vigilance to see that the laws are adapted to the changing circumstances which they have to meet ... It is recognised by all of us that we are working towards the goal of being able to get rid of the system altogether.

(Sir Hilton-Young, Minister of Health 1933)

During the early 1930s there was considerable debate within the party about the role of local authorities in new house building. The catalyst for this debate was the Ray Report of 1932 which called for major cuts in public expenditure including the ending of housing subsidies. Leading Conservatives expressed anxiety about 'the trend of recent events, which tend to turn our local authorities into owners and still more managers of small house properties' (quoted in Yelling 1992). There was a call for the involvement of public utility associations – a form of housing association – in the rehabilitation of properties on the borderline of unfitness and, where necessary, in new building on cleared sites. In 1933 the Moyne Committee was set up to consider houses 'which are neither situated in an area suitable for clearance . . . nor suitable for demolition . . .' and to consider 'what, if any, further steps are necessary or desirable to promote the supply of houses for the working class, without public charge, through the agency of public utility societies . . .'. The committee came to the conclusion that housing associations should be involved in the reconditioning of the older housing stock, leaving new building for general needs to private enterprise and the clearance of slums to local authorities (Garside 1994). Opposition from local authorities and the National Federation of Housebuilders – who believed that such a course of action would discourage private investment – meant that no action was taken on the housing association elements of the Moyne Committee proposals. The Housing (Financial Provisions) Act of 1933, ended the Wheatley subsidy but retained the Greenwood subsidy for building arising from slum clearance. The Conservative Party justified the withdrawal of 'general needs' assistance by alleging that state subsidy to local authorities was preventing the movement of private enterprise into building homes for the working class. 'If you wish to provide the supply of houses that we need,' argued Sir Hilton-Young, when introducing the bill to end central assistance to local authorities for building for general needs, 'then the most obvious course is the withdrawal of the subsidy' (quoted in Branson and Heinemann 1973).

Although the Housing Act of 1935 added overcrowding to unfitness as a proper object of state involvement, it is clear that the Conservative strategy in the late 1930s was to confine the state to removing 'pathological' conditions, leaving private enterprise the role of building the vast majority of new dwellings on 'greenfield' sites (Harloe 1995). In the late 1930s local authorities concentrated their efforts on building dwellings for the inhabitants of the slums. During this time the quality of the new dwellings declined with a higher proportion of dwellings being provided in the form of walk-up flats. The average cost of a council house declined from 77 per cent of the cost of an owner-occupied house in 1934 to 50 per cent in 1939 (Cleaver 1984). Branson and Heinemann provide an account of the design of many of these developments:

For the most part the blocks built at this time were severely utilitarian in character. Often five storeys high, they were usually served by concrete staircases with outside balcony access making one side dark and noisy. The bleak paved yards were not often relieved by trees or grass . . . Built as though to last a hundred years, some of these blocks seemed to emphasise that they were rough places for rough people.

(Branson and Heinemann 1971: 211)

Owner-occupation and the growth of suburbia

Although the percentage of owner-occupied dwellings in 1914 has not been firmly established (it was not until 1961 that a question on tenure was included in the Census), most authorities quote 10 per cent. If this figure is accurate then there was a substantial growth in owner-occupation between the wars – up to 35 per cent by 1939 (Swenarton and Taylor 1985). State subsidies were available for inexpensive houses built for owner-occupation; the persistence of rent control encouraged some landlords to sell when they secured vacant possession and local authorities were allowed to guarantee mortgages (Forrest, Murie and Williams 1990) but the growth of home ownership was not a consequence of direct state intervention. The extension of suburban railways and the provision of better bus services meant that it was possible for more people to live at some distance from their place of work. This trend – together with the absence of restrictive planning regulations – allowed builders to erect dwellings on cheap 'greenfield' sites, making the price of houses affordable to more people.

The recession of the inter-war period did not affect all groups equally. As Mowat has explained, 'some of the saving in cost was at the expense of the men in the building trades: much building was done at cut rates, by men who camped out in the half-finished houses they were constructing' (Mowat 1968: 459). Finance for house purchase became more readily available because savings invested with building societies increased rapidly, and an agreement with developers protected the societies from potential losses from mortgage default. The numerous building society offices offered a convenient and generally safe haven for the capital of the middle class and the skilled working class. The continuance of rent control had made a traditional repository of such savings – direct investment in houses to be let – less attractive. The result was:

> Over two and a half million houses were built for private sale within twenty years. Houses were relatively cheap – a typical 'semi' could be bought for as little as £450, about twice the annual salary of an average professional man. Mortgages were available on easy terms, with an average interest rate of 4.5 per cent and repayments that came well within the range of most of the middle classes and a substantial portion of the better-off working class. Deposits on new homes could be as low as £25, particularly towards the end of the thirties when the number of house completions topped 350,000 and gave the market a more competitive edge.
>
> (Stevenson 1984: 223)

Planning control

The rapid development of suburban owner occupation did not meet with universal approval. Community control of the built environment in the period between the wars was limited. In 1909 local authorities had obtained the power to prepare town planning schemes for any land that was being developed or appeared likely to be developed (extended to all land in 1932) but few authorities chose to use these powers and those that did encountered problems of enforcement and compensation. The Restriction of Ribbon Development Act 1935 was aimed at controlling the spread of building along main roads but Hall (1992) maintains that a minority of thinking people were still alarmed at the consequences of rapid suburban growth and the inability of the state to control this expansion.

They included both town planners, who by then existed as a profession (the Town Planning Institute had been incorporated in 1914), and rural conservationists. They were concerned at the fact that the development was uncontrolled by any sort of effective planning. Though Acts of Parliament had provided for local authorities to make town planning schemes for their areas – in 1909, in 1925 and then, most decisively, in 1932 – basically these Acts gave them no power to stop development altogether where such development was not in the public interest . . . and this, the planners and conservationists argued had two bad effects. First, it was using up rural land – the great majority of it agricultural land – at an unprecedented rate . . . Secondly, the critics argued that the effect on the townsman was equally bad . . . traffic congestion in cities appeared to be growing; and journeys to work, it was assumed, must increase . . .

(Hall 1992: 27–28)

These concerns were explored by a Royal Commission set up in 1937 under the chairmanship of Sir A. Montague-Barlow to investigate the problems of the distribution of the industrial population, and the Scott Committee on Land Utilisation in Rural Areas (1942). The Barlow Report (1940) supported the notion that the inter-war pattern of development had produced undesirable consequences of which 'not least grave . . . is transport congestion, which . . . often involves serious loss of time and money and probably some impairment of health'. It called for a central planning authority to be established. The Scott Report took the view that the countryside and its agriculture were priceless national assets that should have special protection. It made proposals for firm controls on development to preserve agricultural land, green belts, nature reserves and national parks. The Barlow and Scott reports, together with the Uthwatt Report on Compensation and Betterment (1942) were to have a significant influence on housing provision after the war.

Conclusion

Substantial progress was made in improving general housing conditions in the inter-war years. Housing investment, which had hovered around 19 per cent of total domestic investment between 1870 and 1914, increased to 26 per cent between 1920 and 1929 and to 33 per cent between 1930 and 1938 (Glynn and Oxborrow 1976). Four million houses were completed: 1,330,000, in the public sector, 470,000 in the private sector with state aid, and 2.5 million by unsubsidised private enterprise. 250,000 unfit properties were demolished and Rowntree (1941) found that overcrowding in York had been reduced by two-thirds since 1900. Slum property had decreased from 26 per cent of the housing stock in 1900 to 12 per cent in 1936.

References

Barlow Commission (1940) *The Royal Commission on the Distribution of the Industrial Population*, Cmd 6153, HMSO, London.

Beevers, R. (1988) *The Garden City Utopia: a critical biography of Ebenezer Howard*, Macmillan, London.

Burke, G. (1981) *Housing and Social Justice*, Longman, London.

Burnett, J. (1986) *A Social History of Housing*, Routledge, London.

Branson, N. and Heinemann, M. (1973) *Britain in the Nineteen Thirties*, Panther, St Albans.

Cherry, G. E. (1993) *Cities and Plans*, Edward Arnold, London.

Cleaver, M. (1984) 'Housing Milestone and Trends 1934–1984', *Housing Review*, September-October, 33 (5).

Cole, T. and Furbey, R. (1994) *The Eclipse of Council Housing*, Routledge, London.

Craig, F. W. S. (1970) *British General Election Manifestos 1918–1966*, Political Reference Publications, Chichester.

Damer, S. (1980) 'State, Class and Housing: Glasgow 1885–1919', in Melling, J. (ed.) *Housing, Social Policy and the State*, Croom Helm, London.

Daunton, M. J. (1983) *House and Home in the Victorian City, working class housing 1850–1914*, Edward Arnold, London.

Daunton, M. J. (1987) *A Property-owning Democracy? Housing in Britain*, Faber, London.

Dennis, R. (1989) '"Hard to Let" in Edwardian London', *Urban Studies*, (26), pp. 77–89.

Englander, D. (1983) *Landlord and Tenant in Urban Britain, 1838–1918*, Clarendon Press, Oxford.

Flinn, M. (ed.) (1965) *Edwin Chadwick, Report of the Sanitary Conditions of the Labouring Population of Great Britain*, Edinburgh University Press, Edinburgh.

Forrest, R., Murie, A. and Williams, P. (1990) *Home Ownership: differentiation and fragmentation*, Unwin Hyman, London.

Garside, P. (1994) 'Housing Issues in the 1930s: slum clearance, overcrowding and the role of housing associations', *Housing Review* 43 (5) September–October.

Gauldie, E. (1974) *Cruel Habitations: a history of working-class housing 1780–1918*, Allen and Unwin, London.

George, H. (1979) *Progress and Poverty*, Hogarth Press, London. (First published in 1879.)

Gilbert, B. B. (1970) *British Social Policy 1914–1939*, B. T. Batsford, London.

Glynn, S. and Oxborrow, J. (1976) *Interwar Britain: a social and economic history*, George Allen and Unwin, London.

Hall, P. (1992) *Urban and Regional Planning*, 3rd edn, Routledge, London.

Harloe, M. (1995) *The People's Home?*, Blackwell, London.

Hennock, E. P. (1987) *British Social Reform and German Precedents*, Clarendon Press, Oxford.

Hobhouse, L. T. (1911) *Liberalism*, Williams and Norgate, London.

Holmans, A. (1987) *Housing Policy in Britain: a history*, Croom Helm, London.
Howard, E. (1902) *Garden Cities of Tomorrow*, Faber, London.
Johnson, P. B. (1968) *Land Fit For Heroes*, University of Chicago Press, Chicago.
McKenna, M. (1991) 'The Suburbanisation of the Working-class Population of Liverpool Between the Wars', *Social History* 16 (2), pp. 173–89.
Malpass, P. (1990) *Reshaping Housing Policy*, Routledge, London.
Morgan, N. (1993) *Deadly Dwellings: The shocking story of housing and health in a Lancashire cotton town*, Mullion Books, Preston.
Morton, J. (1991) *'Cheaper Than Peabody'* : *local authority housing from 1890 to 1919*, Joseph Rowntree Foundation, York.
Mowat, C. L. (1968) *Britain Between the Wars, 1918–1940*, Methuen, London.
Orbach, L. (1977) *Homes For Heroes*, Seely Service, London.
Ravetz, A. (1986) *The Government of Space*, Faber and Faber, London.
Rowntree, S. (1941) *Poverty and Progress: a second social survey of York*, Longman, London.
Rule, J. (1986) *The Labouring Classes in Early Industrial England 1750–1850*, Longman, London.
Scott Committee (1942) *Report of the Committee on Land Utilisation in Rural Areas*, Cmd 6378, HMSO, London.
Short, J. R. (1982) *Housing in Britain, the post-war years experience*, Methuen, London.
Skilliter, R. K.(1993) 'The Role of Public Utility Societies in Early British Town Planning and Housing Reform, 1901–1936', *Planning Perspectives*, 8 (2), pp. 125–165.
Stevenson, J. (1984) *British Society 1914–45*, Penguin Books, Harmondsworth.
Swenarton, M. (1981) *Homes Fit For Heroes: the politics and architecture of early state housing in Britain*, Heinemann, London.
Swenarton, M. and Taylor, S. (1985) 'The Scale and Nature of the Growth of Owner Occupation in Britain Between the Wars', *Economic History Review*, 38 (3), pp. 373–392.
Uthwatt Committee (1942) *Final Report of the Expert Committee on Compensation and Betterment*, Cmd 6386, HMSO, London.
Wohl, A. S. (1983) *Endangered Lives*, Methuen, London.
Yelling, J. A. (1992) *Slums and Redevelopment, policy and practice in England with particular reference to London*, UCL Press, London.

CHAPTER 3

The politics of housing policy: towards 2000

The Labour Government 1945 to 1951: a Fabian solution?

An emergency programme

The advance of the Conservative Party towards the restoration of a free market in housing was curbed by the outbreak of the Second World War. The experience of 1915 had been absorbed and this time the government did not wait for social unrest before putting controls into place: rents were frozen in 1939 for the duration of hostilities.

Despite the progress made between 1918 and 1939 there was still a serious shortage of satisfactory homes. The war intensified the problem; 458,000 houses were destroyed and 250,000 badly damaged (Foot 1973). When the war was over household formation accelerated and the birthrate increased. Housing became *the* political issue and a squatting movement developed with homeless people, sometimes led by the Communist party, taking over disused army camps and empty luxury flats. Despite these problems there was no housing equivalent of the Beveridge report on social security. This absence of a comprehensive review of housing policy may have been a reflection of the obvious nature of the problem – a massive shortage of houses – and the self-evident nature of the solution: state-directed production that had been so successful in meeting the needs of the war economy. The *Daily Mirror* declared in 1945 that 'Housing will have to be tackled like a problem of war. We make, as if by miracle, tanks, aircraft, battleships, pipelines, harbours! Are we then, then incapable of building houses?'.

1944 brought the introduction of an emergency project to build 500,000 temporary prefabricated homes with a ten year life using surplus airfield construction plant for site preparations and aircraft factories for component assembly. The standard 'prefab' had a fridge, hot water, two bedrooms, an indoor lavatory and a large garden. The Ministry of Health produced plans to authorise local authorities to acquire and prepare sites for 300,000 permanent houses, negotiations were started with local authorities on subsidies, and the Dudley Committee reported on the standards that should be established for the construction of new homes. The War Cabinet Reconstruction Committee 'allotted 127,000 man-years and £56 million each year of peace to building new houses; 81,000 man-years and £36 million to all other types of new building – industrial, infrastructure,

public utilities, educational buildings, health and R and D establishments' (Barnett 1986). However, such plans were restricted to an
'emergency period' and there is evidence that the battle lines were
being drawn up on the respective roles of local authorities and private
enterprise when the emergency period was over.

The case for private enterprise was put forward by the Private Enterprise
Subcommittee of the Central Housing Advisory Committee of the Ministry
of Health in its report (known as the Pole report) published in 1944. It
argued that private enterprise could play the major role in meeting
housing needs if it concentrated on building houses to let, received the
same subsidies as municipal housing, and developed a method of safeguard-
ing the quality of the new houses. E. D. Simon (1945) put the case
against private enterprise, which he called 'speculative' building. He
asserted that jerry-building had been far too common in the inter-war
period, that governments could insist on the use of mass production
methods by local authorities, that speculative builders would not be
willing to manage large estates of poor tenants from the slums, that
subsidies might be used to boost profits and that local authorities could
plan neighbourhood units and guarantee a stable building programme.

Planning the new Jerusalem

The victory of the Labour Party in the 1945 general election meant that
arguments similar to Simon's held sway. Aneurin Bevan, the minister
responsible for the housing programme, favoured local authorities because
they were, in his words, 'plannable instruments' and could meet, in a
direct manner, the need of poor people for homes to rent. The Labour
Party tackled the post-war housing shortage with pure Fabian principles.
The 1947 Town and Country Planning Act imposed taxes of between
40 per cent and 100 per cent on the 'betterment' value of land used for
development, set up a Central Land Board with powers to purchase
land compulsorily, made provision for grants to be paid to local government for land assembly, placed a duty on local authorities to prepare
development plans for their areas, allowed local authorities to acquire
land by compulsion for planning purposes and made it a requirement
that most development should have planning permission.

The New Towns Act of 1946 made provision for the establishment
of new towns as a method of relieving congestion in the major cities
and providing workers with homes in a planned environment. Central
government offered local authorities a new flat rate subsidy for houses
built for general needs in the Housing (Financial and Miscellaneous
Provisions) Act 1946, made it mandatory to make a contribution from
the rates to house building, allowed local authorities to borrow from
the Public Works Loans Board at a rate of interest below the market
rate and introduced a strict system of building licences to control the
use of materials by the private sector.

Bevan wanted to ensure that new housing schemes promoted mixed communities (see Document 6, page 207) and demanded that three out of four new houses should be owned by local authorities. He also claimed that 'we shall be judged for a year or two by the number of houses we build. We shall be judged in ten years time by the type of houses we build', and so the new homes should be of high quality. In the face of opposition from other members of the government he insisted on higher standards than had been provided in the inter-war period and included a water closet, both upstairs and downstairs, in each family dwelling. In 1948 he ended the programme of building prefabricated bungalows started in 1944 arguing that such homes were 'rabbit hutches' of insufficient quality and limited space.

The Conservatives and housing policy 1951–64

The people's house

Despite Eden's pronouncement in 1946 that the Conservative aim was a 'nation-wide property-owning democracy', in the years immediately following the end of the war the Conservatives did not advance strong objections to the concentration of house building in the public sector. However in the late 1940s they began to blame the slow progress in house construction on the involvement of the state, arguing that restrictions on the private sector and the taxation of land values were impeding the housing drive. At the Conservative Party Conference in 1950 the delegates passed a resolution – against the wishes of the leadership – calling for a target of 300,000 houses per year and started a political 'numbers' auction that was to last until the early 1970s (see Document 7, page 208). The Conservative government that came to power in 1951 had little hope of meeting their target through private enterprise alone – the private sector had built only 26,000 dwellings in the previous year – so, for a time, they continued to rely on local government. By reducing standards – 'the people's house' was 15 per cent smaller than those built in the 1940s – encouraging terrace building (Sim 1993) and increasing subsidies so that the new homes would absorb about 10 per cent of the income of working people, Harold Macmillan, the minister responsible, was able to hand over the key of the 300,000th house built in 1953. This use of the public sector by the Conservatives demonstrates how the political need to build homes took precedence over any ideological considerations related to the desirability of different tenures. Nonetheless a shift towards home ownership was started by the ending of licences for building and the promotion of land release through the abolition of the tax on 'betterment' value.

Rachmanism

In a series of measures introduced in the middle 1950s – reminiscent of the strategy pursued in the late 1930s – the Conservatives took some tentative steps towards the application of free market principles to housing. The policies were heralded by a White Paper, *Housing: The Next Step* (1953), which acclaimed home ownership as 'the most satisfying to the individual and most beneficial to the nation'. Local authorities were forced to borrow from the capital markets at higher rates of interest than had been available from the Public Works Loan Board, subsidies to local authorities to build for general needs were withdrawn and the available central resources were concentrated on dwellings erected as a result of slum clearance or for the 'special' housing needs of elderly and disabled people. The statutory contribution from the rates to council housing was ended. An attempt was made to persuade local authorities to charge more 'realistic' rents and to introduce differential rent schemes (Malpass 1990).

Private sector solutions to the problem of unsatisfactory dwellings were encouraged by the introduction of mandatory improvement grants for the installation of basic amenities. Rent control and security of tenure were modified by the 1957 Rent Act. Rents of dwellings above a rateable value of £30 were decontrolled and 'creeping decontrol' was introduced through the ending of rent control when a house became vacant. This experiment in free market economics was a political fiasco. Decontrol failed to increase the pool of private rented houses and did not even stop the decline. In 1957 there were 4.5 million privately rented homes but by 1965 the total had fallen to 3.5 million. The consequences of the decontrol of rents generated a political storm as the vicious tactics used by a small number of slum landlords to secure vacant possession added a new term to the English language – 'Rachmanism' – named after Perec Rachman, the most notorious practitioner of the abuses, who attracted media attention in 1963 because of his association with Mandy Rice-Davies and the Profumo Affair (Timmins 1995).

Taxation and home ownership

In an attempt to ease the housing problem and cool the political controversy, 'general needs' subsidies were restored to local authorities in 1961 and the following year owner-occupation was stimulated by the abolition of Schedule A Tax on resident owners. Schedule A had been levied on the rental income that all owner-occupiers were assumed to have paid to themselves and ensured that a home owner was treated in the same way as a private landlord who had to pay tax on rental income. As part of the package involved in the payment of Schedule A, owner-occupiers had been allowed to deduct their mortgage interest payments from their income tax liability. When Schedule A tax was abolished for resident owners the tax relief on mortgage interest continued and thereby a substantial subsidy to home owners was created, a subsidy which was to have profound implications for the future development of the tenure system in Britain and for the 'tax expenditures' of the state.

The Labour Government and housing 1964–70

Despite the emotional atmosphere in which the housing issue was debated during the 1964 election campaign, the policies of the two major parties were similar. The Conservative Party, although not prepared to show enthusiasm for local authority housing, had to give it a role because of lack of alternatives in the provision of homes for rent. Private landlordism had been totally discredited by the publicity given to the activities of Rachman and an attempt, started in 1962, to create a 'third sector' of non-profit landlords through cost-rent societies needed time to make an impact. The ten year plan described in the White Paper on Housing (Cmnd 2050, 1963) promised 400,000 houses each year – a substantial portion being local authority homes. Labour outbid the Conservatives by setting a target of 500,000 houses per year. The party had a stronger commitment to public housing than its rival but thought it necessary to declare its support for owner-occupation by a promise to reduce the interest rate on mortgages to 4 per cent.

The Labour Government of 1964–70 attempted to adopt an even-handed approach to local authority tenants and home owners. Its five year housing programme (Ministry of Housing and Local Government 1965), promised that new building would be split 50/50 between the two sectors and that interest rates for home owners and local authority tenants would both be held at 4 per cent. Labour's growing taste for home ownership was reflected in the declaration that the expansion of the public sector was a response to 'exceptional needs' whereas 'the expansion of buildings for owner occupancy . . . is normal' (Ministry of Housing and Local Government 1965). Owner-occupation was stimulated by the introduction of an 'option mortgage' scheme allowing a person with a low income who did not benefit from tax relief on mortgage interest to receive a low interest loan. Gradually Labour began to restore the balance between public and private sector building which had tipped in favour of owner-occupation in the late 1950s and early 1960s. The gap between the two sectors narrowed from 96,000 in 1964 to 23,000 in 1969 but as Dunleavy (1987) has commented:

Yet, if Labour's strategy was successful in terms of the numbers of public housing completions, it contained the seeds of its own demise in the type of housing being completed. Nationally 25 per cent of the dwellings being produced by 1966–7 were in high-rise blocks. In big cities, the proportion was much higher, reaching 70 per cent in Greater London and other conurbations. Over 60 per cent of all high flats were being built by industrialised systems (compared with less than a third of other types of housing).

(Dunleavy 1987: 24)

Cities in the sky

The story of high-rise is complicated with a number of interacting factors contributing to their use. Technical advances in the inter-war period made tower blocks possible, and in the 1930s the architectural profession came under the spell of 'modernism'. The Bauhaus School argued that structural form should reflect the functional mechanisms within the building and hence dwellings should have clear, angular lines and incorporate materials such as glass, steel and concrete. Le Corbusier maintained that houses should be 'machines for living in' with well-spaced tower blocks providing homes with equal access to daylight; links between blocks by 'streets in the air' would allow the area around and beneath the blocks to be used as parkland (see Document 8, page 209 for one view of the impact of such schemes). The major building firms, who possessed the techniques for systems building, regarded high rise as a source of profit and used their influence on the National Building Agency and with senior politicians to promote tower blocks. Central government wanted housing units to be built quickly and regarded system-building as a way of achieving this objective. Many city authorities demanded more homes within their boundaries in order to retain rateable value and 'civic status' (Glendinning and Muthesius 1994) whereas suburban authorities – assisted by the green belt policy of central government – resisted most attempts to move the 'overspill' people from clearance schemes into their areas.

Extra central subsidy for high-rise was introduced in 1956 by the Conservatives and tower block construction gained momentum in the 1960s. It did not start to decline until after the collapse of Ronan Point in 1968 when seven people were killed. Other forms of housing design and estate arrangement were introduced in the 1960s. Deck access, in which entry to flats was attained from walkways so as to enhance social interaction, became established (Sim 1993) and many low-rise estates were designed on Radburn principles which kept vehicle and pedestrian access separate by cul-de-sacs for traffic attached to parking/garage areas at the rear of the dwellings. Both these forms of estate design were to produce problems in the future because of their lack of private, defensible space.

The unfurnished private landlord sector now provoked little party political controversy. The Labour Party set up new mechanisms to regulate rents giving tenants and landlords the opportunity to ask Rent Assessment Committees to determine a 'fair' rent (one that ignored scarcity value) for a property. Consensus was also generated around a switch in emphasis from clearance to improvement based on a degree of targeting of funds on special status areas. The Labour government promoted this change in emphasis as a positive measure, stressing the ways that clearance disrupted established communities, but the policy was also a response to the financial crisis of 1967; rehabilitation was cheaper than demolition and new building.

The Conservatives and housing policy 1970–1974

'Fair' rents and rent rebates

It is possible to interpret the Housing Finance Act 1972 – the most significant housing legislation of the Heath administration – in two ways. In opposition the Conservative Party became increasingly influenced by the ideas of free market liberalism as expounded by the Institute of Economic Affairs. The Housing Finance Act, with its extension of 'fair rents' to the local authority sector, may be interpreted as a move towards the restoration of a market in renting, especially if one accepts that there was a potential link to be made between 'fair' rents and market rents. Alternatively the Act can be seen as a rational/technical measure designed to make more effective use of available resources. It was presented in this way in the White Paper *Fair Deal For Housing* (1971) which stated 'the present system provides subsidy for housing authorities which do not need it. It gives too little to authorities with the worst problems of slum clearance and overcrowding'. Civil servants in the Ministry of Housing had been concerned about the distribution of subsidies which reflected historical entitlements under earlier legislation rather then current need and had tried to persuade Richard Crossman, Minister for Housing between 1964 and 1966, to adopt similar legislation (Crossman 1971).

Perhaps the Housing Finance Act was introduced because it seemed to satisfy all elements within the Conservative Party – the market advocates and the 'consensus' politicians – the 'drys' and the 'wets' as these two factions in the party later came to be labelled. The Act introduced a national rent rebate and allowance scheme which at least offered the possibility that some low-income households would be able to afford to live in the better quality local authority dwellings, and that the tenants of private landlords would be able to afford a rent sufficient to keep their houses in reasonable repair. However, the merits of the Act need to be considered in the context of its potential impact. 'Fair rents' meant higher rents for a large number of tenants, the extension of means-testing and, in some areas, the use of council housing to produce a large surplus over costs which had to be returned to the Treasury (Crosland 1971). The Labour Party opposed the 'fair rent' provisions of the Act to the point of non-compliance with the law by certain local authorities. Many tenants identified with the campaign against the Act and, as part of Heath's U-turn on economic policy, the rent increases planned to bring local authority rents to 'fair' levels were modified. Extending the availability of improvement grants was an additional element of Heath's reflationary policy but the temporary nature of this gesture was demonstrated by the introduction of a White Paper *Better Homes – The Next Priorities* (1973) which was aimed at promoting the refurbishment of older private sector property on a more selective basis.

Labour 1974 to 1979: the party's over

Labour recast the policy contained in the 1972 Housing Finance Act. The national system of rent rebates and allowances was retained but local authorities were instructed to charge only 'reasonable' rents and a new form of central government subsidy was introduced by the 1975 Housing Rents and Subsidies Act that consolidated all existing assistance and granted a subsidy of 66 per cent of loan charges for new capital investment. The ideas contained in the Conservative White Paper *Better Homes – The Next Priorities* were adopted and incorporated into the Housing Act 1974. Housing associations were given a major role by the legislation. They were encouraged to concentrate on rehabilitation in the 'stress areas' and associations registered with the Housing Corporation became entitled to Housing Association Grant (HAG) designed to pay, as a capital sum, the difference between the cost of a project and the amount that could be raised by charging 'fair' rents. Between 1974 and 1976 local authorities and housing associations were provided with resources to purchase and refurbish properties owned by private landlords. These measures, combined with the financial impact of the more generous improvement grant regime and high interest rates produced a dramatic increase in public expenditure on housing. National and local contributions to the costs of council housing almost doubled in real terms between 1973–74 and 1976–77 and total public expenditure on housing (including mortgage interest tax relief) increased from 3.3 per cent of the Gross Domestic Product in 1973–74 to 4.1 per cent in 1976–77 (Hills 1990).

The sterling crisis of late 1976, and the agreements made with the International Monetary Fund, produced big cuts in capital expenditure. Anthony Crosland, Secretary of State for the Environment, declared that 'the party's over' and capital investment in housing declined from £8.6 billion in 1974–75 to £5.3 billion in 1978–79. However, revenue spending to support rents was left untouched and by 1979 central subsidies to council housing had doubled; rents as a percentage of average earnings declined from 7.8 per cent in 1973–74 to 6.3 per cent in 1978–79. Crosland set up a major review of housing finance which concluded:

The Government believe that the objectives of housing policy must be rooted in the traditions and reasonable expectations of the nation, but must also reflect present realities . . . we should no longer think about (housing conditions) only in terms of national totals; we must try to secure a better balance between investment in new houses and the improvement and repair of older houses, with regard to the needs of the individual and the community, as well as cost . . .; we must increase the scope for mobility in housing . . . and we must make it easier for people to obtain the tenure they want.

(Secretary of State for the Environment 1977: 7)

The realities of the economy and the growing popularity of owner-occupation – described in a Green Paper as a 'basic and natural desire of all people' – had combined to modify Labour's traditional faith in public housing. The Department of the Environment adopted the notion that there was no longer a *national* housing problem but a number of *local* problems, and introduced a new system to control the building of new homes by local authorities through the housing strategy process. The 1977 Green Paper described this system as 'a means of controlling public expenditure while allowing resources to be allocated selectively with regard to variations in local requirements.' (Secretaries of State 1977). Local authority construction was cut back from 110,000 units in 1975 to 47,000 in 1979 and housing association production fell from 27,000 in 1976 to 14,000 in 1979.

The New Right and housing 1979 to 1987

In 1975 the Conservative party acquired a leader with firm anti-collectivist beliefs. Ranelagh (1992) records Mrs Thatcher's first and only visit to the Conservative Research Department.

Another colleague had also prepared a paper arguing that the 'middle way' was the pragmatic path for the Conservative Party to take, avoiding the extremes of Left and Right. Before he had finished speaking to his paper, the new Party leader reached into her briefcase and took out a book. It was Friedrich von Hayek's *The Constitution of Liberty*. Interrupting our pragmatist, she held the book up for all of us to see. 'This,' she said sternly 'is what we believe,' and banged Hayek down on the table.

(Ranelagh 1991: ix)

By 1975 there were years of experience of state intervention in housing against which the ideas of the neoclassical economists could be tested. It was the predictions made by such theorists as Hayek that made their arguments so powerful. In 1960 Hayek had warned that subsidised state housing would result in uncontrollable expenditure and the increase in state subsidies to council housing in the late 1970s could be interpreted as confirmation of the accuracy of Hayek's prediction. The experience of state housing also created concern about lack of consumer influence in the local authority sector. Local authority architects had set out to design dwellings that were different to those provided by the specula-tive builder (Oliver, Davis and Bentley 1981). Simon (1945) sum-marises the views of a private developer on local authority housing:

the architect of the local authority has known all through the inter-war period that there would be no difficulty in letting all the houses he could build, and he has, therefore, been in a position, to a considerable extent, to design the house according to his own views and in particular to lay a lot of stress on the external appearance.

(Simon 1945: 74)

The developer gave two examples of the lack of consumer orientation in local authority housing: the use of cul-de-sacs, which he had abandoned because they were hard to sell because the housewife wanted to be on a road so as to have something of interest to watch; and the installation of small windows so as to make the overall design of the estate more attractive, whereas the private developer built homes with larger windows reaching nearly to the floor to give lighter rooms with better views.

Such limitations on consumer involvement were not serious in the inter-war period. In the hands of people such as Raymond Unwin, influenced by William Morris and John Ruskin before he joined the Fabian Society, the connection between planning and local authority housing produced design on a human scale. Some municipal architects, adopting Unwin's rejection of 'embellishments' in favour of clean 'aesthetic' lines, produced uniform, drab estates without local amenities, but most of the properties built for 'general needs' in the inter-war period were agreeable for their time. In the 1930s planning began to be influenced by the 'modernist movement' and by the late 1970s the high-rise, system-built dwellings that such ideas helped to produce were widely believed to have been a disaster that could be attributed to the lack of consumer influence in public sector housing. The negative features of state housing were contrasted with the positive aspects of owner-occupation which, so it was argued, encouraged personal responsibility, gave people a capital stake in society and contributed to greater equality in the distribution of wealth.

The sale of council houses began to feature more strongly on the political agenda. Selling council houses was not a new idea. It had started as early as the late nineteenth century but had been limited up to the early 1970s despite central government granting a general consent to sell in 1952. In the election campaign of 1974 the Conservatives promised to allow council tenants of three or more years a right to buy at 33 per cent less than the market value, and in 1975 Peter Walker suggested that council tenants who had occupied council houses for 20 years should be given their homes. According to Gilmour (1992: 142) 'Mrs Thatcher feared that those on the Wates estates, the least well-off owner occupiers, whom she regarded as "our people" would have resented council house occupiers being given something for nothing . . .' and hence the proposal of an outright gift was changed to the discount system of 1974 but on more generous terms. Walker's initial suggestion caused great concern in Harold Wilson's kitchen cabinet and a scheme for the sale of council homes was prepared by Labour (Haines 1977). However, despite endorsement by some Labour members of Parliament (Field 1975), when Crosland's housing review was published in 1977 there was no mention of any new scheme for council house sales. Instead proposals were put forward to enhance the status of tenants by offering more involvement in the management of council housing and giving more legal rights to tenants. These proposals were incorporated into a bill introduced into Parliament in 1979. The bill fell with the defeat of the government but its provisions were included by the Conservatives in the Housing Act of 1980.

The ambivalent attitude of the Labour Party to the sale of council houses was not mirrored in the views of the Conservative Party. The idea (put into practice by many Conservative-controlled local authorities in the 1970s) was embraced at national level and became the central theme of Conservative policy on housing. The party was on firm political ground; opinion surveys conducted in the late 1970s revealed that less than 20 per cent of council tenants under 55 stated that their ideal choice of tenure in two years time was the council sector, and 59 per cent of council tenants gave negative reasons for living in their present accommodation (Coles 1989). Even the letter sent in 1979 by Mrs Thatcher's private secretary to a tenant who had complained about the condition of her home probably demoralised as many council tenants as it angered. It said:

I hope you will not think me too blunt if I say that it may well be that your council accommodation is unsatisfactory but considering the fact you have been unable to buy your own accommodation you are lucky to have been given something which the rest of us are paying for out of our taxes.

(quoted in *The Times*, 9 April 1979)

The privatisation of council housing was neatly linked with the notion of tenant's rights in the right to buy provisions of the 1980 Housing Act and the Tenants' Rights Etc. (Scotland) Act. Tenants were given an individual right to purchase their homes at a substantial discount on the market value: up to 50 per cent in the early stages of the policy and then extended to 60 per cent on houses and 70 per cent on flats. Tenants of non-charitable housing associations were given similar rights. Such a policy seems distant from the philosophy of free markets advocated by Hayek – a true marketeer would have sold the houses on vacant possession at full market value – but, despite her respect for market principles, Margaret Thatcher had such a strong belief in the virtues of home ownership as a source of self-respect and social stability that pure market philosophy was put into abeyance. The push of higher rents was added to the pull of discounts and eligibility for housing benefits was restricted so that by 1988 only households on less than 50 per cent of average male gross earnings were able to claim, compared to 110 per cent of average male gross earnings in 1983 (Ungerson 1994).

The establishment and promotion of the mechanisms to encourage the sale of council houses absorbed most of the energies of the Conservative governments between 1979 and 1987. Its success – 745,977 were sold in England and Wales between 1980 and 1987 – created scope for new expenditure. The capital receipts generated from the sales – financed by building societies – were recycled into improvement, but the Treasury soon claimed a share of the income to pay for tax cuts and other programmes. Central government subsidies to local authority housing were reduced, resulting in higher rents (until the majority of local authorities lost entitlement to subsidy), and some experiments in the decontrol of private sector rents were introduced. A number of innovative but limited schemes to promote low cost home ownership were set up and in 1983 Mortgage Interest Relief at Source (MIRAS) was introduced, allowing lenders to deduct the value of tax relief from actual mortgage repayments, a measure that removed the need for the option mortgage scheme. An attempt was made to limit the spending of local authorities on building new council homes and on subsidising council rents from rate contributions. This policy was met by vigorous opposition from a small number of 'big city' authorities controlled by groups labelled the 'New Left'.

The New Left alternative

The term 'New Left' embraces a variety of political ideas developed in the 1960s and 1970s. These were founded on a Marxist analysis of the nature of the local state and its potential for radical action. During the first phase of the analysis, emphasis was placed on the negative aspects of the operation of the local state. It was argued that local bureaucrats helped the capitalist class to control ordinary working-class people and that the professionals working within the local state 'disabled' their clients by acting for them rather than with them in an equal partnership. Such an analysis posed the question of how workers employed by the local state but committed to socialist values should operate. The answer was to look downwards to the local community as the worker's primary source of legitimacy and to identify and articulate the demands of working-class communities. Within this general community orientation ethnic minorities and women were to be specifically targeted on the grounds that they had not yet been fully incorporated into the system and therefore retained radical potential.

The notion that it might be in control of parts of the local state was not a prominent aspect of early New Left thinking but in the early 1980s the New Left gained political control in a few urban areas. The political programme of the New Left emphasised local economic strategies, equal opportunities, 'going local' in service delivery and strong opposition to cuts in services imposed by the central government. These themes were a reflection of the battles between the New Left, the labourist 'old guard' and the town hall bureaucracy. They also incorporated a theoretical reformulation of the relationship between the local state and capitalism. The notion of the 'dual state' serving capitalism through the process of production but responsive to working-class demands through the process of consumption provided hope that the local state could influence life chances through its role in distribution. Reaction against 'labourism' and the traditional town hall bureaucracy produced an emphasis on the incorporation of disadvantaged groups into the policy machinery. 'Going local' would help to win public support for welfare provision in the struggle for resources against central government, and a local economic strategy would act as a demonstration exercise as to what socialist economic ideas could achieve if applied at the national level.

None of these ideas stood alone; they were inter-related so that progress on one front would be accompanied by progress on others. In power each of the New Left authorities pushed forward the overall strategy in a different way. In housing great emphasis was placed on the decentralisation of local authority management, equal opportunities policies based on targets for recruitment, the promotion of housing cooperatives and resistance to attempts by the Conservative government to increase council house rents and reduce investment in public housing. Increases in rents were modified by use of the rates to subsidise council housing and capital expenditure was maintained by what was called 'creative accounting', the use of the assets of the local authority as security for new loans.

Taming the town halls and reviving the private landlord

The 1987 Conservative Party Manifesto was the result of a major reappraisal of policy and strategy. It was aimed at a further reduction of the role of local authorities as suppliers of housing and at using market forces, underpinned by a more selective system of housing assistance, to promote the supply of private rented accommodation. Home ownership retained its dominant position in the ideology of the party, but the new policy initiatives were directed mainly to the rented sector. This switch in attention from home ownership to renting may have been the result of the consequences of the expansion of home ownership becoming more apparent. The successful programme of council house sales had made a substantial contribution to an increase in home ownership (up from 57.4 per cent in 1979 to 65.6 per cent in 1987). However, officially recorded homelessness was increasing rapidly and the cost of home ownership to the Treasury in the form of tax relief on mortgage interest had increased from £2.050 billion in 1981–82 to £4.7 billion in 1985–86 (Heseltine 1987). A White Paper was published (DoE 1987) which gave more detail on the policy outlined in the 1987 manifesto. The paper set out the government's view of the impact of the policies of the past (see Document 9, page 210) and gave four aims for the future:

First to reverse the decline of private rented housing and improve its quality; second to give council tenants the right to transfer to other landlords if they choose to do so; third to target money more accurately on the most acute problems; and fourth to continue to promote the growth of owner occupation.
(DoE 1987: 3)

Private landlordism was to be promoted by removing controls on new private sector lettings and allowing investors in private landlordism to claim up to 40 per cent of their investment against their tax liability through the Business Expansion Scheme. In future housing associations were to be regarded as part of the 'independent' rented sector and would have to obtain more of their capital resources from the private sector. Nonetheless housing association tenants were linked to the local authority sector as tenants of subsidised 'social' housing, a curious term which implied that only occupants of homes owned by local authorities and housing associations received assistance from the state. A statutory procedure would be established to enable local authority tenants to change landlords, and Housing Action Trusts would be set up to take over local authority estates, improve them and then sell the stock into a variety of tenures. Grants for home improvement would be means-tested and each local authority's housing revenue accounts would be 'ring fenced' to prevent the use of local taxation to subsidise rents and, as had happened in some authorities, the use of rents to subsidise rates. Tighter controls on local authority capital expenditure, and measures to bring local authority rents more directly under central control, were to be introduced.

The 1988 Housing Act and the 1989 Local Government and Housing Act gave these proposals legislative backing but, as Margaret Thatcher (1993) recognised in her memoirs, the implementation of these acts proved troublesome. Despite extensive publicity, tenants showed little interest in leaving their local authority and few alternative landlords came forward to buy council estates. Housing Action Trusts, a vital part of the government's housing policy, encountered local opposition and gained modest momentum in seven areas only when tenants were given the right to return to their local authority when the improvements had been carried out. Between 1988 and 1995 moves towards the elimination of local authorities from the provider role came more from local authorities using large-scale *voluntary* transfer than from tenants concerned about the quality of local authority management. Large-scale voluntary transfer was promoted by local authorities, not by central government. The sale of council homes to a housing association set up to receive the dwellings allowed local authorities to keep homes for rent in their areas and produced substantial capital receipts. Between 1989 and 1995, 41 councils transferred over 185,000 homes to the housing association sector.

The crisis in owner-occupation

A distraction to the policy of privatisation was created by a crisis in owner-occupation. The active promotion of home ownership in the middle 1980s by the removal of restrictions on borrowing (Forrest and Murie 1994) produced a leap in house prices (see Table 3.1); the buyer of an average-price new house in 1980 could have expected to sell it for a profit of £50,000 in the late 1980s. Feeling confident and affluent on the basis of the current value of their dwellings, many home owners began to spend on consumer durables. In addition a large amount of equity – estimated at over £50 billion between 1985 and 1989 (Wilcox 1994) – was taken out of the accumulated value of housing by inheritance, remortgaging, downmarket moves and other conduits. The rise in consumer spending and the subsequent use of interest rates to dampen

Table 3.1 **House prices 1986–95: United Kingdom**

Year	Real change (%)
1986	11.1
1987	11.4
1988	17.0
1989	3.8
1990	−2.2
1991	−4.8
1992	−6.5
1993	3.7
1994	0.3
1995[1]	−6.3

Note:
[1]First quarter
Source: *Housing Finance* (1995)

the boom (the mortgage rate reached 15.4 per cent in February 1990), produced high mortgage payments with the house price/earnings ratio rising to 4.56 in 1989 and first-time buyers having to pay 44.2 per cent of their earnings to buy a home. A slump in house prices started in some areas, take-up of the right to buy declined (see Tables 3.2 and 3.3), repossessions escalated and 'negative equity' (homes worth less than the amount borrowed) emerged as a significant problem. In order to prevent a further downward spiral in house prices, the government introduced a 'housing market package' which provided finance to housing associations to purchase unsold homes built for owner occupation.

The Conservative Party manifesto for the 1992 general election promised to introduce a new nation-wide 'rent to mortgage' scheme enabling

Table 3.2 **Council house sales: Great Britain 1980–94**

Year	Number of sales
1980	568
1981	79 430
1982	196 430
1983	138 511
1984	100 149
1985	92 230
1986	89 250
1987	103 309
1988	160 568
1989	181 370
1990	126 214
1991	73 365
1992	63 986
1993	60 107
1994	63 241

Sources: *Housing and Construction Statistics* (1994), Wilcox (1995)

Table 3.3 **Value of dwellings sold by local authorities 1981–82 to 1993–94[1]**

Year	Value of sales (net of discounts) £ million
1981–82	1 241
1982–83	1 769
1983–84	1 316
1984–85	1 108
1985–86	1 061
1986–87	1 237
1987–88	1 697
1988–89	2 653
1989–90	2 700
1990–91	1 616
1991–92	1 086
1992–93	891
1993–94	1 034

Note:
[1]Excluding receipts from block transfers
Source: *Hansard*, October 1994 p. 533.

council tenants to take a part share in their home, gradually stepping up to full ownership; to enable housing associations to manage properties on behalf of landlords; and to allow home owners to rent rooms to lodgers free of tax. All these pledges were given legislative backing in the period 1992 to 1994 and, in addition, arrangements were made to 'market test' local authority housing management through competitive tendering. The most noteworthy change in approach came from the response of the government to the large Public Sector Borrowing Requirement caused by the recession in the 1990s. The 1992 manifesto pledge to 'maintain mortgage tax relief' was dented by the reduction of the relief to 20 per cent in 1994–95 and to 15 per cent in 1995–96. In the middle 1990s the market in owner-occupation remained stagnant despite the steep fall in house prices since 1989 and the reductions in the mortgage interest rate, which cut the cost of buying a home to less than 15 per cent of the average married couples' take-home pay. The turnover of houses in 1994 was less than half of its peak in 1989 and the number of first-time purchasers aged 25 or under had declined from 224,000 to 103,700. In 1994 the real value of the owner-occupied housing stock was down by 30 per cent on its value five years earlier (Nationwide 1995) and more than 25 per cent of those who purchased after 1987 owed more on their mortgage than could be raised by selling their homes. In addition 151,181 mortgage holders had arrears of more than 12 months (Eldridge 1994). Nonetheless, in the White Paper *Our Future Homes: Opportunity, Choice and Responsibility* (DoE 1995) the Conservative government promised to maintain its support for 'sustainable home ownership' and declared that an additional 1.5 million households would become home owners in the next ten years, assisted by a new grant to enable the tenants of housing associations to buy their homes.

Labour and the Liberal Democrats

Labour's housing policies were revised in the 1980s. The Party was opposed to the right to buy in the early years of the decade but this position gradually changed to one of supporting sales to tenants (including rent into mortgage) but insisting that the capital receipts generated should be used to replace the homes lost to the rented sector. On tax relief on mortgage interest the Party adopted the curious position of supporting it more strongly than the Conservatives, although the 1992 manifesto promised to 'seek new arrangements to enable first-time buyers to concentrate relief in the early years'. In contrast to the growing reliance of the Conservatives on selective 'personal subsidies' through the housing benefit system, Labour has placed more emphasis on direct producer subsidies (Blake and Dwelly 1994). In the 1990s Labour's attitude to private landlordism changed beyond recognition from its position in the 1980s. The Party began to see merit in a circumscribed role for the private landlord and to contemplate state support in the form of tax breaks and subsidies to landlords renting at the lower end of the market.

The Liberal Democrats have expressed a commitment to the long-term goal of abolishing tax relief on mortgage interest to new buyers and its replacement by 'housing cost relief' which would be available to both renters and buyers. Some of the savings from the abolition of tax relief on mortgage interest would be devoted to making 'housing cost relief' more generous than housing benefit. They support the right to buy but have their own version of rent into mortgage. Receipts from council house sales would be used to help to finance the 500,000 social housing units that the Party's 1992 manifesto thought it would be necessary to produce over the next five years. They have adopted similar proposals to Labour on private landlordism and would create 'partnership housing' involving state subsidies to investment in private renting accompanied by greater regulation of the sector.

A new consensus?

Housing was never integrated into the post-war consensus on social policy. The Conservatives were prepared to use local authorities to help to make good the housing shortage caused by the Second World War, but demonstrated a yearning for a market in rented accommodation in the middle 1950s and early 1970s, extolled the virtues of home ownership in an aggressive manner in the 1980s and pushed towards a free market in housing in the 1990s. Labour accepted home ownership in the late 1960s but maintained its traditional hostility to private land-lordism and in the 1980s was forced to defend council housing against a robust attack from the Conservatives. Party divisions are now less extreme and there appears to be a stronger consensus about housing issues than at any time in the past. The divisions between the parties now relate to the form and amount of state subsidy to be allocated to housing and the use of the capital receipts generated from the right to buy rather than to the promotion of a specific tenure. Labour and the Liberal Democrats want to retain an element of general producer subsidies across all tenures but specific proposals from the opposition parties became scarcer after the 1992 General Election.

In the early 1990s the Conservatives favoured a market in housing mitigated by selective subsidies to the poor, although there are tensions in the Party concerning the withdrawal of general subsidies to home ownership and a concern about the explosion in expenditure on housing benefit. This concern was reflected in *Our Future Homes* (1995), and the drive to put up rents and let housing benefit 'take the strain' was curbed in the decisions made about local authority rents for 1996–97.

References

Barnett, C. (1986) *The Audit Of War*, Macmillan, London.

Blake, J. and Dwelly, T. (1994) *Home Front*, Roof, London.

Coles, A. (1989) 'Satisfying Preference', *Housing Review*, 38 (4).

Crosland, A. (1971) *Towards a Labour Housing Policy*, Fabian Society, London.

Crossman, R. H. S. (1971) *The Diaries of a Cabinet Minister*, Vol. 1, Hamish Hamilton and Jonathan Cape, London.

Department of the Environment (1973) *Better Homes, the Next Priorities*, HMSO, London.

Department of the Environment (1987) *Housing: the government's proposals*, Cm 214, HMSO, London.

Department of the Environment and the Welsh Office (1995) *Our Future Homes: opportunity, choice, responsibility*, Cm 2901, HMSO, London.

Dunleavy, P. (1987) *Public Housing in Urban Change and Conflict*, Unit 26, The Open University, Milton Keynes.

Eldridge, B. (1994) 'Commentary On The Fourth Quarter', *Housing Finance* No 21, February.

Field, F. (1975) *Do We Need Council Houses?*, CHAS Occasional Papers 2, CHAS, Liverpool.

Foot, M. (1973) *Aneurin Bevan 1945–1960*, Davis-Poynter, London.

Forrest, R. and Murie, A. (1994) 'Home Ownership in Recession', *Housing Studies*, 9 (1), pp. 55–74.

Gilmour, I. (1992) *Dancing With Dogma: Britain Under Thatcher*, Simon and Schuster, London.

Glendinning, M. and Muthesius, S. (1994) *Tower Block: modern public housing in England, Scotland, Wales and Northern Ireland*, Yale University Press, New Haven, Connecticut.

Haines, J. (1977) *The Politics of Power*, Cape, London.

Heseltine, M. (1987) *Where There's A Will*, Hutchinson, London.

Hills, J. (ed.) (1990) *The State Of Welfare: the Welfare State in Britain since 1974*, Oxford University Press, Oxford.

Malpass, P. (1990) *Reshaping Housing Policy*, Routledge, London.

Nationwide (1995) *Housing Finance Review*, No. 1. April.

Ministry of Health (1944) *Private Enterprise Housing (The Pole Report)*, HMSO, London.

Ministry of Housing and Local Government (1965) *The Housing Programme 1965 to 1970*, Cmnd 2838, HMSO, London.

Oliver, P., Davis, I. and Bentley, I. (1981) *Dunroamin, the suburban semi and its enemies*, Barrie and Jenkins, London.

Ranelagh, J. (1991) *Thatcher's People*, Fontana, London.

Secretary of State for the Environment and the Secretary of State for Wales (1971) *Fair Deal For Housing*, Cmnd 4728, HMSO, London.

Secretary of State for the Environment and the Secretary of State for Wales (1977) *Housing Policy: A Consultative Document*, HMSO, London.

Sim, D. (1993) *British Housing Design*, Longman, London.

Simon, E. D. (1945) *Rebuilding Britain – a twenty year plan*, Victor Gollancz, London.

Thatcher, M. (1993) *The Downing Street Years*, HarperCollins, London.

Timmins, N. (1995) *The Five Giants*, HarperCollins, London.

Ungerson, C. (1994) 'Need, Equity, Ownership and the Economy' in George, V. and Millar, S. (eds) *Social Policy Towards 2000*, Routledge, London.

Wilcox, S. (1994) *Housing Finance Review 1994/5*, Joseph Rowntree Foundation, York.

CHAPTER 4

The institutional framework

Central government

The Department of the Environment

The Department of the Environment (created in 1970) is the principal government department involved in supervising the housing programme in England although its responsibilities overlap with the Department of Health and the Department of Social Security with regard to community care and housing finance. The Treasury, of course, is in the foreground of all decisions involving public expenditure.

The Department of the Environment is under the political control of the Secretary of State for the Environment, who has three ministers to assist in giving political guidance to officials. The headquarters of the department are in London and there are ten centres with offices in the regions that they oversee. In 1994 these centres were integrated with the regional offices of other departments to form the Government Offices for the Regions. The Scottish and Welsh Offices perform similar functions to the DoE for their areas but, for a number of reasons, policies can differ in emphasis to those promoted in England. The Secretaries of State for Wales and Scotland control budgets across a range of service areas and have political discretion in shaping policies according to local factors (e.g. the high proportion of local authority tenants in Scotland), national identities and regional economic circumstances (Maclennan and More 1995, Smith and Williams 1995). Wales and Scotland have been used as testing grounds for policies under consideration for introduction in England. Scottish Homes (the equivalent of the Housing Corporation in England) and the Development Board for Rural Wales pioneered the 'rent into mortgage' programme and a system of 'gro-grants' was introduced in Scotland that allowed private developers access to government grants to encourage them to build affordable accommodation. This scheme is to be introduced in England and Wales in 1996 (DoE, Welsh Office 1995).

Prior to 1971 the housing function in Northern Ireland was discharged by 66 local authorities, three new town commissioners and the Northern Ireland Housing Trust set up after the Second World War to supplement the house building activities of local government. Following the civil rights marches and the subsequent intensification of violence in 1968–69, the Cameron Commission (1969) was set up to inquire into the disturbances. It concluded that a major cause of the troubles was 'a rising sense of continuing injustice and grievance among large sections of the Catholic population in particular in Londonderry and Dungannon' centred around the 'unfair methods of allocation of houses built and let by such authorities, in particular refusals and omissions to adopt a points system'. The findings of the Cameron Commission led to the establishment of an appointed Northern Ireland Housing Executive, which by 1973 had assumed responsibility for all housing functions in the area except the registration and financing of housing associations. The Northern Ireland Housing Executive is under the direct political control of the Westminster Parliament and now manages 160,000 dwellings (Pollock 1993).

The Department of Social Security

This department has an important role in housing because it determines policy on the benefits designed to help people to pay their housing costs.

Housing benefit: In the 1980s housing benefit became a vital form of state assistance to people who rent their dwellings. Prior to 1973 there was no national mechanism available to adjust rents to income in either the public or private rented sectors although the supplementary benefits system paid the 'reasonable' rent of economically inactive people. The 1930 Housing Act contained a provision allowing local authorities to operate rent rebates – called 'differential rents' at the time – but few authorities adopted such schemes. Opposition to the means test from the working class was strong and some local authorities believed that the concentration of subsidies on the poor would lead to housing finance becoming the responsibility of the ratepayer because poor relief could be interpreted as a public assistance matter – a traditional responsibility of local government (Malpass 1990).

Despite encouragement from the Conservatives in the 1950s, rent rebate schemes made limited inroads into local authority procedures, and so the introduction of a national scheme of rent allowances and rent rebates in 1973 marked an important change in housing policy.

Housing benefit, as rent rebates and allowances came to be called, has had a troubled history and was reformed twice in the 1980s. The 1988 reform produced a scheme that was simpler than its predecessors but less generous in that the entitlement of students was abolished, young people under 18 were denied access to the scheme, those under 25 had their rights reduced and a steeper income 'taper' of eligibility was introduced. Despite these restrictions the cost of housing benefit increased. In 1987 housing benefit accounted for 35 per cent of total public expenditure on housing but by 1992 its share had climbed to 57 per cent (Hills 1993); total housing benefit expenditure grew from £4.6 billion in 1985–86 to £12.3 billion in 1994–95 (Department of Social Security 1995). Part of this increase was caused by the recession of the early 1990s – the number of recipients of housing benefit increased by 585,000 between May 1988 and February 1995 – but the main reason for the dramatic growth in expenditure was the government policy of allowing rents to increase and letting housing benefit 'take the strain'. Between 1988 and 1994 the average housing benefit paid to council tenants increased by £17.32 and private sector tenants received an additional £34, more than double the amount paid in 1988.

Housing benefit is administered by local authorities in accordance with rules set by the Department of Social Security. It covers only those who rent their homes and was received by 4.6 million households in 1993–94, about 62 per cent of all tenants. It has been estimated that about 17 per cent of those eligible to claim do not do so (Burrows, Phelps and Walentowicz 1993). Eligibility is determined in accordance with a threshold of income similar to that used for income support. If a claimant's income is equal to or less than this threshold then housing benefit will cover 100 per cent of the rent but for every pound of income above the threshold, housing benefit is reduced by 65 per cent. Those people with more than £16,000 in capital cannot receive housing benefit. Capital up to £3,000 is ignored in calculating eligibility but that between £3,000 and £16,000 is assumed to give a 'tariff income' of £1 for every £250 of capital.

For the purpose of housing benefit calculations, rent excludes certain charges (e.g. fuel) but includes some payments for services such as lifts, entry phones, cleaning of communal areas and emergency alarm systems in accommodation designed or adapted for elderly, sick or disabled people. There are complex procedures for determining the amount of private sector rent on which housing benefit will be paid and many claimants have discovered that the rent on which benefit is assessed is not the rent demanded by the landlord (Burrows, Phelps and Walentowicz 1993).

'Perverse' incentives: Until the current housing benefit scheme was introduced in April 1988 beneficiaries had to pay a proportion of any increase in rent following a move to a better house with a higher rent but, after 1988, all the additional rent became eligible for housing benefit if the tenant's income was low. Some commentators believed that this created a 'perverse incentive' for 'upmarket' moves into more expensive accommodation but a study of 39 private tenants who had moved home demonstrated that 'the availability of benefit was not the main reason why people moved and generally it acted as a constraint' (Kemp *et al.* 1994: 2). This research scotched the notion of 'upmarketing' but a new 'perverse incentive' was identified by market economists. It was alleged that tenants claiming full housing benefit had no inducement to bargain with their landlords (Clark 1994) and therefore the market in rented housing was not working efficiently. This idea was accepted by the Chancellor of the Exchequer and local caps on housing benefit were announced to be implemented in early 1996. Full housing benefit

will be paid only if the rent is in the bottom half of the local rental market. Prospective tenants can apply for a 'pre-tenancy determination' to discover whether their potential claim for housing benefit will be restricted by the regulations, and are expected to use this information to bargain with the landlord.

Income support: The payment of the mortgage interest of home owners receiving national assistance was introduced in 1948. Today the interest paid by income support is calculated on the amount originally borrowed to purchase the home or to undertake repairs and limited improvements. Remortgages are not eligible for assistance.

In the late 1980s the government began to reduce the help available to mortgage holders claiming income support. In 1987, only 50 per cent of interest payments became eligible for income support for the first 16 weeks of a claim and in the early 1990s the ceiling on the mortgage eligible for support was lowered. Nonetheless the estimated annual 'expenditure' on mortgage interest continued to grow (from £553 million in 1990 to £1,217 million in 1993). The budget statement of November 1994 announced that from April 1995 the statutory limit on loans eligible for assistance would be £100,000. In addition anyone taking out a new mortgage after October 1995 would no longer have their mortgage payments covered by income support for the first 39 weeks of a claim; they would be expected to insure against loss of income. Existing borrowers receive no help for the first two months, then half the full interest is paid for the next 18 weeks.

Housing agencies

The central government has a limited role in the supply of accommodation. It owns accommodation for prison officers, medical staff and the armed forces. In 1989 it also owned 22 resettlement units for homeless single people but, through the Resettlement Agency, most of these units have been closed and replaced by housing association provision (Resettlement Agency 1995). Thus, in order to ensure that the housing needs of its citizens are met, the central state must work through a number of semi-autonomous agencies.

The financial institutions

The origins of building societies can be traced to the land buyers' society formed in Norfolk in 1640 to buy large tracts of land by means of a group of people 'laying their purses together' and then dividing the land into small plots so that cottages could be built. The idea of pooling resources in order to secure home ownership was revived in the late eighteenth century through working class self-help groups known as 'terminating societies'. A number of workers formed a society and agreed to pay into a fund to build houses. When sufficient finance had been raised to acquire a house (many were erected by the labour of the members) lots were drawn to determine which member of the society should move into the new dwelling. Payments into the fund continued until every member of the society was able to own a house and then the society was terminated. In order to speed up the housing of its members some societies allowed people who did not require homes to join the association and paid interest on the investment. These societies were called 'permanent' and had become the most common form of building society by the start of the twentieth century.

Building societies were successful in attracting the savings of working people; offices were accessible and links were made between saving with a society and the opportunity to obtain a mortgage when needed. In 1900 there were 2,250 building societies but by 1994 – through mergers and the occasional financial collapse – their number had declined to 81.

The growth of owner-occupation helped building societies become major financial institutions but in the 1970s criticisms of their activities were voiced. It was alleged that their mutuality had become a myth and that unaccountable directors rather than savers and mortgage-holders controlled the movement (Boddy 1980). The societies were accused of being too cautious in granting mortgages, of wasting resources through the proliferation of branch offices, of a reluctance to lend in certain geographical areas and of operating a cartel in fixing the mortgage interest rate. The Conservative government attempted to deal with some of these criticisms by exposing the societies to more intense competition from banks, specialist mortgage companies and other financial institutions. In June 1980 the restriction on bank lending for house purchase (the so-called 'corset') was ended.

The movement of the banks and specialist mortgage lenders into the mortgage market led to the breakdown of the building society cartel; by 1987 building societies were responsible for only 51 per cent of net mortgage lending compared to 79 per cent in 1980 (Boleat and Taylor 1993). The societies argued that if banks were to be allowed into their business, then societies should be granted more scope to diversify. The Building Societies Act 1986 enabled such diversification to develop: societies were allowed to raise more funds from wholesale markets (i.e. to borrow from institutions as well as individuals), to purchase land, to act as developers, to set up estate agencies and to offer cheque clearing facilities.

The emphasis placed on the spirit of competition in lending helped to produce the crisis in the housing market; in 1991 75,540 property repossessions were carried out because of mortgage default. The government attempted to reduce repossessions and restore confidence in the housing market by agreeing a package of measures with the financial institutions. Provision was made for mortgage interest payments, paid as part of income support, to be sent directly to the lending agencies and funds earmarked for housing associations were brought forward to allow associations to purchase unsold properties. In return lenders agreed not to repossess properties where income support paid mortgage interest and to introduce a number of mortgage rescue schemes. This agreement between the mortgage lenders and the government illustrates how the financial muscle of the state (in this case its control over housing association finance and income support) can be used to influence the operation of the housing market. It was not the first time that the state had intervened directly to assist the building societies in coping with fluctuations in the housing market. In 1974 the government provided the societies with bridging loans to keep the rate of interest stable and in the late 1970s, in order to prevent house price inflation, government imposed an annual ceiling on new loans.

When the market share of the building societies in lending to home owners began to decline in the middle 1980s, they started to show an interest in what they called 'special housing markets' (Smallwood 1992). Nationwide Anglia helped to finance Quality Street, an organisation set up in 1987 to supply rented accommodation at market rents. The Halifax and Nationwide Anglia societies formed a partnership with the Lovell Group to set up PROBE, which sought to provide finance and expertise for urban renewal. Some societies became involved in funding housing associations to enable them to obtain the private sector resources demanded by the 1988 Housing Act. Between 1989 and 1993 building societies provided £1109.2 million in loans to housing associations (Pryke and Whitehead 1993).

Building societies have traditionally been mutual organisations. Mutuality means that the association is owned by its customers (borrowers and lenders) who are entitled to vote at the annual general meeting. In fact mutuality is somewhat of a myth because the size of the majority of societies (see Table 4.1) makes it difficult for the members to exercise any real control over 'their' society and few societies make it easy for members to participate in the activities of the movement.

Table 4.1 **Building Societies: 1994**

Number of Societies	Assets £m	% of total
5	177 345	58.8
5	70 717	23.4
10	36 708	12.2
20	13 096	4.3
41	3 893	1.3
Total 81	310 759	100.0

Source: Adapted from BSA estimates (1995)

Private landlords

At the end of the nineteenth century over 90 per cent of households rented from private landlords. By 1989 only 8.6 per cent did so; a low rate of private renting compared to other European countries (Stephens 1994). Rent control played an important role in the decline of private landlordism but other factors have made a contribution. The tax regime in which private landlordism has operated has been austere in comparison to investment in owner-occupation and other forms of assets; in the past landlords have been subject to tax on rental income (abolished for owner-occupiers in 1963), they have had to pay capital gains tax and they have been unable to claim the depreciation allowances available on other forms of investment. The poor reputation of private landlordism has also contributed to its decline; it is still associated in the public mind with the harassment of tenants, insecurity of tenure, high rents and poor standards of maintenance.

The Conservative Party made a lukewarm attempt to revive the private landlord sector in the early 1980s. The Housing Act 1980 transferred all remaining controlled tenancies (about 400,000) into regulation and in a move calculated to attract major builders and financial institutions into private renting, 'approved' landlords, who built new properties for rent, were allowed to let them as 'assured' tenancies. 'Assured' tenants had a form of security based on that for business premises but could not apply for the determination of a 'fair' rent. In contrast 'protected shorthold' tenancies could be offered by all private landlords. They were subject to 'fair' rents and at the end of the fixed term of letting – which had to be more than a year – the presumption was that the landlord was entitled to vacant possession.

Assured tenancies were not immediately successful in attracting major institutional investors into the rental market and by 1984 only 210 properties had been let on this form of tenure (Smith 1989). The Housing and Planning Act 1986 extended the 'assured' tenancies of 'approved' landlords to improved properties but radical reform of the tenancy law was postponed until the 1988 Housing Act.

Landlords and tenants: A study by the Office of Population Censuses and Surveys provides an account of private landlordism as it existed prior to the 1988 Housing Act. It revealed that in 1988 there were 1.7 million private tenancies with 40 per cent to be found in London and the South East. The most common type of landlord was an individual who was not resident in the property (53 per cent) and 25 per cent of tenants rented from an employer. There was great diversity in the sector but the progressive decline of private landlordism had left it operating in only two significant markets. Private landlords provided accommodation for elderly people with long-term tenancies: 'the typical tenant in a regulated tenancy with a registered rent was a female over 60' (Gay 1991). The more profitable sector consisted of renting to single people and couples without children. These geographically mobile groups were either unable to afford home ownership or were willing to accept lower levels of space in return for living close to their place of work or study and being free of the substantial transfer costs that home owners are obliged to pay when they move house. There was a rapid turnover of tenants in this sector, and only a small minority of people taking up new tenancies in 1987–88 (6.8 per cent) had registered a 'fair' rent.

The 1988 Housing Act allowed the vast majority of lettings made after 15 January 1989 to be either 'assured' or 'assured shorthold'. Although the former system of 'approved' landlords was abolished, 'assured' tenancies seem to have been designed for the housing association and company landlord sector. Market rents are payable but the landlord can only gain repossession on the mandatory or discretionary grounds specified in the Act which, although more extensive than allowed by former legislation, do provide the tenant with some protection. 'Assured shorthold' tenancies must be for more than six months and at the end of the specified term a court must grant vacant possession to the landlord as long as the tenant has been given two months written notice of the ending of the tenancy agreement. Rents are determined by the free market but in certain circumstances the tenant can apply to a rent assessment committee for the determination of what the market rent ought to be, taking into account the limited security of tenure available to the tenant.

A revival in private landlordism?   In the early 1990s a new scheme was introduced to stimulate the sector. The Housing Associations as Managing Agents programme (HAMA) enables housing associations to manage properties acquired in a safe and acceptable condition on behalf of a private landlord. Such properties are let to homeless households and the landlord is given a guarantee that the rent will be paid, vacant possession will be available when required and the property will be returned in good order. Under HAMA PLUS, housing associations lease properties in need of repair from the owners for a period of two to three years and let them directly to homeless people nominated by the local authority. The owner does not receive a full market rent for such properties because the housing association has to carry out essential repairs and improvements.

There appears to have been a modest revival of private renting in the 1990s. Although the figures need to be interpreted with caution because the definition of privately rented includes rent-free dwellings attached to jobs and holiday lets (Downs, Holmans and Small 1994) the Department of the Environment has estimated that the number of private rented homes in England increased from 1.7 million in 1988 to over 2 million in 1994 (*Hansard* 26/5/94; DoE, Welsh Office 1995). Whether this is due to the positive measures introduced by the government or to the crisis in owner-occupation – with owners letting unsaleable property on a short-term basis – is difficult to determine. Research by Crook, Hughes and Kemp (1995) has revealed that about one in ten of all current letting are the homes of individual landlords that they have been unable or are reluctant to sell.

The future of private landlordism appears rosier than at any time since 1915. Many of the tax advantages of its major competitor, home ownership, have been eroded, the fall in house prices has dented confidence in the investment value of owner occupation, the Labour Party has showed signs of abandoning its traditional hostility to the sector and there are indications that young people are more favourably disposed to private renting than in the past. In 1989 only four per cent of people in their early twenties saw private renting as their ideal tenure but this figure had risen to 11 per cent in 1993 (Coles and Taylor 1993).

Housing associations

In order to understand the character of housing associations today it is necessary to explore the forces that have shaped what has been called the 'third arm' of housing.

Diversity has been an important element in the development of voluntary housing (Baker 1976). This is reflected in the different financial orientations and the multiplicity of purposes represented in the housing association movement today.

Some associations have their origins in charitable activity (e.g the Peabody Trust, the Guinness Trust); others in the voluntary restriction of the return on investment to 5 per cent; and a few are the product of 'exchange' professionals, such as solicitors and estate agents, who established 'cost-rent' societies in the early 1960s. The list of the objectives pursued by different housing associations is a long one. In the nineteenth century benevolent manufacturers established housing trusts in the conviction that a healthy, contented workforce was a productive one; visionary planners established 'public utility' societies to promote the garden city idea; and charity workers, who believed that the urban working class needed moral guidance, also became involved in the movement. In the twentieth century associations began to specialise in making provision for various categories of people in housing need (e.g. elderly people, disabled people, single women over 40) and mutual aid organisations started to develop.

Housing associations and the state: Throughout most of its history the voluntary housing movement received little direct assistance from the state. In 1866 the Labouring Classes' Dwellings Act permitted the Public Works Loan Commissioners to make loans to associations at a low interest rate. The 1919 Housing and Planning Act allowed local authorities to transfer their central government subsidies to associations, and the 1936 Housing Act gave local government wide powers to provide financial assistance to the sector, including grants and loans. Few local authorities used this 'enabling' procedure.

In the early 1960s, in an attempt to demonstrate that dwellings could be provided for rent without direct subsidy, loan capital was made available at a preferential rate to stimulate cost-rent and co-ownership societies. This resource was distributed by the National Federation of Housing Societies in order to reduce reliance on local authorities as a source of capital. The Housing Corporation was created in 1964 to supervise the activities of the associations and to distribute loans, but it was not until the early 1970s that the housing association movement received substantial assistance from the state. The 1974 Housing Act represented a watershed in the history of housing associations and was described by the Department of the Environment as a new 'charter for the housing association movement'. It introduced a range of capital and revenue subsidies, the most important being Housing Association Grant (HAG), designed to cover any deficit between the costs of a scheme and the income that could be generated by charging 'fair' rents. In order to be eligible for such grants housing associations had to register with the Housing Corporation in accordance with the Corporation's rules on management. The 1974 Act had a dramatic impact on the fortunes of the voluntary housing movement. Smith comments:

The new system triggered off remarkable activity – the associations soon exceeded the Housing Corporation's target of some 30,000 new dwellings, built or improved, for the financial year 1975–76; and, together with housing association schemes approved by local authorities, the voluntary movement obtained the go-ahead to start no fewer than 53,000 homes, a record figure that has not been repeated.

(Smith 1989: 231)

The groundwork for the 1974 Housing Act had been laid by a Conservative government, but the act was steered through Parliament by Labour. Although the two parties may have had different expectations of a voluntary housing movement they were in agreement that a non-profit rental sector, independent of local government, was necessary. This consensus was not shared by the Conservative government led by Mrs Thatcher. In the 1980s the housing association development programme was cut, producing a decline in housing production (see Table 4.2), associations were directed towards low cost home ownership schemes and the tenants of non-charitable housing associations were given the right to buy, with only an amendment in the House of Lords preventing a similar right being granted to the tenants of charitable associations. The government regarded housing associations as part of the 'unproductive' public sector with their loans from the Housing Corporation contributing to the Public Sector Borrowing Requirement and their capital grants adding to the burden of taxation.

The 1988 Housing Act transformed the nature of housing associations and paved the way for the expansion of their role as part of the 'private' sector. The Act placed all new housing association tenants under the legal regime governing tenant–landlord relationships in the private landlord sector; pleas from the National Federation of Housing Associations for a special housing association tenure were ignored. The right to buy was abolished for new housing association tenants, making

Table 4.2 **Housing associations: new completions and
total rented stock 1985–94**

	New completions	Total rented stock
	(000s)	
1985	13.1	548
1986	12.6	565
1987	12.6	586
1988	12.8	614
1989	13.9	651
1990	16.9	706
1991	19.7	737
1992	25.2	801
1993	34.2	870
1994	34.2	943

Source: Housing Finance (1995)

private sector investment in housing association stock more attractive,
and housing associations had to rely on private finance for a proportion
of their investment. These measures, together with the reduction in the
rate of HAG, meant that housing associations began to assume the
characteristics of private landlords.

Affordability: The intention of the government in introducing the
1988 Housing Bill into Parliament was clear: it wanted market rents
with housing benefit available to ensure that market rents were affordable to low income groups. However, lobbying by the National Federation of Housing Associations managed to secure agreement to the
introduction of the 'Tenants' Guarantee'. This guarantee, issued by the
Housing Corporation, stated:

where housing accommodation has been provided with the help of public
subsidy . . . it is intended to be accessible to people on low incomes, whether
or not they are in paid employment or in receipt of housing benefit. Associations are therefore expected to set and maintain their rents at levels which are
within the reach of those in low paid employment. This will usually entail
setting rents below market level. Associations should not discriminate in their
rent setting between those who are eligible for housing benefit and others.
                                                    (Housing Corporation 1991: 6)

In the absence of any precise definition of 'accessible to people on low
incomes' from either the government or the Housing Corporation, the
National Federation of Housing Associations supplied its own specification. Gross rents (without taking housing benefit into account) should
not, in general, absorb more than 22 per cent of net household income.
This figure was adopted because it was just below the average percentage of income spent by owner-occupiers on housing at the time and it
was argued that social sector tenants should not pay more than owner-
occupiers.
    The Federation hoped that its measure of affordability would persuade

the government to maintain the value of the grants paid as producer subsidies to housing associations. The strategy failed and housing association grant was reduced in the 1990s. The government argued that housing benefit enabled households with low incomes to afford higher rents and refused to give any formal, specific definition of affordability although the Housing Minister did state in April 1993 that the DoE assumed, when making decisions on grant rates, that 35 per cent of a housing association tenant's income should be spent on rent. The Housing Corporation (1993: 1), in line with the stance of the government about the role of housing benefit, has claimed that 'it is the rent actually paid after the receipt of targeted benefit which is of prime interest and relevance to housing practitioners' and therefore affordability should be assessed by comparing rents minus housing benefit with income.

The National Federation of Housing Associations adopted a new measure of affordability in 1993. Rents are affordable 'if the majority of working households taking up new tenancies are not caught in the poverty trap (because of their dependency on housing benefit) or are paying more than 25 per cent of their net income in rent'. Using this measure 70 per cent of housing association rents failed the affordability test in the second quarter of 1995 (NFHA 1995).

Residualisation: In response to the homelessness crisis of the late 1980s housing associations were encouraged by the government to target their activities on helping homeless people and to produce more dwellings for each pound of government subsidy. The injection of private finance into housing associations, the 'housing market package' and the voluntary transfer of stock from local authorities combined to boost the number of homes owned by housing associations (see Table 4.2). Associations moved away from provision for elderly people and single people below pension age towards the provision of family accommodation. In 1989–90 29 per cent of new lettings were made to adults with children but by 1992–93 this figure had increased to 42 per cent (Housing Corporation 1994) and the proportion of lettings to statutory homeless people increased from 12 per cent in 1990–91 to 25 per cent in 1993–94 (Wilcox 1995). There is evidence that the space standards of new housing association dwellings declined. Research by Karn and Sheridan (1994) disclosed that the number of dwellings built at below the standards set down in the Parker Morris report (1961) had increased from 53 per cent in 1988–89 to 62 per cent in 1992.

In 1994 there were 2,179 associations – excluding co-ownership societies – registered with the Housing Corporation in England (Housing Corporation 1995). They owned 778,000 homes and managed 57,300 dwellings for other landlords. The largest association, North British, managed 31,790 dwellings but 91 per cent of housing associations owned less than a thousand properties. The 13 largest associations with over 10,000 homes owned a quarter of all the housing association stock.

Local authorities

Public rented housing reached its zenith in 1979 when 31.5 per cent of the housing stock was owned by local authorities. The right to buy, combined with reductions in the capital available for new houses, reduced public housing to 22 per cent of the national stock in 1995 (see Table 4.3). In 1994 only 500 new local authority homes were started. Even so, local authorities are still the major suppliers of rented housing and provide accommodation for a far higher proportion of the population than in most other western European countries (Stephens 1994). In 1993 there were 457 local authorities in England, Wales and Scotland with housing powers although, by 1998, this figure will change as new unitary authorities are created (Jackson and Lavender 1995).

Local authorities are multi-purpose organisations with many responsibilities. In the unitary districts in England and in the London boroughs they have powers relating to education, housing, personal social services, leisure services, highways, physical planning and environmental health, powers that are divided in county/district areas. In relationship to housing the most significant aspect of the current allocation of powers between the tiers in county/district areas is the administrative separation of the housing and social services functions.

Strategic enablers?   The White Paper *Housing: The Government's Proposals* (1987), having reviewed the history of local authority housing (see Document 9 on page 210), announced that 'provision of housing by local authorities should gradually be diminished, and alternative

Table 4.3 **Dwellings constructed: England and Wales 1919–94**

Years	Local authority	Private builders	Total
1919–24	176 914	221 543	398 457
1925–29	326 353	673 344	999 697
1930–34	286 350	804 251	1090 601
1935–39	346 840	1269 912	1616 752
1940–44	75 500	75 500	151 000
1945–49	432 098	126 317	558 415
1950–54	912 805	228 616	1141 421
1955–59	688 585	623 024	1311 609
1960–64	545 729	878 756	1424 485
1965–69	761 174	983 338	1744 512
1970–74	536 560	830 047	1366 607
1975–79	640 658	667 430	1308 088
1980–84	294 002	573 630	867 632
1985–89	90 355	858 137	948 492
1990–94	29 142	772 251[1]	801 393

Note
[1] including housing association dwellings
Sources: Halsey (1988), Housing and Construction Statistics

forms of tenure and tenant choice should increase'. Since the publication of this paper the movement of local authorities away from direct provision has been encouraged in a number of ways:

- The imposition of compulsory competitive tendering for housing management services: under the Local Government Act 1988 all local authorities must subject their housing management system to 'market testing' by dividing the 'client' function from the 'service' function and inviting tenders for the 'service' function from the private sector.
- The use of the discretionary powers of the Secretary of State for the Environment to penalise local authorities who continue to promote the provider role and to reward those who champion the 'enabling' role.
- The introduction of a statutory 'rent to mortgage' scheme under the Housing and Urban Development Act 1993, which complemented the right to buy by enabling tenants to buy part of their home on payment of an initial sum which must be at least the amount they can borrow on a mortgage with repayments equal to their existing rent.
- Restrictions on capital expenditure on the local authority housing stock to promote the voluntary transfer of dwellings so that finance can be made available for improvement.
- The White Paper *Our Future Homes* (DoE/Welsh Office 1995) gave support to the establishment of local housing companies to take over local authority houses, stating that such companies 'would need clearly to be in the private sector'.

All these initiatives have been designed to move local authorities away from providing dwellings, but local government has been granted only limited additional powers to assist in the fulfilment of a strategic enabling role. Local authorities have been expected to use their existing capacities and assets in order to discharge their assigned functions. The Audit Commission (1992: 23) has provided guidance on how this might be done. It recommends that since 'a knowledge of local needs is an essential foundation of an effective housing strategy' then local authorities should develop an information base to cover rehousing needs. Having assessed local needs in a comprehensive manner, the local authority should explore all the potential sources for funding new initiatives, including the sale of its land holdings. It should also examine all the methods available of making the best use of the existing 'social' housing stock, including action to reduce voids, better use of housing association nominations, selective stock transfer, and cash incentives to encourage tenants to move, thereby creating vacancies for people in housing need. The cost/benefit effectiveness of these measures should be considered in relationship to an examination of ways to increase the supply of low cost housing and to improve conditions in the private sector.

Housing cooperatives

Housing cooperatives can take a variety of forms and it is difficult to make firm distinctions between the different types of co-op and to decide where cooperatives end and other forms of housing organisation begin. In essence a cooperative consists of a group of people who own or manage their homes on a collective basis. The purest form is a 'par-value' cooperative where each member owns an equal nominal share in the capital of the organisation.

Housing cooperatives have received some encouragement from all the main political parties because each party has seen virtue in the cooperative form of organisation. The Conservative Party sponsored coownership societies in the early 1960s as a method of spreading owner occupation; it was thought that some of the people unable to secure an individual mortgage might have more opportunity to become home owners if they pooled their resources. Most of these coownership societies were wound up in the 1980s and their assets were sold to the individual members. The 1986 Housing and Planning Act – in a move calculated to assist in the break-up of local authority housing and to create a number of small organisations competing in a market economy – provided start-up finance for co-ops and required local authorities to respond to any group of tenants who wished to form a co-op.

In the early 1970s Labour declared a commitment to cooperatives, seeing them as an embodiment of anti-capitalist values, and some Labour controlled authorities, notably Islington, promoted co-ops in the 1980s as symbols of the communitarian ethic of participatory socialism. The Liberal Democrats have also given co-ops local support as part of their commitment to a participatory democracy. Nevertheless, despite the all-party endorsement of co-ops the 'sector has grown slowly and unevenly' (Clapham and Kintrea 1995). An estimate made by the Department of the Environment in 1986–87 (using a comprehensive definition of a cooperative but excluding self-build organisations) found that there were only 487 co-ops in existence in England and Wales (McCafferty and Riley 1989). A range of causes for this slow progress can be put forward (Clapham and Kintrea 1995) but foremost is the historical supremacy of owner-occupation in the Conservative Party and state housing in the Labour Party. Whereas the dominant political parties in Britain during the twentieth century have offered support to the co-operative ideal, they have not given it a place at the centre of housing policy. The communitarian philosophy at the heart of the cooperative ideal has not had the same political appeal as individualism and municipal collectivism.

Most of the development finance for housing cooperatives comes through the Housing Corporation or its equivalents in Scotland and Wales. In return for this finance, cooperatives must conform to the monitoring procedures established by the Housing Corporation.

Estate management boards

The cooperative housing movement tends to blame the shortage of co-ops on the lack of support from central government, but it would be unrealistic to suppose that a large percentage of tenants desire the level of involvement in management necessary to run an organisation according to the purest cooperative principles. The Priority Estates Project developed a less intensive form of tenant involvement – estate management boards. These involved a formal partnership between tenants and the local authority, with the local authority retaining ownership of the dwellings but tenants and local councillors managing an estate as a joint venture with local authority officers often seconded to work for the EMB. The precise responsibilities of the EMB were subject to local agreement but they usually involved the use of an estate budget – negotiated with the council – for carrying out repairs, collecting rents and recovering arrears.

In 1994 estate management boards and tenant management cooperatives were subsumed under a wider government initiative known as the Right to Manage – a relaunch of a scheme first introduced in 1986. Regulations issued under the Leasehold Reform, Housing and Urban Development Act 1993 proclaimed a 'right to manage' for tenant management organisations. Under these regulations any properly constituted tenant-run body with an acceptable constitution serving a defined geographical area and with a membership of at least 20 per cent of tenants in the area can serve a right to manage notice on the authority. Serving a valid notice starts a programme of training and support for the creation of a tenant management organisation (TMO). Following a feasibility study and a development programme, assisted by an agency from the Department of the Environment's approved list, the appropriate local authority, using specified criteria, decides whether or not a proposed TMO is competent to assume management responsibilities. A ballot of tenants is then conducted and if there is a majority for the TMO then it can start to operate (Scott *et al.* 1994). Officers cannot be seconded from the local authority to help to manage an estate, which has meant that the spirit of partnership, a characteristic of EMBs, has been diluted (Crossley 1995).

Resource distribution

The annual public expenditure round

The government determines the total amount of public expenditure, and its distribution between various purposes, on a rolling three year programme. The process begins in early summer with reports to the Cabinet from the Treasury ministers on trends in public expenditure, the state of the economy and the implications for taxation of projected public expenditure. A global figure for public expenditure is agreed and bilateral meetings between the Chief Secretary to the Treasury and the spending ministries begin in order to agree the allocation to each sector. Any disputes are settled by a Cabinet committee or, if necessary, by the full Cabinet. Civil servants expect ministers to fight for the programmes of their ministries. During his period of office as Secretary of State for the Environment Kenneth Baker resisted an attempt by the Treasury to cut £650 million from the local authority housing maintenance programme, declaring that it was his job 'to make sure that colleagues understood the housing crisis facing the country' (Baker 1993: 145). Even Nicholas Ridley, not known for his enthusiasm for public expenditure, attempted to ensure that the capital receipts generated by the sale of council houses were used for housing purposes (Lawson 1992). When agreement has been reached, the Department of the Environment has to allocate its resources between competing objectives and agencies. Only an outline of this complex, opaque and fluid process can be presented here.

Capital programmes: Since 1977 each local housing authority has been obliged to submit a housing investment programme to the Department of the Environment. This programme sets out the housing needs of the area and the action proposed by the authority to meet these needs in the form of a housing strategy and a bid for a borrowing approval. The sum of local authority bids for resources has always exceeded the funds that the Treasury is prepared to devote to housing and hence the Department of the Environment has had to devise a number of rationing mechanisms. In the past the major instrument for resource allocation was the General Needs Index (GNI): a computation of the relative need of each area for housing provision, which took into account such factors as the number of unfit properties and the number of homeless people in an area. The regional officials of the Department of the Environment were allowed some discretion to depart from the GNI in order to allow for some of the unquantifiable factors in the generation of housing need and the peaks and troughs in local housing programmes. However, during the 1980s, the GNI became less relevant to the resources at the disposal of each local authority to meet housing needs.

When the right to buy gained momentum in the early 1980s, and building societies started to provide mortgages to tenants who wished to buy their houses, local authorities found that they were receiving substantial capital resources. The Treasury took action to ensure that an increasing proportion of these capital receipts were deducted from the global sum available to local government in borrowing approvals but local authorities could use their capital receipts for capitalised repairs, spend the interest on accumulated receipts and the 'cascade' principle enabled remaining receipts to be used, although not in the year that they were generated. The impact of this system was to delay and channel the spending of receipts rather than to stop their use.

The main weakness of the procedures (apart from the fact that they were so complex that few people understood their impact) was that there was no effective mechanism to ensure that the allocation to individual local authorities reflected its ability to generate income from land and council house sales. The result was that housing expenditure in the middle 1980s had almost no relationship to housing need. This situation was partially rectified in 1986 by 'top slicing' of the total sum available for national borrowing approvals to finance special initiatives such as the Estate Action programme but it was not until the passing of the 1989 Local Government and Housing Act that a clear legal basis was available on which the Department of the Environment could adjust borrowing approvals to the sums raised in capital receipts by each local authority. Unfortunately those local authorities who felt that their resources would automatically reflect their needs were to be disappointed. In 1990 the role of the GNI in distributing borrowing approvals was diminished. It was announced that, in future, 60 per cent of the borrowing allocation (with the possibility of a move to 100 per cent) would be determined by the discretion of the ministers and that such discretion would be exercised in accordance with efficiency and effectiveness in meeting housing needs. Indicators of efficiency and effectiveness included 'the quality of the proposals submitted, past performance, private sector involvement, commitment to enabling housing association activity and to tenants' participation, as well as specific problems or need and existing commitments' (Department of the Environment, 1994: 93).

Even if the local housing officers are successful in convincing the Secretary of State for the Environment of their competence in conforming to the housing policy of the government and gain a high borrowing approval, this does not necessarily mean that all of the resources obtained will be spent on housing. A local authority does not receive a specific allocation for investment in housing but a sum reflecting the government's assessment of how much it needs and deserves to spend on capital investment across *all* its activities, minus a proportion of the capital receipts that a local authority is anticipated to raise in the relevant financial year. Although some aspects of the housing programme are protected by specific capital grants (clearance and improvement), and by supplementary credit approvals earmarked for a special purpose (usually subject to a competitive bidding process), most of the schemes for housing investment must compete with other projects in the local political arena. There is no research to indicate the success of housing officials in obtaining an appropriate share of the capital resources available at the local level.

Revenue spending: Although the government controls revenue allocations to local authorities through different mechanisms to those used for capital allocations, the distinction between revenue and capital (capital meaning expenditure on durable items and revenue meaning resources consumed during a financial year) is somewhat arbitrary: local authorities can finance capital items from revenue, capital expenditure generates revenue implications in terms of loan charges and capital receipts can be invested to produce revenue (Malpass *et al.* 1993).

Every year the Department of the Environment determines the amount of 'subsidy' it will contribute to the yearly management and maintenance costs (revenue spending) of local authority housing. This process is almost as complex and opaque as that used for capital spending and, once again, only a simplified outline of the procedures can be presented.

Each local authority is required to maintain a Housing Revenue Account (HRA) and is obliged to take all reasonable steps to ensure that it is in balance at the end of the financial year. Until 1990 the HRA was not 'ring fenced'; many local authorities subsidised the HRA from the rates/poll tax and in some local authorities the HRA produced a dividend for the rate and poll tax payers. Under the Local Government and Housing Act 1989, the HRA was 'ring fenced' in England and Wales: any cross-subsidisation was forbidden unless expressly approved by the Secretary of State. However, the issue of what ought to count as a legitimate element of the HRA was not clearly set out and the inclusion of 'welfare' expenditure (such as the costs of warden services) is still a contested issue.

The HRA maintained by each authority consists of a debit side and a credit side. On the credit side are rental income, the interest on capital receipts obtained through sales of land and dwellings, and 'subsidy' from the government. On the debit side are management and maintenance costs, loan charges and, after 1990, the amount spent on the housing benefit awarded to council tenants. The inclusion of housing benefit paid to council tenants aroused controversy on the grounds that it was unfair to force council tenants to meet the cost of 'poverty relief' when other tenants and owner-occupiers are not expected to make a contribution.

The amount of central government 'subsidy' awarded to each local authority is determined, not in accordance with the real HRA, but in relationship to a hypothetical account devised by the Department of the Environment. The Department makes assumptions about the increase in rent that ought to be made by each local authority, taking into account the market value of dwellings in different areas (for 1995–96 the guideline was an average increase of £2.28) and makes an estimate of what each authority ought to spend on management and maintenance. If, after allowing for loan charges, housing benefit costs and other items, the hypothetical account is in deficit then a 'subsidy' is paid. Local authorities know the amount of assistance that they will receive from central government before they finally decide the rent that they will charge their tenants. They are not obliged to follow the rent increase guidelines set out by the Department of the Environment and, in recent years, many authorities have imposed increases above the central guidelines in order to increase spending on the management and maintenance of their stock.

Allocations to housing associations

The assistance given by central government to housing associations consists of an allocation of resources to the Housing Corporation (Scotland and Wales have their own corporations – Scottish Homes and Tai Cymru) in accordance with the Approved Development Programme (ADP). The total government resources allocated to the ADP is announced in the budget statement in November. Allocations have declined from £2,370 million in 1992–93 to £1,028 million in 1996–97. The balance of this programme is determined by the political priorities of the government; housing for home ownership through schemes such as do-it-yourself shared ownership and the tenant's incentive scheme are planned to take a larger share of the available resources in the future: 28 per cent by 1997–98 (Department of the Environment 1995).

The Housing Corporation distributes funds to housing associations. Each summer, as part of the annual spending round, the Department of the Environment determines the grant rate for HAG, that is, the average percentage of the total cost of any housing scheme that will be met by a capital grant from the government: this was set at 58 per cent for 1995–96 and 1996–97. It also fixes Total Cost Indicators (the limits on the cost of different schemes that will be met by HAG) and the cash limit for Housing Corporation spending. When the Housing Corporation receives its cash limit from the government it allocates resources between housing associations and local authority areas. This is done according to criteria such as need as determined by the Housing Needs Index (similar to the GNI used for local authorities); the extent to which housing association bids minimise the demands on HAG by using the association's own resources and negotiated subsidies from local authorities; the priorities set out by local authorities in their housing investment strategies; the total public subsidy involved in a proposed scheme; and, for the first time in 1996–97, the rent to be charged. The balance between these criteria has not been specified, but local authorities have been promised that at least 80 per cent of their entitlement under the HNI formula will be spent in their area.

Since 1992 the Department of the Environment has attempted to achieve closer integration between the housing association programme and local authority activity. The distribution of resources to housing associations is now considered by ministers in conjunction with local authority housing investment bids, and 20 per cent of the allocation to each local authority area is determined by the performance of the local authority as an 'enabler' of housing association activity.

Tax expenditures

Traditionally, decisions about public expenditure have been announced at a different time to changes in taxation; the former have been made in November/December whereas the latter have been made in March/April as part of the budget statement. In 1993, for the first time, an integrated tax/expenditure statement was given in November.

Although government spending is more important to 'social' housing than the pattern of taxation, the fiscal system can have a direct influence on the need for 'social' housing: tax allowances to encourage desirable behaviour offer an alternative to direct state subsidies as a method of achieving housing objectives. The operation of tax allowances can have an important impact on the housing market, as was demonstrated in 1988 when the government restricted tax relief on mortgage interest to £30,000 per property rather than £30,000 per borrower. This measure 'added further fuel to an already booming housing market' (Lawson 1992: 820) as people attempted to become home owners before the restriction started to operate. Tax relief on mortgage interest has been the most significant fiscal intervention in the housing market, but in recent years the fiscal system has been used to encourage private landlordism. The Business Expansion Scheme for private landlord companies, introduced in the late 1980s, allowed investors in homes for rent to set their investment against their tax liability. It produced £3.44 billion in new investment and 40,000 homes but no new schemes were granted tax concessions after the end of 1993 perhaps because the cost of the subsidy – £28,800 per dwelling (Crook, Hughes and Kemp, 1995) – was so great. The Finance Act 1992 allowed furnished rooms to be let free of tax provided that the rental income does not exceed £3,250 a year. The government also gives direct subsidies to the commercial private sector through City Grant and Derelict Land Grant.

Conclusion

The most striking change in the framework within which housing policy is developed and implemented has been the decline in the power of local government. During the late 1970s local authorities had considerable discretion in deciding how much they should borrow for new house building, renovation and clearance and were able to set rents at a level they deemed to be reasonable. Not only has local authority house building been curtailed (see Table 4.3) but central government now controls the level of local borrowing and has considerable influence in setting local rents. It also determines the pattern of local investment through its influence in the housing strategy process, its use of specific borrowing approvals and its control over the Housing Corporation's strategic objectives. This dilution of local autonomy has formed part of a larger project aimed at reducing the domain of collective choice in favour of outcomes determined by market forces.

References

Audit Commission (1992) *Developing Local Authority Housing Strategies*, Audit Commission, London.

Baker, C. V. (1976) *Housing Associations*, The Estates Gazette Ltd, London.

Baker, K. (1993) *The Turbulent Years*, Faber and Faber, London.

Boddy, M. (1980) *The Building Societies*, Macmillan, London.

Boleat, M. and Taylor, B. (1993) *Housing in Britain*, Council of Mortgage Lenders, London.

Burrows, L., Phelps, L. and Walentowicz, P. (1993) *For Whose Benefit? The housing benefit scheme reviewed*, Shelter, London.

Cameron Commission (1969) *Disturbances in Northern Ireland*, Cmnd 532, HMSO, Belfast.

Clapham, D. and Kintrea, K. (1995) 'Housing Co-operatives: potential unfilled' in Pinto, R. (ed.) *Developments in Housing Management and Ownership*, Manchester University Press, Manchester.

Clark, G. (1994) *Housing Benefit: incentives for reform*, Social Market Foundation, London.

Coles, A. and Taylor, B. (1993) 'Trends in Tenure Preferences', *Housing Finance* No. 19, August.

Crook, T., Hughes, J. and Kemp, P. (1995) *The Supply of Privately Rented Homes: today and tomorrow*, Joseph Rowntree Foundation, York.

Crossley, R. (1995) 'Time to give Tenants a Hearing', *Roof*, May/June.

Department of the Environment (1994) *Annual Report 1994*, Cmnd 2607, HMSO, London.

Department of the Environment (1995) *Annual Report 1995*, Cm. 2807, HMSO, London.

Department of the Environment and Welsh Office (1995) *Our Future Homes: opportunity, choice, responsibility*, Cm. 2901, HMSO, London.

Department of Social Security (1995) *Social Security Statistics 1995*, HMSO, London.

Downs, D., Holmans, A. and Small, H. (1994) 'Trends in the Size of the Private Rented Sector in England', *Housing Finance*, May.

Gay, O. (1991) *The Private Rented Sector*, House of Commons Background Paper no. 267, House of Commons, London.

Halsey, A. H. (ed.) (1988) *British Social Trends Since 1900*, 2nd edn, Oxford University Press, Oxford.

Hills, J. (ed.) (1993) *The State of Welfare, the welfare state in Britain since 1974*, Clarendon Press, Oxford.

Housing Corporation (1991) '*The Tenants' Guarantee': guidance on the management of accommodation let on assured tenancies by registered housing associations*, Housing Corporation, London.

Housing Corporation (1993) *The Affordability of Housing Association Rents*, Housing Corporation, London.

Housing Corporation (1994) 'Who do housing associations house?' *Roof*, July/August.

Housing Corporation (1995) *Housing Associations in 1994*, The Housing Corporation, London.

Jackson, P. and Lavender, M. (1995) *The Public Services Yearbook 1995/6*, Chapman and Hall, London.

Karn, V. and Sheridan, L. (1994) *New Homes in the 1990s, a study of design, space and amenity in housing and private sector production*, Joseph Rowntree Foundation, York.

Kemp, P. (1993) 'Rebuilding the Private Rented Sector?' in Malpass, P. and Means, R. (eds) *Implementing Housing Policy*, Open University Press, Buckingham.

Kemp, P., Oldham, C., Rugg, J. and Williams, T. (1994) *The Effects of Benefits on Housing Decisions*, HMSO, London.

Lawson, N. (1992) *The View From No. 11*, Bantam Press, London.

MacCafferty, P. and Riley, D. (1989) *A Study of Co-operative Housing*, HMSO, London.

Maclennan, D. and More, A. (1995) 'Scottish Housing Policy since 1989: contrasts with England', in Smith, M. E. H. (ed.) *Housing – today and tomorrow*, Housing Centre Trust, London.

Malpass, P. (1990) *Reshaping Housing Policy, subsidies, rents and residualisation*, Routledge, London.

Malpass, P., Warburton, M., Bramley, G. and Smart, G. (1993) *Housing Policy In Action*, SAUS, Bristol.

National Federation of Housing Associations (1995) *Core Lettings Bulletin*, NPHA Research, London.

Pollock, L. (1993) 'Irish Eyes Unsmiling', *Roof*, November/December.

Pryke, M. and Whitehead, C. (1993) 'The Provision of Private Finance for Social Housing: an outline of recent developments in funding existing housing associations in England', *Housing Studies*, 8 (4), pp. 274–291.

Resettlement Agency (1995) *Annual Report and Accounts 1994/95*, Resettlement Agency, London.

Scott, S. *et al.* (1994) *Preparing To Manage: frameworks for tenant management work programmes and competencies for tenant management organisations*, Department of the Environment, HMSO, London.

Smallwood, D. (1992) 'Building Societies: builders or financiers?' in Birchall, J. (ed.) *Housing Policy in the 1990s*, Routledge, London.

Smith, M. E. (1989) *Guide To Housing*, Housing Centre Trust, London.

Smith, R. and Williams, P. (1995) 'The Changing Nature of Housing Policy in Wales', in Smith, M. E. H. (ed.) *Housing – today and tomorrow*, Housing Centre Trust, London.

Stephens, M. (1994) *Housing Policy in a European Perspective*, Joseph Rowntree Foundation, York.

Wilcox, S. (1995) *Housing Finance Review 1995/6*, Joseph Rowntree Foundation, York.

PART TWO

Housing Problems

CHAPTER 5

Homelessness

Destitution in the nineteenth century

The concept of homelessness as it is understood today did not exist in the late nineteenth century. Pauperism and destitution were the closest approximations: pauperism referring to a state of dependency and destitution to the absence of the means for physical survival. The prevention of destitution and pauperism was accomplished through charity for the 'deserving' poor and the deterrent Poor Law, especially the workhouse, for the 'undeserving' poor. Families with a local connection were offered shelter in the workhouse but there was little demand for this form of provision. Conditions in the workhouse were meant to be less eligible than the situation of 'the independent labourer of the lowest class' (Checkland and Checkland 1973). A move into the workhouse meant extreme degradation, the possibility of separation from one's spouse and children and great difficulty in finding employment: the work required of a workhouse inmate and the restrictions imposed on personal freedom meant that they had limited opportunity to search for a job. Any form of accommodation was regarded as preferable to the workhouse so the system served its purpose – except in Ireland – of preventing death from exposure without undermining the 'independent' character of the working class.

Single men presented a more serious problem. They were admitted to the 'casual ward' attached to the general mixed workhouse (known as the 'spike' after the spikes used to break blocks of stone as a workhouse task) but not before 4 p.m. in winter and 6 p.m. in summer. They slept in hammocks, on straw mattresses or on wooden planks and were required to be detained for two days to perform some task of work. Despite these deterrent principles the demand for such accommodation was high.

To these 638 Casual Wards, placed all over the country at intervals of a few miles there resort nightly from 7,000 to 17,000 persons according to the season, the weather and the badness of trade. They represent an army 'on tramp' estimated to vary, according to the same influences, from 30,000 to 80,000 separate individuals who resort to the Casual Wards from time to time. Four-fifths of them are men, who are sometimes accompanied by women, and occasionally by young children. The number of single women in the Casual Wards is infinitesimal.

(Minority Report of the Royal Commission on the Poor Law 1909: 1080)

In addition to the casual wards of the workhouse this 'army on tramp' slept in the open, in commercial common lodging houses and in hostels provided by charitable organisations such as the Salvation Army. The

Minority Report of the Royal Commission recognised the connection between destitution and the national shortage of housing. It referred to the problem of the 'houseless' poor and saw the solution as the reorganisation of the labour market and the rehabilitation of those who had become used to an unsettled way of life by the creation of a specialist state employment agency.

The single/family homelessness divide

The system governing what we now call the problem of homelessness continued into the 1930s, but mass unemployment placed great strain on the finances of the local authority public assistance committees which had replaced the Boards of Guardians in 1929. Rateable values in poor areas were insufficient to pay for cash benefits to the long-term unemployed and in 1935 an Unemployment Assistance Board, run by the central government, was established which assumed responsibility for the unemployment duties of the local authority public assistance committees. This change created confusion about responsibility for unemployed and homeless single people. The Unemployment Assistance Board had a statutory duty to promote the welfare of its applicants and began to pay grants to voluntary organisations to resettle those 'in whom the habits of vagrancy are not too deeply ingrained', but many unemployed single men still used the casual wards of the workhouse run by local authorities.

The 1948 National Assistance Act

The National Assistance Act 1948 consolidated the division of responsibility for single and family homelessness: single homelessness was regarded as an employment/resettlement issue and family homelessness as a welfare issue. Under this Act payments (including payment of rent) to all people with no source of income became the responsibility of the National Assistance Board, which also gained control of the casual wards of the workhouse with an additional obligation to 'make provision whereby persons without a settled living may be influenced to lead a more settled life' and to provide and maintain centres 'for the provision of temporary board and lodgings for such persons' (National Assistance Act 1948). As Nelson, Sternberg and Brindley (1982) have observed:

> The problem of homelessness was still seen as the problem of idleness. Temporary accommodation was only afforded the homeless by the State on the condition that they work, either doing task duties, as in the casual wards of the workhouse, or as residents of reception centres, doing many more hours supposedly as preparation for life in the world outside.
> (Nelson, Sternberg and Brindley 1982: 23)

Public assistance committees were renamed welfare committees and became responsible for various forms of residential care, including residential provision for homeless people. The National Assistance Act imposed a duty on local authorities to provide 'temporary accommodation for persons in urgent need thereof, being need arising in circumstances that could not reasonably have been foreseen or in such cases as the authority may in any particular case determine'. The legislation was not intended to give any right to permanent accommodation and indeed no such absolute right was possible in the severe housing crisis at the end of the war. The duties contained in the National Assistance Act were designed for emergencies and were not seen as a replacement for the allocation of homes according to relative need as revealed by the waiting list kept by each authority. People in extreme housing difficulties were to be helped but only on a temporary basis by welfare authorities which in county areas were located at a different administrative level to the housing authority.

The movement for reform

Local authorities interpreted their duties under the National Assistance Act in a restrictive way. To them 'circumstances that could not reasonably have been foreseen' meant fire and flood or other natural disaster; 'other causes' were a signal that the applicant wanted to jump the housing queue. People without children had little hope of assistance as it was assumed that, if anybody had responsibility for them, it was the National Assistance Board. In Greater London 75 per cent of all homelessness applications were rejected (Holman *et al.* 1970). If accommodation was offered to a homeless family then it was often a caravan or communal accommodation of a low standard and many authorities did not allow a man to live with his family. The system had all the characteristics of the 'less eligibility' of the Poor Law from which it had descended: indeed some of the communal accommodation was in a former workhouse (see Document 10, page 212). If, after spending time in the temporary accommodation, the family was unable to secure permanent housing, then the children might be taken into the care of the local authority.

Jeremy Sandford's and Ken Loach's drama/documentary, first shown on television in 1966, focused national attention on the homelessness problem. *Cathy Come Home* told the story of how the homelessness of a young couple led to the end of their relationship. Cathy had to live with her children in a squalid dormitory for homeless families, and eventually her children were taken into the care of the local authority. Prompted by publicity from Shelter and a Ministry of Housing circular, conditions in temporary accommodation improved a little. However the taint of the Poor Law still remained strong enough for one academic researcher to think it necessary to insist that it was the shortage of accommodation rather than the personal characteristics of the homeless that was the basic cause of homelessness (Greve 1971).

It was not until the middle 1970s that reform of the system was undertaken. When social services departments were established in 1972 the duty to provide temporary accommodation to homeless families was replaced by a discretionary power. Voluntary organisations concerned with homelessness objected to this and the Department of Health and Social Security issued a circular (13/74) which imposed a duty on local authorities to provide temporary accommodation but placed it on social services departments rather than on housing departments. The voluntary sector argued that assigning the responsibility to social services suggested that homeless people needed social work help to deal with their personal problems, whereas the real problem was lack of access to permanent homes, a situation over which social services departments had no control. This argument was accepted by the government and a joint Department of the Environment/Department of Health and Social Security circular (18/74) urged local authorities to shift responsibility for homelessness from social services departments (the successors of welfare departments) to housing, and set out a list of priority groups for whom 'the issue is not whether but by what means, local authorities should provide accommodation themselves or help those concerned to obtain accommodation in the private sector'. Unfortunately this circular was advisory and many local authorities ignored its guidance. According to Somerville (1994) such defiance prompted the Department of the Environment to impose its will by legislation. A bill on homelessness was prepared but the lack of parliamentary time prevented its introduction. Stephen Ross, a Liberal MP, drew a place for the introduction of a private member's bill and his Housing (Homeless Persons) Bill became an Act with the support of the government. This Act, now incorporated into the Housing Act 1985, has had a profound influence on the system of local authority housing allocations and has provided the context for the statistical information that forms the basis of the contemporary debate on homelessness.

The Housing (Homeless Persons) Act 1977 and the Housing Act 1985

In order to pinpoint a distinct problem of homelessness and thereby direct local authority attention to overcoming this specific problem it was necessary to define homelessness. This was done by designating persons as homeless if they have no legal right to occupy accommodation, in the words of the Act if there 'is no accommodation which s/he could occupy by virtue of an interest or estate, or contract, together with anyone else who normally resides with her/him either as a member of the family or in circumstances in which it is reasonable for that person to reside with him/her'. In addition, a person is homeless if he or she has a legal right to occupy accommodation but 'cannot secure entry to it or it is probable that occupation will lead to violence from some other person residing in it, or to threats of violence from some other person residing in it who is likely to carry out such threats'.

Following the case of *R v LB Hillingdon ex parte Pulhofer* (1985), which cast doubt on the meaning of the term 'accommodation', the Housing and Planning Act 1986 inserted additional clauses into the Housing Act 1985 stating that 'a person shall not be treated as having accommodation unless it is accommodation that, following proper enquiries by the authority, it would be reasonable for him/her to occupy having regard to the general circumstances prevailing in relation to housing in the area'. The definition of homelessness in terms of the absence of a legal right to occupy also covers those threatened with homelessness within 28 days.

The local authority associations made it clear to the Government that they would not be able to cope with all the people defined as homeless and so criteria were included that homeless people have to satisfy in order to be eligible for assistance.

Priority need

People are judged to have a priority need for accommodation if the authority is satisfied that they come within any one of the following categories:

1 They have dependent children who are residing with, or might reasonably be expected to reside with them.
2 They are homeless or threatened with homelessness as a result of any emergency such as flood, fire or any other disaster.
3 They, or any person who resides or who might be reasonably be expected to reside with them, are vulnerable because of old age, mental illness, handicap or physical disability or other special reason.
4 They are pregnant, or they reside or might reasonably be expected to reside, with a pregnant woman.

Intentional homelessness

People become intentionally homeless if they deliberately do or fail to do anything in consequence of which they cease to occupy accommodation.

Local connection

In the 1960s and 1970s it was common for local authorities to refuse to help homeless applicants on the grounds that they had a 'local connection' with another area. The 1977 Act attempted to modify the practice of pushing homeless people from one authority to another with no authority being willing to accept that a family had a 'local connection' to its area. The Act made the local authority to whom the homeless person applies responsible for temporary accommodation until an agreement was reached with another local authority about long-term responsibility. There is a system of arbitration for resolving disputes between local authorities. The Department of the Environment has issued a code of guidance on the interpretation of the homelessness legislation in an attempt to 'ensure a fairer, more consistent service'. An extract from this guidance covering the meaning of homelessness is given as Document 11, page 214.

If homeless people are in priority need but are found to be intentionally homeless then the local authority has a duty to make accommodation available for a period sufficient to allow them to secure their own accommodation, usually interpreted to mean 28 days. However, if a homeless person satisfies all the requirements of the Act then the local authority must 'secure that accommodation becomes available for his/her occupation'. Until July 1995 this phrase was construed as imposing a requirement on local authorities to make available 'long-term settled, commonly referred to as permanent, accommodation' (DoE 1994). However, the case of *London Borough of Brent ex parte Awua* raised serious doubts about this interpretation of the law when the House of Lords ruled that accommodation can include temporary accommodation (Campbell 1995).

The homelessness legislation imposed specific duties on local councils and so the routine statistical information on homelessness is structured around the provisions of the Act. A selection of the official information is given in Tables 5.1 and 5.2. Such statistics have been criticised from a number of perspectives on the grounds that they give a partial and misleading impression of the nature and causes of homelessness. Each of these criticisms represents an attempt to construct the homelessness problem in a way that implies a particular notion of causation.

Laissez-faire economics

The definition of homelessness

Laissez-faire economics regards the free market as the appropriate mechanism to overcome the housing problem. How then does it view the nature and causes of homelessness and what cures does it propose? We can find some clues as to how economic liberals might define homelessness in the work of Friedrich Von Hayek. Hayek has attempted to demonstrate that deprivation should not be defined in relative terms because to do so implies that the poor have some claim to a relative share of the wealth of a nation whereas, in fact, it is a matter of luck, not desert, which nation one is born into (Hayek 1960). Applying this notion to homelessness would suggest that the concept should be defined according to standards as absolute as can be achieved. The most absolute concept suggested is 'rooflessness'. The Conservative Party has moved towards interpreting the concept of homelessness in

Table 5.1 **Local authority homelessness acceptances: Great Britain 1978–94**

Year	Number of acceptances
1978	63 003
1979	68 562
1980	73 951
1981	80 601
1982	86 564
1983	89 397
1984	95 226
1985	108 768
1986	119 804
1987	127 490
1988	133 189
1989	144 376
1990	165 369
1991	171 480
1992	172 946
1993	159 974
1994	150 501

Sources: Newton (1994), DoE homelessness statistics

Table 5.2 **Homeless households in temporary accommodation: England, 1980–94**

	Bed and breakfast	Hostels	Other[1]	Total
1980	1 330	3 380		4 170
1981	1 520	3 320		4 840
1982	1 640	3 500	4 200	9 340
1983	2 700	3 400	3 740	9 840
1984	3 670	3 990	4 640	12 300
1985	5 360	4 730	5 830	15 920
1986	8 990	4 610	7 190	20 790
1987	10 370	5 150	9 240	24 270
1988	10 970	6 240	12 890	30 100
1989	11 480	8 020	18 400	37 900
1990	11 130	9 010	25 030	45 170
1991	12 150	9 990	37 790	59 930
1992	7 630	10 840	44 600	63 070
1993	4 900	10 210	38 470	53 580
1994	4 330	10 020	33 410	47 760

Note
[1] Includes private sector leasing and 'homeless at home'.
Sources: Newton (1994), Wilcox (1995).

these terms. The Department of the Environment no longer uses the term homelessness to describe the statistical returns resulting from the operations of the Housing Act 1985; it labels such statistics as 'persons accepted as homeless by local authorities under the Housing Act 1985'.

Those who support the view that the homelessness figures exaggerate the 'true' nature of homelessness would add that local authorities interpret the 1985 Housing Act in a wide variety of ways. In 1994 the acceptance rate (the percentage of people accepted by the local authority in relationship to the number of applications) varied from 3.7 per cent to 96.6 per cent (Mason 1994). Bramley (1993) could explain only 60 per cent of the overall variation between local authorities in homelessness acceptances by social and economic factors. Evans and Duncan (1988) discovered that 17 per cent of local authorities accepted young single people as 'vulnerable' homeless on the basis of age alone. Adherents to public choice theory also point out that the agencies involved in making provision for homeless people have an interest in exaggerating the extent of the problem. This phenomenon has been called 'lying for justice' (Jencks 1994) and implies that figures produced by the voluntary sector should be treated with caution. Public choice theorists add the charge that since the indicators used by the Department of the Environment to allocate resources to local government were heavily weighted towards homelessness then an incentive existed for some local authorities to maximise the number of people classified as homeless. In 1994 a consultation paper declared that it seemed 'wrong to put a substantial weight on a measure affected so much by authorities' administrative decisions as this puts authorities under inappropriate and perverse incentives . . .' (DoE 1994b). Later the point was added that the use of homelessness statistics as a basis for resource distribution rewarded those authorities that 'put little effort into preventing problems arising' (DoE 1995).

The causes of homelessness

Leaving home: The necessity for collective action on the problem of homelessness can be reduced by making a connection between rooflessness and the changes taking place in the nature of the family. *Laissez-faire* economists have little to say about the family but their approach links to neo-conservatism which makes changes in family life a central element of the diagnosis of poverty and homelessness. According to this analysis, state welfare has created 'perverse incentives' that have caused the breakdown of traditional family life. With regard to young people it has been argued that if they think they can secure independent accommodation then they will be less concerned about leaving the parental home. Hence the Social Security Act 1988 withdrew all rights to income support for under 18s (limited discretionary payments were made available in cases of proven hardship), restricted access to financial assistance for the purchase of furniture and reduced housing benefit for those aged 18–25 by 25 per cent of the rate for those over 25.

Single parents: Single parenthood became an important issue for the New Right in the late 1980s. Charles Murray (1984, 1988, 1990) argued that welfare payments to single mothers have produced a breakdown of the traditional bonds between young men and young women who no longer need each other for mutual support in the rearing of children, and Ridley (1991: 91) commented that 'a young lady with a child is in "priority housing need" – one without one is not. It became a way of living for some to have one or more children by unknown men, in order to qualify for a council house. The rent and rates were paid by benefit'.

During Ridley's period of office at the Department of the Environment a review of the homelessness legislation was started, amid speculation that it was the intention of the government to redefine homelessness as rooflessness. The results of this review were not as dramatic as forecast. The existing legislation was given qualified endorsement but the issue was soon to return to the political agenda. At the Conservative Party Conferences of 1992 and 1993, emphasis was placed on the the 'perverse incentives' that encouraged the breakdown of the traditional family. Sir George Young asked, 'How do you explain to the young couple who want to wait for a home before they start a family that they cannot be rehoused ahead of the unmarried teenager expecting her first, probably unplanned, child?'

This theme of 'perverse incentives' was taken up in a 1994 consultation paper which, having reviewed the recent history of homelessness legislation (see Document 12, page 215) came to the conclusion that:

By giving the local authority a greater responsibility towards those who can demonstrate 'homelessness' than towards anyone else in housing need, the current legislation creates a perverse incentive for people to have themselves accepted by a local authority as homeless within the meaning of Part III of the Housing Act 1985. In the great majority of cases, someone accepted as homeless is in fact occupying accommodation of some sort at the time he or she approaches the authority ... While in some cases there will be an undeniable need for alternative accommodation, there is a growing belief that the homelessness provisions are frequently used as a quick route into a separate home.

(Department of the Environment 1994c. 4)

The idea that the provision of special routes into permanent housing encourages homelessness has received cautious endorsement from Christopher Jencks, a respected American commentator on social policy. He tells the story of New York's homelessness policy. During the 1980s most of the city's homeless families were housed in welfare hostels where they had to spend more than a year before they were offered permanent accommodation. These hostels were 'nasty and dangerous places' so only the most desperate families stayed long enough to qualify for the permanent homes. Under pressure from the courts and the media the authorities reduced the length of stay in the hostels. The result was that 'as the waiting period for permanent housing shortened, more families began entering the system ... and the number of families in welfare hostels climbed again.' (Jencks 1994: 105.) A similar relationship was identified in Lambeth by Jeffers and Hoggett (1995) who state that

'Lambeth housing department had attempted to cope with its financial crisis by giving more emphasis to rehousing homeless families living in bed-and-breakfast accommodation than those living with relatives and friends. Within a matter of months, the effect was to increase the proportion of homeless families requiring B&B' (Jeffers and Hoggett 1995: 337).

Legislative reform

In order to eradicate the 'perverse incentive' alleged to exist in Britain, the 1994 consultation paper recommended that local authorities should be required only to provide 'emergency assistance' for a 'limited period' to those 'who have no accommodation of any sort available for occupation, provided this situation has arisen unintentionally'. However, following consultation, the government announced that temporary accommodation would be provided for 12 months during which time homeless people would take their place in the housing queue with other people on local housing registers. These registers 'should reflect the underlying values of our society' and should 'balance specific housing needs against the need to support married couples who take a responsible approach to family life, so that tomorrow's generation grows up in a stable home environment' (DoE 1995: 36).

The social reformist approach

Defining homelessness

The definition of homelessness contained in the 1985 Housing Act is broadly acceptable to the social reformist approach, which recognises that too broad a definition of the problem may distract attention from a specific problem that requires focused attention. However, supporters of the approach maintain that the official statistics generated through the operations of the 1985 Housing Act do not provide a full picture of the extent of homelessness: local authorities have no obligations to house childless people except in special circumstances, so homeless single people are unlikely to apply for help or, having applied, will not be recorded in the statistics as homeless.

The 1994 figures produced by the Department of the Environment do not give a national total of the number of applications but it is possible to calculate this national figure from local returns. In the second quarter of 1994, 34 per cent of the households applying as homeless were accepted compared to 39 per cent in the same period in 1993, 43 per cent in 1992 and 49 per cent in 1991 (Mason 1994). This suggests that the drop in the 'headline' figure for homelessness may be the outcome of local authorities adjusting their criteria for acceptance rather than any improvement in the availability of homes. Moreover, even if statutorily homeless people are rehoused quickly and their encounter with homelessness is brief, the experience of losing a home is traumatic and has affected more than one million households since 1981 (Greve 1991). According to the social reformist perspective a comprehensive assessment of the number of homeless people should include:

- Those sleeping rough – a count of rough sleepers on the night of the 1991 Census (21–22 April) found 2,824 people in England, Wales and Scotland sleeping in the open air but this is likely to be a serious underestimate: only 1,312 known sites were examined and no homeless people were discovered in Birmingham and Cardiff!
- Single people living in hostels, squats, bed and breakfast hotels, short-life housing and private sector leased units: 55,800 people according to an estimate made by the Catholic Housing Aid Society in 1994.
- Those households with children in temporary accommodation.
- People due to be discharged from institutionalised accommodation in the near future.
- Households involuntarily sharing accommodation: 3 per cent of the households interviewed for the Department of the Environment's Housing Attitudes Survey (Hedges and Clemens 1994) stated that there was someone in the household who needed a separate home but could not obtain one.
- Split households who would like to live together.
- People living in households where living conditions are intolerable.

Using criteria similar to those described above, Burrows and Walentowicz (1992) estimated that there were 1,712,000 homeless people in Britain in the early 1990s.

The causes of homelessness

In contrast to the neo-conservative perspective, social reformers see changes in family life as the product of economic and social forces such as the increased desire for independence, especially amongst women, reductions in the opportunities for employment with reasonable wages, the shortage of affordable houses and the increased need for mobility in a capitalist/*laissez-faire* economy. They believe that social policy has to adapt to these changes rather than resist them. Academics working within the perspective make a number of points aimed at refuting the 'perverse incentive' argument of the New Right.

First, the notion that young people leave home almost at whim because the state pays for their accommodation does not fit the facts as revealed by social research. Studies by Randall (1988), Hudson and Liddiard (1991) and O'Mahony (1988) have revealed that between 22 per cent and 40 per cent of homeless young people have been in local authority care. Investigations at Centrepoint, Soho – a voluntary agency specialising in working for the young homeless in London – revealed a correlation between the levels of unemployment in Scotland and the North of England and the proportion of young people from these regions who use the Centrepoint night shelter (Randall 1988). This finding reinforces Crowther's historical research (1981) which identified a relationship between unemployment rates and recorded vagrancy.

Many reasons for leaving their former accommodation were given by the 318 homeless single people aged between 16 and 24 interviewed by members of the Centre for Housing Policy at the University of York (Anderson, Kemp and Quilgars 1993). Only 14 per cent of the reasons given were classified by the researchers as 'positive decisions' to leave home; the remaining reasons were mainly 'push' factors such as conflict with parents and eviction. Recent research in Scotland (Jones 1994) has revealed that, despite the reductions in social security benefits, a higher proportion of young people leave the parental home. The research demonstrated the impact of family dynamics on homelessness. Although 25 per cent of homeless young Scots had a step-parent, the report went on to say that 'it is not only in step-families that young people and their parents do not get on'. Altogether 60 per cent of homeless young Scots had left home because they did not get on with their families; many had experienced violence or abuse at home and left because of it.

Secondly, the idea that a significant number of young women become pregnant to qualify for a local authority home is not supported by research evidence:

housing policies which give priority to families with children have led some commentators to suggest that young women deliberately become pregnant in order to obtain a council flat. There is no systematic evidence for this and it seems more likely to be a rational explanation for what happened, offered by some young mothers after the event.

(Stewart and Stewart 1993: 30)

It is also pointed out that in 1992–93 only 31 per cent of local authority lets were allocated to homeless households, only 2 per cent of households housed as homeless were headed by a person aged between 16 and 19 and that a very limited number of council homes are occupied by single young women: 13,000 women under 20 or 0.3 per cent of the total number of council tenants in 1993 (Wilson 1994). In 1993–94 52 per cent of lone mothers under 20 lived with their parents (Green and Hansbro 1995).

Finally, the increased rate of divorce and separation is the consequence of men and, more particularly, women being unwilling to tolerate unhappy marriages which, in the case of women, have often been based on unequal relationships of power.

Government housing policy is the principal reason given by adherents of the social reformist perspective for the explosion in homelessness acceptances by local authorities. The state has been withdrawn from a significant role in the delivery of housing at an affordable price. The right to buy has meant that 1.5 million homes have been lost from the rented sector – the tenure that is most accessible to low income households with children – with the result that by 1991–92 'the number of families accepted as homeless exceeded the number of suitable local authority lettings in 43 per cent of local authorities in England. In 11 per cent of local authorities family acceptances were more than double the number of suitable dwellings' (Rowntree Foundation 1994). Many low income households became obliged to become owner-occupiers in the 1980s due to the lack of available alternatives. The rapid increase in house prices in the middle 1980s, followed by high interest rates, resulted in an increase in the number of mortgage foreclosures. In addition increases in the rent have meant that families with an income marginally above eligibility for housing benefit have struggled to meet their payments and hence the likelihood of eviction has increased. Social reformist explanations of the increase in the incidence of single homelessness concentrate on the continued decline of the private landlord sector in the 1980s and changes that have been made in the benefits system (Hudson and Liddiard 1994).

The Marxist political economy approach

Although the ideas outlined below have been designated as Marxist many of the points made are shared by commentators who adopt a more radical stance than social reformism but who would not wish to see the introduction of a fully socialist economic system.

Defining homelessness

Marxists believe that the function of the state is to promote a representation of homelessness that ensures the solution is not located in major structural change. The history of homelessness in Britain provides ample ammunition for this perspective. The linking of homelessness to the system of poor relief automatically made a problem of the housing market into a problem of the character of those who resorted to assistance from the state. It was not until the 1970s that family homelessness became the responsibility of housing departments with a duty to provide accommodation rather than a duty imposed on welfare authorities whose 'core business' was changing individual behaviour. The 1977 Housing (Homeless Persons) Act, despite its denunciation as 'a scroungers charter', gives homeless people with children no individual right to accommodation. Its provisions relate to the duty of the local authority to provide accommodation – a duty owed to the community rather than to the individual homeless person – so the decisions of local authorities can only be challenged by the complex process of judicial review. Individual rights such as those contained in the right to buy a council house are not reflected in the homelessness legislation. The Act is riddled with tests reminiscent of the Victorian Poor Law: homeless people have to establish that they are not intentionally homeless and they also have to demonstrate a local connection. Even if these obstacles are surmounted then they are eligible for a permanent home only if one is available; they go to the head of the queue but then have to wait for an offer. Childless people without homes are not even protected by the legal duties placed on statutory authorities; they have to rely on the charitable motivations of voluntary organisations.

The statistics presented by the government on homelessness minimise the true extent of the problem and present it as a 'personal trouble' rather than a social evil. The official statistics on homelessness do not include those who are living in overcrowded dwellings, unfit accommodation, in lodgings or with tenancies that do not have long-term security, who have a justifiable claim to be considered homeless. Moreover the official reasons given for homelessness may be only the presenting symptoms. Thus the category 'family and marital breakdown' used in the official figures can disguise economic causes of homelessness such as stress caused by problems of debt.

The causes of homelessness

Marxists do not expect housing provision in a capitalist economy to prevent homelessness. The logic of capitalism dictates that housing standards must be related to the productivity of the worker for capitalism. The necessity of maintaining the relativity of rewards and imposing strong sanctions on those who do not achieve in a capitalist system requires some level of homelessness.

Homelessness policies in the 1990s

Although Conservative governments have been inclined to take the view that homelessness is a residual problem linked to undesirable changes in family life, attempts have been made to target resources on the most extreme and visible manifestations of the problem: 'rough sleepers' and families living in 'bed and breakfast' accommodation.

The Rough Sleepers Initiative

The reduction in housing benefits to young people in the middle 1980s did not have the anticipated deterrent impact and by 1989 considerable media attention was focused on the growth of 'cardboard cities' and the increase in begging, especially in central London. Mrs Thatcher was not prepared to restore the value of benefits to the under-25s, arguing

that 'it was vital that we should not add to the already too evident lure
of the big city for young people'. She wanted young people 'back with
their families, not in London living on benefits' (Thatcher 1993: 603)
and urged the DoE to bring in the voluntary sector to solve the problem.

The Rough Sleepers Initiative was announced in June 1990. It consisted
of a programme run by voluntary organisations who contacted homeless people in central London, developed emergency hostel places and
then offered more permanent 'move on' accommodation. £96 million
was made available for the initiative and in 1993 the Department of the
Environment stated that the initiative had reduced the numbers sleeping out in central London from between 1,000 to 2,000 in 1990 to
about 290 in late 1994 (DoE 1995). The Homeless Mentally Ill Initiative for London was launched by the Department of Health in 1990. It
consisted of a multi-disciplinary community health team to identify
clients and provide assistance, specialist hostels and move-on accommodation. A year after identification, 53 per cent of client cases were
closed satisfactorily (Craig *et al.* 1995). The success of these schemes
illustrates what can be done if resources are devoted to a problem, but
it is important to emphasise that the project had limited objectives and
was evaluated only in terms of these objectives; it was restricted to
central London and to rough sleepers. The scheme was due to end in
1993 but the government made an additional £86 million available to
continue the scheme for three more years with an emphasis on providing permanent self-contained accommodation. The White Paper *Our
Future Homes* (DoE/Welsh Office 1995) announced that 'the Government will consider assisting the development of the RSI model in areas
where sleeping rough can be demonstrated to be a major problem'. The
Homeless Mentally Ill Initiative suffered from a failure to provide the
move-on accommodation required, and 18 per cent of clients were lost
to the team in the follow-up period.

Bed and breakfast hotels

Local authorities have used a variety of temporary housing for homeless families: short life accommodation, hostels, mobile homes, private
sector leasing and 'homeless at home'. The use of one form of temporary
accommodation – bed and breakfast hotels – has attracted particular
criticism on the grounds of cost (the total cost of bed and breakfast in
England increased from £22 million in 1984–85 to £143 million in
1987–88 and was as high as £259 per family per year in one London
borough); the risk to health (Health Visitors Association and British
Medical Association 1989); and the lack of amenities (Niner 1989).
Miller (1991), who interviewed a number of the homeless mothers in
bed and breakfast hotels:

was shocked by the conditions they lived in, by the way they were bullied by
hotel managers and ignored by the local authorities who were supposed to be

responsible for them and by the Department of Health and Social Security. I met children aged two or three who were obviously unhealthy. They could hardly talk at all and played with a terrible passivity. Most of the mothers were clearly depressed and run down.

(Miller 1991: 1)

In response to such concerns the DoE launched its 'homelessness initiative' at the end of 1989, aimed at reducing the number of families living in bed and breakfast hotels. The initiative consisted of special borrowing approvals targeted on local authorities in London and the DoE's South East and Eastern regions. The money was spent on creating hostel accommodation, the rehabilitation of local authority and private sector dwellings purchased by housing associations and on cash incentives (average payment £15,816) to sitting tenants to help them buy a home, thereby creating a vacancy for a homeless family (White and Low 1992). Although it is difficult to assess the independent impact of this special scheme the number of households living in bed and breakfast hotels declined by 7,440 between 1991 and 1994. A contribution to this reduction came from the use of the 'homeless at home' procedure, which has been defined as 'any arrangement for a household which has applied to be or has been accepted as homeless to remain in the accommodation from which they are being made homeless, or in other accommodation found by the applicant, on a strictly temporary basis, until such time as other temporary or permanent accommodation is secured by the housing authority' (London Housing Unit 1993). The majority of 'homeless at home' families live with their parents.

Private sector leasing, whereby a local authority leases a private property either directly or through a housing association, and guarantees the rent and the return of the property in good order at the end of the lease, has also helped to reduce the number of homeless families in bed and breakfast accommodation. In London most homeless households (58 per cent) were placed in homes rented from the private sector (Edwards 1995). The consultation paper on homelessness (DoE 1994c) expressed the view that more homeless families should be accommodated in the private landlord sector, and the legislative changes proposed in the paper were designed to remove any doubts about the legality of regarding private landlord accommodation as a permanent home.

Training hostels

A programme of linking hostel provision for homeless single people to employment and training opportunities was started in 1991. The aim of providing these hostels was to break the 'no home, no job, no home' cycle. The idea was imported from France where 500 *foyers* exist that offer 'an integrated referral system to young people to move around the country for employment or training with guaranteed accommodation' (Wilson 1994b). The British programme is coordinated by the Foyer

Federation for Youth and in 1994 the network contained more than 1,000 beds in 22 schemes with over 20 new projects in development. An examination of training hostels by Quilgars and Anderson (1995) found that 'most young people found the support services useful and the foyer approach reached young people who might not have used more formal, employment services' and that 'mostly this was achieved without making use of the services a condition of residence'.

Making more efficient use of the housing stock

At a particular time, a number of dwellings will be empty because of a change in occupier or because the house needs substantial repairs. In 1993 70,000 local authority dwellings were vacant (Rowntree Foundation 1994). If the void interval (the time a house is empty) could be reduced, then more properties would be occupied at a specific time and hence the incidence of homelessness could be reduced. The Audit Commission's report *Managing the Crisis in Council Housing* (1986) proposed a performance target on re-let time for local authority dwellings of six weeks in London and three weeks elsewhere. By 1990–91 66 per cent of local authorities had failed to achieve this target and, according to the Audit Commission, this resulted in 26,000 lettings not being available. Performance had not improved in 1994 (Audit Commission 1995) but whether or not such targets are realistic for all authorities is questionable. Local authorities now have a low void rate (1.9 per cent) – less than that for housing associations (2.4 per cent) and for property owned by the government (15 per cent) – and pressures to reduce void rates may result in insensitive rehabilitation schemes and inappropriate allocations. However there is a substantial number of empty dwellings in the private sector (764,000) some of which might be brought back into use by housing associations letting on behalf of the owner through increased funding of the HAMA and HAMA PLUS programmes, and by converting space above shops into flats.

In some areas there is a serious shortage of family accommodation but a more adequate supply of smaller dwellings with the result that waiting times are longer for the larger dwellings suitable for families. If the people now underoccupying dwellings could be persuaded to move then more homes suitable to families would be made available. Barelli (1992) has attempted to assess the extent of underoccupation and the contribution that a proactive policy aimed at reducing underoccupation might make to alleviating the problems of homelessness and overcrowding. Using a standard specifically devised for the purpose of measuring underoccupancy she calculated that in the social rented sector 'somewhere around a half to three quarters of each "at risk" bedsizes (3 and 4+) are less than fully occupied'. However, as Barelli points out, this does not mean that the spare bedrooms are not used. Many people use the spare room for a variety of purposes such as a storage area or to accommodate visitors. Thus, unless there is to be a policy of compelling people to move, the scope for using the additional living space is limited to those who wish to live in smaller accommodation: about 17 per cent of underoccupying tenants.

Conclusion

. . . homelessness must be regarded as a condition rather than as an event. It is tempting to treat it simply as the loss of a roof or shelter but homelessness is more than this. It occurs usually within a broader process of marginalisation which involves not just housing or financial inadequacy but an inability to participate in the quality of life and opportunities enjoyed by the rest of society.
(European Observatory on Homelessness 1992: 2)

The substantial increase in homelessness since the late 1970s cannot be isolated from the changes in Britain's economic and social structure. Unemployment increased from an average annual rate of 2.5 per cent in the period 1960 to 1976 to an average annual rate of 9.3 per cent between 1976 and 1992. Unemployment also became concentrated in particular groups such as those aged 18–25, single parent families and ethnic minorities. Low pay has followed the same pattern as unemployment and both low pay and unemployment have become more concentrated in particular geographical areas. The prevention of homelessness requires policies to ensure that those marginalised by the economic and social structure are reintegrated back into the mainstream economy.

References

Anderson, I., Kemp, P. and Quilgars, D. (1993) *Single Homeless People*, HMSO, London.

Audit Commission (1986) *Managing the Crisis in Council Housing*, HMSO, London.

Audit Commission (1992) *Developing Local Authority Housing Strategies*, HMSO, London.

Audit Commission (1995) *Local Authority Performance Indicators*, HMSO, London.

Barelli, J. (1992) *Underoccupation in Local Authority and Housing Association Housing*, HMSO, London.

Bramley, G. (1993) 'Explaining the incidence of Statutory Homelessness in England', *Housing Studies*, 8 (2), pp. 126–47.

Burrows, L. and Walentowicz (1992) *Homes Cost Less Than Homelessness*, Shelter, London.

Campbell, R. (1995) 'Back to no Future', *Roof*, September–October.

Checkland, S. G. and Checkland, E. O. A. (1973) *The Poor Law Report of 1834*, Penguin, Harmondsworth.

Craig, T., Bayliss, E., Klein, O., Manning, P. and Reader, L. (1995) *The Homeless Mentally Ill Initiative*, HMSO, London.

Crowther, M. A. (1981) *The Workhouse System 1834–1929: the history of an English social institution*, Batsford, London.

Department of the Environment (1993) *The Rough Sleepers Initiative The Next Three Years: A discussion paper*, HMSO, London.

Department of the Environment (1994a) *Annual Report 1994*, Department of the Environment, HMSO, London.

Department of the Environment (1994b) *Fundamental Review of the Generalised Needs Index (GNI) and the Housing Needs Index (HNI)*, Department of the Environment Consultation Paper, DoE, London.

Department of the Environment (1994c) *Access to Local Authority and Housing Association Tenancies: A consultation paper*, DoE, London.

Department of the Environment (1995) *Provision For Social Housing – background analysis*, Department of the Environment, HMSO, London.

Department of the Environment and the Welsh Office (1995) *Our Future Homes: opportunity, choice, responsibility*, Cm 2901, HMSO, London.

Department of the Environment, Department of Health, Welsh Office (1994) *Homelessness Code Of Guidance for Local Authorities* (revised 3rd edn), HMSO, London.

Edwards, R. (1995) 'Making Temporary Accommodation Permanent: the cost for homeless families', *Critical Social Policy*, 15 (5), pp. 60–78.

European Observatory On Homelessness (1993) *Abandoned: profile of Europe's homeless people*, FEANTSA, Brussels.

Evans, A. and Duncan, S. (1988) *Responding To Homelessness: local authority policy and practice*, HMSO, London.

Green, H. and Hansbro, J. (1995) *Housing in England 1993/4*, Office of Population Censuses and Surveys, HMSO, London.

Greve, J. (1971) *Homelessness in London*, Scottish Academic Press, Edinburgh.

Greve, J. (1991) *Homelessness in Britain*, Joseph Rowntree Foundation, York.

Halsey, A. H. (ed.) (1988) *British Social Trends Since 1990*, 2nd edn., Oxford University Press, Oxford.

Hayek, F. A. (1960) *The Constitution of Liberty*, Routledge, London.

Health Visitors Association/British Medical Association (1989) *Homeless Families and Their Health*, HVA/BMA, London.

Hedges, B. and Clemens, S. (1994) *Housing Attitudes Survey*, Department of the Environment, London.

Holman, R , Lafitte, F , Spencer, K. and Wilson, H. (1970) *Socially Deprived Families in Britain*, Bedford Square Press, London.

Hudson, S. and Liddiard, M. (1994) *Youth Homelessness: the construction of a social issue*, Macmillan, London.

Jeffers, S. and Hoggett, P. (1995) 'Like Counting Deckchairs on the Titanic: a study of institutional racism and housing allocations in Haringey and Lambeth', *Housing Studies*, 10 (3), pp. 325–44.

Jencks, C. (1994) *The Homeless*, Harvard University Press, London.

Jones, G. (1994) *Young People in and out of the Housing Market*, Findings Housing Research 108, Joseph Rowntree Foundation, York.

London Housing Unit (1993) *Homeless at Home*, London Housing Unit, London.

Mason, P. (1994) 'The Figures that Flatter to Deceive', *Inside Housing*, 30 September.

Miller, M. (1991) *Bed and Breakfast: women and homelessness today*, The Women's Press.

Murray, C. (1984) *Losing Ground*, Basic Books, New York.

Murray, C. (1988) *In Pursuit of Happiness and Good Government*, Simon and Schuster, New York.

Murray, C. (1990) *The Emerging British Underclass*, IEA Health and Welfare Unit, London.

Nelson, J., Sternberg, A. and Brindley, E. (1982) *Avoiding Institutions*, Nelson's Column Publications, London.

Newton, J. (1994) *All in One Place: the British housing story 1973–1993*, Catholic Housing Aid Society, London.

Niner, P. (1989) *Homelessness in Nine Local Authorities*, HMSO, London.

O'Mahony (1988) *A Capital Offence: The plight of the young single homeless in London*, Routledge, London.

Quilgars, D. and Anderson, I. (1995) 'Foyers For Young People', *Housing Research 142*, Joseph Rowntree Foundation, York.

Randall, G. (1988) *No Way Home: homeless young people in Central London*, Centrepoint, London.

Ridley, N. (1991) *My Style of Government: the Thatcher years*, Fontana, London.

Rowntree Foundation (1994) 'Findings', *Housing Research* 117, July 1994, Joseph Rowntree Foundation, York.

Royal Commission on the Poor Laws and Relief of Poverty (1909) Cd 4499, HMSO, London.

Somerville, P. (1994) 'Homelessness Policy in Britain', *Policy and Politics*, 22 (3), pp. 163–79.

Stewart, G. and Stewart, J. (1993) *Social Work and Housing*, Macmillan, Basingstoke.

Thatcher, M. (1993) *The Downing Street Years*, HarperCollins, London.

White, J. and Lowe, A. (1992) *Cash Incentives Review: the first two years of local authority cash incentive schemes 1989/90 and 1990/1*, HMSO, London.

Wilson, W. (1994a) *Lone Parents and Housing*, House of Commons Research Paper 94/11, House of Commons, London.

Wilson, W. (1994b) *Single Homelessness*, House of Commons Research Paper 94/89, House of Commons, London.

CHAPTER 6

Unfit and overcrowded dwellings

The slum

In the nineteenth century the term 'slum', which may have been a contraction of 'slump' (Kirby 1979), was applied to an entire area of social pathology as well as to an individual dwelling unfit for human habitation. As Mellor (1977: 67) explains, 'the slum was the locale of vice, crime, delinquency and disease, a disorderly gathering of people beyond society and without community.'

Attempts were made to deal with the 'nuisance' of individual unfit dwellings in the 1830s but it was not until 1868 that even modestly effective legislation was enacted. The Artisans' and Labourers' Dwellings Act, generally known as the Torrens Act after the back-bench MP who introduced it into Parliament, granted local authorities the power to require owners to repair or demolish unfit houses, but imposed no obligation on the landlord to replace the property or to rehouse the displaced tenant. The 1875 Artisans' and Labourers' Dwellings Improvement Act (known as the Cross Act) made provision for the eradication of the slum *area*. The aim of the legislation was to use state funds to eliminate the threat to public welfare posed by the slums and minimise the cost by selling the cleared site to philanthropic, 'model dwelling' housing associations. These associations claimed to be able to build new homes without public subsidy and even make a limited return of 5 per cent for investors. The Cross Act did little to improve the welfare of the poor. The cost of demolition with compensation to the slum landlord at market value was far greater than the amount housing associations were prepared to pay for the cleared sites. The call on public funds soon outstripped the resources earmarked for the task and the promise that all the slums in London could be cleared at a cost to the rates of two million pounds (Yelling 1982) was demonstrated to be unfounded.

The idea at the heart of this initiative – using the enhanced value of the cleared site to finance future clearance – was abandoned, and throughout the late nineteenth and early twentieth century municipal clearance activity was limited. Although the Cross Act had placed a duty on local authorities to arrange for new dwellings to be built on or near the cleared site, sufficient to rehouse the displaced persons (reduced to 50 per cent in 1882), this provision was often ignored and when housing associations did build new properties they had to let them at rents which were well beyond the incomes of the former inhabitants of the slum. The poor were forced to move into adjacent areas of overcrowded and low quality housing. Such displacement was justified by the claim that occupation of the new 'model dwellings' by the more affluent 'artisan' would release accommodation for the poor: a justification that failed to take into account the continuing growth in household formation in the cities and towns and the additional loss of dwellings caused by the clearance necessary to make way for the new railways and stations (see Document 13, page 216).

The clearance drive in the 1930s

The slum issue was placed in abeyance after 1919 while efforts were made to rectify the national shortage of dwellings caused by the virtual ending of house building during the First World War. The 1919 Housing, Town Planning, etc., Act established that compensation for an unfit house should be at site value only but, although Chamberlain's Act of 1923 contained provisions for clearance, few houses were demolished. Local authorities had to meet 50 per cent of the cost and there was strong opposition from tenants because 'there had generally been no suitable alternative accommodation on or near the site, and tenants in many cases objected to being moved from the site, and in other cases were terrified of having to pay too high rents' (Simon 1933: 36).

The Labour Government of 1929–31 started the major slum clearance drive of the 1930s. The Housing Act 1930 offered additional subsidies on condition that for every five persons removed from the slum one three-bedroomed house would be built. The Act also marked the first attempt to deal with *areas* in which the houses were on the borderline of unfitness. Improvement areas could be declared and grants were available to encourage repair.

When in 1933 the Conservative government abolished the subsidy available for general needs introduced by Wheatley, almost all local authority housing building activity was directed towards need arising from clearance. The minister responsible, Sir Hilton-Young, declared that slum clearance was 'a public health problem . . . not a first line problem of housing; it is a problem of ridding our social organism of radiating centres of depravity and disease'. Accordingly, subsidies were 'appropriate in this region as a measure for the protection and preservation of the public health'. The ending of the 'abnormal and artificial machinery' of the Wheatley subsidy meant a return to the forms of provision which were 'normal and natural to the economic life of the country' (Hilton-Young 1932, quoted in Yelling 1992).

During the 1930s over 250,000 houses were demolished or closed and over a million people were displaced. Attention was focused on the difficulties of rehousing the people affected by this clearance drive. Lack of land within the boundaries of city authorities caused problems but the main concern centred on the ability of the former inhabitants of the slum to pay the cost of their improved living standards. Figures produced by A. R. Holmes in 1947 (quoted in Yelling 1992) demonstrated that over 20 per cent of those rehoused through clearance schemes in Bethnal Green, Shoreditch and Southwark paid over four shillings (20p) more for their new accommodation than they had paid for their former dwelling. A study of council tenants in Stockton who had been rehoused from the slums demonstrated a rise in mortality connected with malnutrition (Ineichen 1993) and an examination of a clearance area in Hulme (Manchester) revealed that only 31 per cent of the people rehoused on the new estate were living there three years after the initial move. Yelling (1992: 74) maintains 'that the principal cause of this was undoubtedly rent. The old four-room houses had gross rents of 6s. 6d. [32.5p] to 8s. 6d. [42.5p], while the new A3 type house rented at 15s. 10d. [79p]'. Although this affordability problem was more frequently ignored than tackled (filtering theory again being used as the excuse), some experiments in what were then called 'differential rents' were introduced. Central government subsidies and the value of homes built in earlier years were pooled and used to offer lower rents to the poorest while increasing the rents of those above the poverty line. Such schemes met with fierce opposition from more affluent tenants and an alternative strategy – reducing the standard of the homes built for former slum dwellers – became more common in the late 1930s.

The bulldozer returns

Between 1939 and 1945 the Luftwaffe provided all the demolition thought to be necessary and it was not until late in 1953 that clearance returned to the political agenda. The Minister of Housing and Local Government, Harold Macmillan, announced that 'the time had come to take the slum problem up again as a great national effort'. One million dwellings were demolished in Britain in the years 1954 to 1975 as part of a large-scale urban renewal exercise. For the first few years this clearance drive provoked little controversy, the most significant objection being its limited scale in relationship to the true magnitude of the problem (Cullingworth 1960). However, in the early 1970s the rationale of clearance began to be questioned. The vast majority of the dwellings demolished in the 1950s and early 1960s were grossly unfit and the tenants living in them were excluded from the formal mechanisms of appeal against a local authority decision on clearance.

By the late 1960s local authorities were beginning to deal with a different type of area in which not all the dwellings were seriously unfit and where there were more home owners, former tenants who had purchased their homes from their landlords. Objections to compulsory purchase orders for demolition became more frequent and community activists started to take an interest in the clearance process and to assist local people to devise rehabilitation schemes (Coates and Silburn 1980). Social research began to reveal the hardships created by the protracted clearance procedures that could leave people living in blighted areas for many years (Ungerson 1971, Dennis 1972, Document 14, page 217). The sense of loss of community when people were rehoused in different areas was also highlighted (Ministry of Housing and Local Government 1970), and attention was drawn to the increased cost of living in the new estates, both in terms of rent and the increased expenses of travelling to work from the periphery estates. Some of the people from clearance areas found replacement accommodation in sub-standard private sector housing near to the clearance area that was less expensive than the local authority dwellings on offer (few authorities operated a rent rebate scheme at the time). Coates and Silburn comment on the impact of slum clearance and redevelopment in the St Ann's area of Nottingham:

> Today only one quarter of our original respondents are still living in St Ann's: most of these are living in one of the new houses, although a tiny handful of the people are living in the one or two streets on the edge of St Ann's that were excluded from the redevelopment order in favour of rehabilitation and improvement.
>
> (Coates and Silburn 1980: 52)

As the difficulties of living in some of the new dwellings became apparent the merits of clearance seemed less obvious. Shelter organiser David Mahon commented in 1971 that 'there is a growing feeling that the destructive ride of the bulldozer ought not to be inevitable. People have grown sceptical of the planners' right to wipe away their community'. But despite the growing concern about clearance, many local authorities still made it the central element of their urban renewal strategy for the 1970s. In Greater Manchester, for instance, local authorities estimated that 82,650 dwellings still needed to be demolished (Clark, 1973), and in Britain an average 85,000 dwellings per year were cleared in the early 1970s.

Improvement or demolition?

Although the state concentrated on demolition in the period between the wars, the improvement of older properties was not totally ignored. The Housing (Rural Workers) Act, 1926 gave local authorities outside London the discretionary power to give grants for improvement (two-thirds of the cost up to a maximum of £100 provided that the value of the improved dwelling did not exceed £400). This act promoted extensive refurbishment activity in the inter-war period but in the years from 1945 improvement was neglected as energy was focused on the production of new homes. The Housing Act of 1949 allowed local authorities to offer improvement grants in all areas of the country of 50 per cent of the cost of rehabilitation up to a limit of £600 on condition that the house would have a life of 30 years, that its rateable value was below a specified threshold and that the grant was used for improvements such as the installation of a bath, piped water and a water closet. Only 7,000 grants were issued between 1949 and 1953, mainly because local authorities did not inform the public of their availability. The 1954 Housing Repairs and Rents Act increased the value of improvement grants and the House Purchase and Housing Act 1959 made it mandatory for local authorities to pay grants – now called 'standard' grants – for the installation of basic amenities such as a bath and an internal water closet. Additional discretionary grants – directed at sub-standard rather than unfit properties – were made available to assist owners to improve their dwellings to a standard necessary for a life of 30 years.

This dual strategy – clearance of unfit property and improvement for 'sub-standard' dwellings – was continued in the Housing Act 1964 which revived the notion of improvement areas in which local government would have 'last resort' powers to compel landlords to improve their properties. A National House Condition Survey conducted by the Ministry of Housing in 1967 found that 1.8 million houses were unfit and beyond repair and 3 million dwellings needed major repairs and improvement. The following year, against a background of financial constraint and the devaluation of sterling, the Labour Government published a White Paper *Old Houses into New Homes* (1968). This declared that although:

the need for large new house building programmes will remain for many years ahead . . . the balance of need between new house building and improvement is now changing, so there must be a corresponding change in the emphasis of local authority housing programmes . . . within a total of public investment at about the level it has now reached, a greater share should go to the improvement of older houses.

(*Old Houses into New Homes* 1968)

The 1969 Housing Act increased grant payments, introduced a special grant for the provision of basic amenities in multi-occupied dwellings, and made grants available for environmental measures in what were in future to be known as General Improvement Areas. Great reliance was placed on the 'halo' impact of area selectivity:

The effort and resources devoted to improvement provides a much better return when directed to the up-grading of whole areas – the houses and the environment. People are more likely to find it worth their while to co-operate and to maintain their houses after improvement.

(Ministry of Housing and Local Government, circular 65/69)

The 1971 Housing Act offered a higher rate of grant (75 per cent of eligible costs) in development and intermediate areas. The number of grants approved soared from 108,938 in 1969 to 360,954 in 1973 (Kirby 1979) as a consequence of Edward Heath's attempt to inject demand into the economy and to use home improvement as a means to limit the future need for comprehensive redevelopment and new council housing. The 1969 and 1971 Housing Acts helped to improve the private sector housing stock, but many people with low incomes left their homes as landlords encouraged tenants to move so their houses could be sold to home owners (Balchin 1995) – a process that became known as 'gentrification'. The White Paper *Better Homes: The Next Priorities* (1973) heralded a return to rationing by area selectivity and introduced the idea of the Housing Action Area to complement the existing notion of the General Improvement Area. Housing Action Areas were to be areas of housing and social stress exhibiting some combination of a number of problems: a high proportion of unfit houses or houses with bad external layout, households living at a density exceeding 1.5 persons per room, furnished tenancies, shared accommodation, a high proportion of elderly people and large families and a significant number of homes lacking a hot water supply, a fixed bath or an inside WC.

The Labour government of 1974 adopted many of the principles contained in the Conservative's 1973 White Paper. The 1974 Housing Act made provision for local authorities to declare Housing Action Areas in which they would have powers to make grants for repairs only; to pay 75 per cent and, in cases of hardship, 90 per cent grants for the purpose of improvement; to compel private landlords to refurbish their properties; to ensure that tenanted dwellings were let at a registered rent after a grant had been made; and to acquire rented properties by compulsory purchase. Government circulars on the implementation of the legislation emphasised that local authorities now had a wide range of powers which provided the basis for a comprehensive, corporate and flexible local strategy to tackle the problem of unfit and sub-standard housing and that 'in declaring a clearance area, a local authority will have to establish for example that an HAA declaration is not more appropriate' (Circular 13/75). It was believed that the use of these flexible powers would result in 'a continuous process of minor rebuilding and renovation which sustains and reinforces the vitality of a neighbourhood in ways responsive to social and physical needs as they develop and change' (Circular 13/75: *Housing Act 1974: renewal strategies*).

What went wrong?

Writing in 1981 on the impact of the 1974 Act Gibson and Langstaff stated that 'in numbers game terms the 1974—79 period was dismal'. Slum clearance fell from 309,000 between 1970 and 1974 to 213,000 between 1975 and 1979, reaching 33,000 in 1979, the lowest annual figure since 1955. However, improvement grants also declined from 361,000 in 1973 to 136,000 in 1979 and the number of grants awarded in General Improvement Areas and Housing Action Areas between 1975 and 1979 was only 67,000. This reduction in grants was the result of the tightening up of procedures for discretionary grants outside GIAs and HAAs (part of the 'targeting' objective of the 1974 Housing Act), but one might have expected a corresponding increase in activity in the new 'special status' areas.

What went wrong? The main problem was that the Housing Action initiative got caught in the cutbacks in public expenditure (mainly on capital spending) that resulted from the financial crisis of 1976. Other factors also contributed to the ineffectiveness of Housing Action Areas. Many people in the areas were too poor to find their contribution to the cost of refurbishment and the powers granted to local authorities to compel landlords to improve were cumbersome to operate. Some local authorities, by concentrating a large share of their resources on HAAs, managed to make them work but Monck and Lomas (1980: 133–34) concluded their investigation into the policy by stating that 'the lost opportunities outweigh the examples of best practice, and it is widely known that central government and many local authorities are disillusioned with HAAs'.

Looking back over the years of urban renewal between 1953 and 1979 produces a mixed response. If improvement is measured in terms of the physical condition of the housing stock then progress was made. However, with hindsight, it is clear that many errors of judgement occurred. The clearance procedures, which involved many different local authority departments, were complex and protracted with the result that too many people had to endure years of living in deplorable surroundings. Scant regard was paid to the views of the tenants involved in the redevelopment process and, although too much should not be made of the 'loss of working class communities', some damage to the neighbourhood spirit did occur. Many of the mass housing schemes which replaced the slums were badly constructed, poorly designed and provided inappropriate accommodation. Little attention was given to the economic impact of clearance, and numerous small workshops and businesses were lost in the process of redevelopment. The improvement grant system tended to favour those with the knowledge of its operation and the resources to meet their share of the cost. When the system became more selective in the late 1970s, resources for improvement diminished: a demonstration that selectivity is often used as an excuse for reductions in expenditure rather than as a mechanism to concentrate resources on those in greatest need.

From rehabilitation to retrenchment

Mrs Thatcher's first government (1979–83) displayed a strong commitment to the rehabilitation of older homes. In the late 1970s clearance was automatically associated with council housing and hence the improvement of the private sector stock, in addition to being a useful economic regulator in the recession of the early 1980s, was seen as a mechanism for preventing the need for more local authority building. This commitment to rehabilitation was accompanied by a shift in policy away from area-based renewal towards extending the availability of improvement grants regardless of location. The Housing Act of 1980 enabled tenants as well as landlords and owner-occupiers to apply for grants; annulled the provisions, introduced in 1974, concerning the repayment of a grant when the property was sold; made repair grants for pre-1919 houses available nationwide; and introduced more flexibility into the grant system.

In 1982 the maximum grant rate for repairs and the installation of basic amenities was raised to 90 per cent for all applicants, a move which effectively reduced the advantages of the special status of GIA or HAA. The government also announced that an extra £75 million could be spent by local authorities on private sector improvement, and grants paid to private owners and tenants increased to 293,000 in 1983. Only a small proportion of this grant aid was received by people living in 'special status' areas but there was some targeting of improvement activity through block repair schemes (where the local authority managed the simultaneous provision of grants to a group of properties) and 'enveloping' (the external renovation of a block of terraced houses without cost to the owner, thereby encouraging investment in the interior).

Following the General Election of 1983, reductions in public expenditure were made and improvement grants were badly affected by these cuts. Although the number of grants remained at a high level in 1984 – the legacy of approvals made before the reductions in housing expenditure – the late 1980s were a time of limited local government activity on the housing dimension of urban renewal. The number of grants awarded went down from 229,000 in 1984 to 98,000 in 1989 and clearance declined from 9,400 properties in 1983–84 to 3,200 in 1989–90.

A Green Paper *Home Improvement ─A New Approach,* published in 1985, revealed the thinking of the government concerning the future principles to be applied to the issue of unfit and sub-standard housing. It proposed a switch in responsibility for the older private stock from the government to the owner stating that 'home ownership offers opportunities for individuals to alter and improve their homes as they wish; they must carry the primary responsibility for keeping their property in good repair'. In the future, eligibility for improvement grants would be determined by two criteria: the fitness of the property and the income of the occupiers. In relationship to the fitness standard the Green Paper declared that it believed that 'a policy of raising the minimum standard to match rising social expectations would be inappropriate' and that the existing fitness standard would form the basis of the new legislation. The owner-occupier of any dwelling found to be unfit according to the defined standard would be eligible for an improvement grant but only if the income of the household was below a specified level. This testing of means was justified by the quotation of evidence that a significant proportion of the grants available had been claimed by more affluent groups. The new grant would cover only the cost of making a dwelling fit; additional expenditure to give a house a 30-year life would be covered by an equity-sharing loan whereby, in return for a loan, the local authority would acquire a share in the value of the property.

The Local Government and Housing Act, 1989

No action was taken on the principles outlined in the Green Paper until the 1989 Local Government and Housing Act, and in the interim the idea of equity-sharing loans was abandoned. One of the purposes of the 1989 Act was to simplify both the system of improvement grants and the process of area-based renewal, but procedures remained complicated and only a simplified version of the arrangements introduced under various government circulars is given here.

- A new benchmark for the assessment of unfitness was introduced (See Document 15, page 218).
- Renovation grants became mandatory in that local authorities had to award a grant to home owners if a dwelling did not meet the fitness standard and the local authority was satisfied that renovation was the most appropriate way of dealing with the faults in the property.
- Renovation grants, sufficient to bring a property up to a fitness standard, became subject to a test of means. The grant covered the cost of making a property fit but additional grants, given at the discretion of the local authority, became available for work such as providing more living space.
- Disabled facilities grants were made available; it was mandatory for essential works to enable a disabled person access into and around their dwelling but discretionary for other purposes.
- Minor works grants for repairs and adaptations costing less than £1,080 were introduced to assist elderly people in receipt of a means-tested benefit to stay in their own homes and for anyone claiming a means-tested benefit to use for insulation work.
- Declarations of Housing Action Areas and General Improvement Areas were abolished but local authorities were allowed to introduce group repair schemes and designate renewal areas. Group repair schemes could only be introduced where 75 per cent of the dwellings were in poor repair and one third of the owners was in receipt of a means-tested benefit. Renewal areas could be declared only after the local authority had carried out a neighbourhood renewal assessment, a comprehensive appraisal of the options for an area with a cost/benefit analysis of these options. The area concerned must have more than 300 dwellings, 75 per cent must be unfit, 75 per cent in private ownership and at least 30 per cent of the households should be mainly dependent on means-tested benefits.
- The declaration of clearance areas was permitted only when a local authority had carried out a detailed cost/benefit appraisal of the options for the area.

The new regime for urban renewal produced disappointing results because insufficient resources were available to enable the system to operate effectively. The notion of a mandatory grant to households with a low income living in unfit property implies that such households have a right to the grant but the central government has not made the finance available to meet the demand for mandatory grants, especially in areas in which there was a combination of low income and a major problem of unfitness. Local authorities responsible for such areas were forced to remain silent on the mandatory entitlement to a grant and to delay the payments to those who had applied, thus creating uncertainty and frustration amongst applicants. Even with these delaying tactics mandatory improvement grants have taken 90 per cent of the resources available at the expense of area-based renewal initiatives (by June 1993 only 50 renewal areas had been declared, mainly in the North West).

In 1993, the Government issued a consultation paper giving its views on the difficulties presented by the 1989 legislation and offering proposals for change. The paper included statistics from the 1991 English House Condition Survey to justify the assertion that 'useful progress' had been made in recent years in dealing with the worst condition housing stock, but the paper maintained that 'it has become clear that, despite more effective use of resources brought about by improved targeting, a growing number of authorities are finding it difficult to operate the system within the resources allocated to it.' All the suggestions for change involved cutbacks in the scope of the scheme (tighter means testing, the abolition of mandatory grants, requiring local authorities to find a bigger share of costs, a reduction in mandatory grants, the introduction of loans), in order to bring projected expenditure into line with the anticipated reduction in resources. Some of these measures were introduced in 1994; local authorities had to absorb 40 per cent of expenditure on grants and the maximum grant was reduced from £50,000 to £20,000 (£24,000 in Wales). The White Paper *Our Future Homes* (1995) announced that legislation would be introduced to make renovation grants discretionary.

The future of housing renewal

The extent of the problem

In 1991 there were 1.7 million dwellings unfit or below the tolerable standard (the measure used for unfitness in Scotland) in the United Kingdom (Leather, Mackintosh and Rolfe 1994); 13.3 per cent of dwellings in Wales were unfit (Welsh Office 1994); 8.8 per cent in Northern Ireland and 4.7 per cent in Scotland. According to the 1991 English House Conditions Survey, 1,498,000 dwellings were unfit for human habitation, that is, 7.6 per cent of the total stock. The average cost of making these dwellings fit was £3,301 at 1991 prices with a range of less than £500 for the one-third of unfit dwellings with minor problems to £15,000 for the 7 per cent of dwellings with five or more defects. Progress had been made since 1986. Using a standard comparable to that of 1991, it was estimated that the number of dwellings lacking basic amenities had decreased by 258,000 in England (DoE 1993a) and by 50,000 in Wales (Welsh Office 1994). Nonetheless a significant problem of unfitness remains and because much of the progress between 1986 and 1991 was the result of the buoyancy in the housing market – allowing owners to use the asset value of their homes to finance repairs – then housing conditions are likely to get worse in the future.

Clearance and improvement

A circular issued under the 1989 Local Government and Housing Act giving advice on area renewal and unfitness indicated that the Department of the Environment wished to see more clearance, and the 'thorough appraisal' of the various options before a renewal area can be declared (including an economic assessment of the costs and benefits of clearance relative to area improvement) was designed to stimulate clearance. This device did not produce the desired result; only 3,856 dwellings were closed or demolished in England in 1993–4 and at the present rate of clearance each new dwelling in Britain will have to last for over 3,300 years (Leather, Mackintosh and Rolfe 1994). The necessity for demolition can be postponed by ensuring that investment is made in older homes which, if preserved, are an asset for future generations. The amount spent on the improvement of older property declined from £764.6 million in 1984 to £232 million in 1992 (at 1982 prices) and the biggest fall occurred after the implementation of the 1989 Act. Leather and Mackintosh (1994 7) point out that in overall terms, the number of grants provided in England has fallen from almost 100,000 in the last full year of the old system (pre 1990) to 'only 34,928 mandatory renovation grants, 16,728 disabled facilities grants and 29,337 minor works grants' in 1992. Housing associations also reduced their renovation work: from 18,000 homes rehabilitated in 1984 to 6,000 in 1993. The reasons for this reduction are complex but the risks involved in rehabilitation when compared to new build, and the costs involved, have been two important factors (NFHA 1994).

It seems that the 1989 Act was a rationing rather than a targeting measure. Further reductions in expenditure have been announced and, if the government is unwilling to make the resources available to implement a mandatory grants system plus an area-based system renewal strategy it is a sensible decision to abandon mandatory grants and concentrate existing resources in renewal areas at least until the 440,000 dwellings identified as being in the worst condition and located in areas with a poor environment (DoE 1993a) have been treated.

Ideally some of the measures taken to modernise the housing stock should be part of a comprehensive strategy for economic development. In this respect the idea of concentrating resources, which lies at the heart of the City Challenge and the Single Regeneration Budget initiatives, has considerable potential, but such a strategy would leave the owners of unfit dwellings outside the designated target areas without assistance. An additional set of rationing mechanisms have been proposed by Leather and Mackintosh (1994: 27). They suggest that if resources cannot be provided, the emphasis of grant aid should be shifted. 'The amount of assistance per household should be limited in order to provide help to a larger number of those in need'. In addition, 'grant aid should be concentrated on basic aspects of housing conditions which are important to safeguard the health and comfort of residents'. These are sensible methods of targeting the restricted resources available for housing renewal but it must be remembered that in 1989 the means-testing of grants was to be the primary method of targeting. The fact that yet more rationing mechanisms are now required demonstrates that a policy of selectivity and targeting does not mean more resources for the poor; it simply leaves them exposed to further cuts because they lack the economic and social power to protect their interests.

Overcrowding

Blaming the victims

Overcrowding is a neglected issue. This neglect is connected to the lack of a realistic statutory definition of the problem, complacency at the progress that has been made in reducing its incidence and the relationship between overcrowding and 'race'.

During the nineteenth century overcrowding was given an importance almost equal to unfitness as a proper object of state action; both overcrowding and unfitness were described in the 1875 Public Health Act as 'statutory nuisances'. Overcrowding caused concern because it was believed that lack of ventilation caused disease and because crowded conditions were associated with immorality. 'If human beings are crowded together' declared the Reverend John Montgomery in 1860, then 'moral corruption takes place, as certainly as fermentation or putrefaction in a heap of organic matter' (Montgomery 1860, quoted in Wohl 1983). The greatest anxiety focused on the common lodgings houses, in which straw mattresses and beds could be rented on a nightly basis. Overcrowding in common lodgings houses occurred on a massive scale. In Leeds in 1851 'the Commissioner of Police in one small area found 222 lodging houses in which lived 2,500 people, averaging two and a half persons per bed!' (Hodgkinson 1980: 10, see Document 16, page 219). Unfortunately the cause of overcrowding was believed to be located in the behaviour of the poor who were thought to prefer overcrowded conditions to paying an appropriate part of their income for more spacious accommodation. The consequence of this belief was that action taken to overcome the problem consisted of regulations issued under the Act for the Regulation and Inspection of Common Lodging-Houses 1851, which was aimed at controlling the number of people occupying a dwelling. The police or sanitary inspectors made periodic visits to lodging houses to evict any surplus inhabitants.

It was, of course, the construction of additional dwellings rather than control measures that alleviated the problem, but in the 1930s a serious level of overcrowding remained. The 1931 census recorded seven million people living at densities of more than 1.5 persons per room and 397,000 households at more than 2 persons per room. The Moyne Committee, established in 1933 to explore the issue of the 'reconditioning' of older houses and the 'facilitation of the efforts of public utility societies', made a number of references to overcrowding and its findings convinced officials that overcrowding was a more serious menace to health than deficiencies which can be met by reconditioning. But overcrowding presented a troublesome issue for the Conservative Party because it was more difficult to set clear boundaries to state action than in the case of slum clearance. Hilton-Young, the minister responsible, neatly side-stepped this difficulty by arguing that overcrowding should be dealt with by 'rehousing on the overcrowded and slum sites', thereby presenting the issue as an inner-city, redevelopment matter rather than a general housing issue that might interfere with the operations of private enterprise in the suburbs (Yelling 1992: 105).

The Housing Act 1935 set out a framework for tackling overcrowding by defining overcrowding and giving local authorities additional powers to take action against landlords. Recognising the futility of attempting to control overcrowding without the provision of additional accommodation, the Act also offered subsidies to assist the building of new homes. However, these subsidies were to be 'strictly limited to areas where rehousing is effected on or near the central sites by means of blocks of flats', although in special cases dwellings could be erected elsewhere. The major attack on overcrowding was to follow the completion of the task of eradicating the slums, but the outbreak of the Second World War prevented any significant action.

After the Second World War no specific initiative was directed towards mastering overcrowding; the problem was regarded as one element of the overall housing issue to be overcome by building more homes. The 1957 Housing Act, in establishing the duties of local authorities in relationship to the allocation of council houses, stated that they should give reasonable preference to 'persons who are occupying insanitary or overcrowded houses, have large families or are living under unsatisfactory housing conditions'. The definition of overcrowding given in the 1957 Act was based on the Housing Act of 1935 and 'was, even in 1935, a very limited one' (Cullingworth 1979). The problem of overcrowding took second place to slum clearance in the 1950s, 1960s and the early 1970s, and since 1977 it has had a lower priority than statutory homelessness.

The extent of overcrowding

Estimates of the extent of overcrowding are related to the criteria used to measure its incidence. There are a number of measures available.

The Census standard: The census reports provide statistics on levels
of occupancy since 1911 but interpretations of the meaning of these
figures over time are bedevilled by the periodic changes that have been
made in the definition of a room (see Halsey 1988); Table 6.1 should
therefore be interpreted with caution.

The statutory standard: This standard is used to determine whether
or not an occupier of a dwelling who causes or permits it to be overcrowded
is guilty of an offence and as such it provides the baseline for any
official action that may be taken. Two standards are specified: a room
standard and a space standard. The room standard relates to sexual
overcrowding and is contravened when:

the number of persons sleeping in a dwelling and the number of rooms available as sleeping accommodation is such that two persons of opposite sexes
who are not living together as husband and wife must sleep in the same room.
For this purpose –
(a) children under the age of ten shall be left out of account, and
(b) a room is available as sleeping accommodation if it is of a type normally
used in the locality either as a bedroom or as a living room.

(Housing Act 1985: Section 325)

The space standard is complicated and compares the number of rooms
and the floor area of these rooms with the number of people permitted
to live in the accommodation. For instance a room of 110 square feet
can be occupied by two persons. No account is taken of children under
one and a child under ten 'shall be reckoned as one-half of a unit'.

This statutory standard is very low and as Ormandy (1991) has observed
'the average two storeyed, terraced house (with three bedrooms, two
living rooms and a kitchen) could be occupied by the equivalent of 10
persons without being overcrowded – and that could mean six adults
and eight children aged between one year and 10 years.'

The bedroom standard: The Bedroom Standard is used for the General
Household Survey and the English House Conditions Survey. It is calculated
as follows:

a separate bedroom is allocated to each cohabiting couple, any other person
aged 21 or over, each pair of young persons aged 10–20 of the same sex; and
each pair of children under 10 (regardless of sex). Unpaired young persons
aged 10–20 are paired with a child under 10 of the same sex if possible or are

Table 6.1 **Number of households with more
than 1.5 persons per room: 1951–91**

Year	No. households
1951	664 000
1971	220 000
1991	109 000

Source: Census returns

allocated a separate bedroom. Any remaining unpaired children under 10 are also allocated a separate bedroom. The calculated standard for the household is then compared with the actual number of bedrooms available for its sole use to indicated deficiencies or excesses. Bedrooms include bedsitters, boxrooms and bedrooms which are indicated as such by informants even though they may not be in use as such.

(DoE 1993a: 33)

The findings of the English House Conditions Survey indicate that 3 per cent (517,000) of households live in overcrowded conditions according to the bedroom standard. As would be expected overcrowding is more prevalent in large families; 13 per cent (263,000) of households where there are three or more dependent children are overcrowded. The English House Conditions Survey comments:

this category encompasses households containing more than one family, of whom some 15% (170,000) are overcrowded. This indicates that extended families and families sharing a household may have particular difficulties in this respect. Around one in four (88,000) households of Asian origin, for whom extended family relationships are an important aspect of home life, are living in overcrowded conditions. Their difficulties lie particularly in the pre-1919 terraced housing available in urban centres, where such households predominantly live, which cannot meet the needs of larger families. Around half of Asian overcrowded households consist of seven or more persons. Around one in twelve (64,000) lone parent households . . . also suffer from overcrowded conditions. For this group the problem is more one of the limitations of flats.

(DoE 1993a: 35)

The importance of overcrowding

There are a number of relationships between overcrowding and life chances; it can influence mental health, physical health and the educational progress of children. Gabe and Williams (1989) found 'a significant and strong "J" shaped relationship' between crowding in the home and psychological distress amongst the women 'which accounted for half of the explained variance in psychological symptoms'. The National Child Development Study (1988) came to the conclusion that:

Those whose families were owner-occupiers at seven, 11 and 16 and similarly those who were not in crowded homes at those ages, were more likely, compared with those who were local authority tenants (or in crowded homes) at all three ages to be in higher-status occupations at 23; to have high family incomes, particularly when family situation is taken into account; to have experienced less unemployment, both currently and since completing education; to have high qualifications; and to rate their health highly.

(National Child Development Study 1988: 25)

Overcrowding increases the risk of the spread of tuberculosis (Hyndman 1990), there is a significant association between overcrowding in childhood and levels of stomach cancer in adults (Barker *et al.* 1990) and overcrowding has been related to high rates of accidental injury and fire (Lowry 1991) as well as to emotional problems in childhood (Arblaster and Hawtin 1994). 'Chronic bronchitis, asthma and emphysema also show significantly high correlations with overcrowding which are not explained by social deprivation factors or smoking' (The Standing Conference on Public Health 1994: 32).

Conclusion

Despite the declaration by the government that 'individuals . . . must carry the primary responsibility for keeping their property in good repair' (Secretary of State for the Environment 1985: 1) a strong case can be made for the involvement of the state in the clearance and improvement of older homes. Living in an unfit dwelling damages your health. According to the Department of the Environment dampness encourages:

the formation of moulds, and the proliferation of moulds and mites in conditions of high relative humidity is associated with ill health. It has been estimated that some 15 to 20 per cent of the population suffer some form of allergic disease, rhinitis and asthma being the most common, and a proportion of these can be attributed to mite and mould allergy. A number of recent studies also conclude that damp and mouldy housing has both direct and indirect effects on physical and mental health.

(DoE 1990: 43)

In addition dampness in clothing and bedding, through the process of cooling by evaporation, may reduce body temperatures, particularly in elderly people and children. Houses in a poor state of repair are difficult to keep warm; dampness can act on the fabric of the building lowering the temperature and making a marginal heating system inadequate (DoE 1990). High heating bills can lead to people with low incomes having to make a choice between adequate heating and nutritional food; deaths from myocardial infarction, strokes and respiratory conditions increase in the winter months. According to The Standing Conference on Public Health (1994: 31) 'there is both epidemiological and experimental evidence to indicate a relationship between exposure to cold and physiological changes that may be implicated in both respiratory disorders and heart disease'.

The health implications of unfitness indicate that it should be regarded as part of a national commitment to ensure that every citizen, regardless of means, is as healthy as possible; it has been estimated that expenditure of £3,000 per household on housing would be justified by the savings made to the National Health Service in reducing the incidence of poor health (Carr-Hill, Coyle and Ivens 1993). State involvement in improvement is also a vital element of community care and can help to reduce the necessity for expensive residential provision. At some point in its life a dwelling becomes worn out, unsuitable to prevailing norms of living, and must be demolished to make space for new accommodation. Since many dwellings in Britain are terraced then it is difficult to undertake clearance on a house by house basis: collective action is required.

A necessary first step in mastering overcrowding is to give the issue its due recognition in the national system of resource distribution. In the past the indicators used by the Department of the Environment to allocate resources to housing associations and local authorities have placed a high value on statutory homelessness and a low value on overcrowding. Whereas the impact of long periods in bed and breakfast accommodation deserves its high priority, it is questionable that some of the other variables used in the construction of national resource distribution indicators should have a higher priority than overcrowding.

References

Arbaster, L. and Hawtin, M. (1994) *Health, Housing and Social Policy*, Social-ist Medical Association, London.

Balchin, P. (1995) *Housing Policy: an introduction*, Routledge, London.

Barker, D., Coggon, D., Osmond, C. and Wickam, C. (1990) 'Poor Housing in Childhood and High Rates of Stomach Cancer in England and Wales', *British Journal of Cancer*, 61, pp. 575–78.

Carr-Hill, R. A., Coyle, D. and Ivens, C. (1993) 'Poor Housing: Poor Health?' Unpublished report.

Clark, D. M. (1973) *Greater Manchester Votes*, Redrose Publications, Manches-ter.

Coates, K. and Silburn, R. (1980) *Beyond the Bulldozer*, University of Notting ham, Nottingham.

Cullingworth, J. B. (1960) *Housing Needs and Planning Policy*, Routledge and Kegan Paul, London.

Cullingworth, J. B. (1979) *Essays On Housing Policy*, Allen and Unwin, London.

Dennis, N. (1972) *People and Planning: the sociology of housing in Sunder-land*, Faber and Faber, London.

Department of the Environment (1990) *Local Government and Housing Act 1989: area renewal, unfitness and enforcement action*, Circular 6/90, 28 March

Department of the Environment (1993a) *English House Conditions Survey*, HMSO, London.

Department of the Environment (1993b) *The Future of Private Housing Renewal Programmes: A Consultation Document*, Department of the Environment, London.

Department of the Environment (1993c) *Monitoring the New Housing Fitness Standard*, HMSO, London.

Department of the Environment and the Welsh Office (1995) *Our future homes: Opportunity, Choice, Responsibility*, HMSO, London.

Gabe, J. and Williams, P. (1993) 'Women, Crowding and Mental Health', in Burridge, R. and Ormandy, S. (eds) *Unhealthy Housing*, E & FN Spon, London.

Gibson, M. A. and Langstaff, M. J. (1981) *An Introduction to Urban Renewal*, Hutchinson, London.

Halsey, A. H. (ed.) (1988) *Social Trends Since 1900, a guide to the changing social structure of Britain*, 2nd edn, Oxford University Press, Oxford.

Hodgkinson, R. (1980) *Science and the Rise of Technology since 1800*, Block V, Unit 10, Open University, Milton Keynes.

Hyndman, S. (1990) 'Could TB return?', *Roof*, March/April.

Ineichen, B. (1993) *Homes and Health: how housing and health interact*, E and FN Spon, London.

Kirby, D. (1979) *Slum Housing and Residential Renewal: the case of urban Britain*, Longman, London.

Leather, P. and Mackintosh, S. (1994) *The Future of Housing Renewal Policy*, Joseph Rowntree Foundation, York.

Leather, P., Mackintosh, S. and Rolfe, S. (1994) *Papering over the Cracks*, National Housing Forum, London.

Lowry, S. (1991) *Housing and Health*, British Medical Journal, Plymouth.

Mellor, J. R. (1977) *Urban Sociology in an Urbanised Society*, Routledge and Kegan Paul, London.

Ministry of Housing and Local Government (1968) *Old Houses into New Homes*, Cmnd 3602, HMSO, London.

Ministry of Housing and Local Government (1970) *Moving Out of a Slum*, HMSO, London.

Monck, E. and Lomas, G. (1980) *Housing Action Areas: success and failure*, Centre For Environmental Studies, London.

National Child Development Study (1988) *A Longitudinal Study of Housing and Social Circumstances in Childhood and Early Childhood*, NCDS, London.

National Federation of Housing Associations (1994) *Winning The Regeneration Game*, NFHA, London (1994).

Ormandy, D. (1991) 'Overcrowding', *Roof*, March/April.

Secretary of State For The Environment (1985) *Home Improvement – A New Approach*, HMSO, London.

Secretary of State For The Environment and Secretary of State For Wales (1973) *Better Homes The Next Priorities*, Cmnd 5339, HMSO, London.

Simon, E. D. (1933) *The Anti-Slum Campaign*, Longman, London.

Standing Conference On Public Health (1994) *Housing, Homelessness and Health*, The Nuffield Provincial Hospitals Trust, London.

Ungerson, C. (1971) *Moving Home: a study of the redevelopment process in two London boroughs*, Bell, London.

Welsh Office (1994) *Welsh House Conditions Survey*, HMSO, Cardiff.

Wohl, A. S. (1983) *Endangered Lives*, Methuen, London.

Yelling, J. A. (1982) *Slums and Slum Clearance in Victorian London*, Allen and Unwin, London.

Yelling, J. A. (1992) *Slums and Redevelopment: policy and practice in England, 1918–45, with particular reference to London*, UCL Press, London.

CHAPTER 7

'Problem' estates

Residualisation

The literature on housing is now replete with accounts of the 'residualisation' of local authority housing (English 1979, Hamnett 1984, Hamnett and Randolph 1987, Willmott and Murie 1988, Williams, Sewel and Twine 1986). This ugly term has been applied to the process by which local authority housing has come to be occupied by people with low incomes, often derived from state benefits rather than market transactions (Forrest and Murie, 1983, 1990, Tables 7.1 and 7.2). In the long term, public housing 'provides only a safety net for those who for reasons of poverty, age or infirmity cannot obtain suitable accommodation in the private sector' (Malpass and Murie 1982). Bentham (1986) has estimated that in 1953 the median income of council house tenants was almost the same as the overall median income but by 1992 it had declined 50.2 per cent (Government Statistical Office 1994).

Residualisation has important implications for the quality of the housing occupied by people on low incomes. Although some politicians argue that 'welfare' housing will be of high quality – targeting available resources on the poorest sections of the community provides funds for a better quality service – the historical evidence indicates a different conclusion. When building for the 'general needs' of the working class, local authorities built good quality homes whereas, during the periods when subsidies were directed towards building for people displaced

Table 7.1 Median weekly income of local authority heads of household and heads of household with partner, at constant 1990 prices relative to mortgaged buyers and all households: Great Britain, selected years, 1975–92

	Local authority		Buying with mortgage		All households	
	Head of household	With partner	Head of household	With partner	Head of household	With partner
	£ weekly		£ weekly		£ weekly	
1975	124.1	n.a.	208.0	n.a.	146.0	n.a.
1980	102.4	120.7	280.3	298.0	153.6	184.6
1985	76.0	150.7	243.8	338.1	149.4	255.6
1990	73.0	84.0	286.0	375.0	175.0	218.0
1992	76.5	86.4	252.0	336.6	151.2	194.4

Source: Newton (1994)

Table 7.2 **Employment status of household heads by tenure: 1981 and 1991**

	In employment full time	Unemployed, sick, retired or disabled	Others
1981	%	%	%
Outright owners	37	49	14
Home buyers	92	6	2
Council renting	43	42	15
Housing association	42	43	15
Unfurnished private	51	36	13
Furnished private	65	15	20
All tenures	58	31	11
1991			
Outright owners	26	65	9
Home buyers	86	10	4
Council renting	25	59	16
Housing association	29	56	15
Unfurnished private	54	37	9
Furnished private	56	17	27
All tenures	54	37	9

Source: Adapted from Wilcox (1994)

from the slums, quality deteriorated. Moreover, as local authority housing was pushed towards 'the tenancy of last resort' during the 1980s its image became tarnished and its political profile diminished.

The process of residualisation

Clearance   The process of residualisation started in the 1930s when local authorities were diverted from 'general needs' provision to clearance and it resumed in the 1950s when 'general needs' subsidies were ended and local government was encouraged to concentrate on provision for people displaced by clearance. Holmans (1987) notes that between 1953–5 and 1963 the proportion of council tenants with low incomes increased significantly.

The popularity of home ownership   Good evidence on 'real' tenure preference over time is difficult to find. Ideally the choices of different age groups should be distinguished and some allowance would be made for the subsidies granted to each sector at different periods. A survey conducted in 1967 by the Opinion Research Centre asked 'what kind of accommodation would you prefer, if you moved from your present house, if you could get it?' The survey found a 66 per cent preference for owner-occupation, 23 per cent for local authority tenure and 11 per cent for private renting. By 1975, according to a survey by the British Market Research Bureau, 21 per cent wanted local authority housing but by 1989 only 12 per cent expressed such a preference (Boleat 1989). The recession in the housing market produced a decline in the popularity of owner-occupation but, in 1991, 37 per cent of council tenants still aspired to home ownership (Coles 1991).

Housing benefit   Prior to 1972 families with a low income found it difficult to afford council housing, but this problem was eased by the 1972 Housing Finance Act which introduced a national system of rent rebates. The financial barriers to a local authority tenancy were further reduced by the reforms to the social security system introduced in April 1988 (Hills1991). Housing benefit – previously related to the rent charged for a property so that a tenant had to pay a proportion of any rent increase – was linked only to the income of the tenant.

Homelessness legislation   The 1977 Housing (Homeless Persons) Act improved the access of homeless people to local authority accommodation. Homelessness is linked directly to financial problems; Duncan and Evans (1988) found that the majority of those accepted as homeless had no earned income.

Polarisation

'Polarisation' is often used as a substitute for 'residualisation'   with emphasis on the 'income gap' between council tenants and home owners – but it also refers to the *spatial* segregation that has accompanied residualisation (Forrest and Murie 1991).

Local authority housing is not a uniformly desirable commodity. Specifications of internal amenity set out in government reports (Tudor Walters 1919, Dudley1944, Parker Morris 1961) have always been high relative to the standard product of the speculative builder, but the overall attractiveness of local authority estates has not always been pleasant. Many of the 'self-contained cottages' built under the Addison and Wheatley Acts, with their bathrooms, internal WCs, hot water and gardens, are still agreeable places in which to live but too often they are somewhat uniform in style, lack local amenities and are in need of refurbishment. Because their designers disliked embellishment and individuality, they can be clearly distinguished from homes built for owner-occupation. When the housing effort switched from 'general needs' to slum clearance and overcrowding in the late 1930s, more flats built at higher densities than the 'cottage estates' were erected and these were frequently placed around courtyards giving an almost prison-like atmosphere. Moreover, because such estates housed people from the slums they sometimes attracted an undesirable reputation from the moment that they were built.

The 'Bevan' houses of the period 1946 to 1951 were well designed and, as Cole and Furhey (1994: 98) comment, 'appropriately maintained and upgraded, the products of these years endure as some of the best of the public housing stock'. Despite the reduction in space standards that took place in the middle 1950s the quality of the homes built in the period was good. It was not until the new clearance drive and the competition between the political parties over the quantity of homes gained momentum that the quality of local authority homes declined. Internal standards remained high but the quality of design and construction deteriorated. High rise, industrial building techniques, deck access, maisonettes and the separation of garages from dwellings began to be common features of new local authority homes. Standards of dwelling design improved towards the end of the 1960s but the application of 'housing cost yardsticks' by central government after 1967 meant that many of the community facilities incorporated in the blueprints for the estates were removed in order to ensure that the schemes received government approval.

Allocation

The variations in the desirability of council homes have been mirrored in the incidence of right-to-buy sales (Forrest and Murie 1991) and are reflected in the outcomes of the processes of allocation used by local authorities. Many studies have documented how the informal and formal procedures for allocating council housing have led to the allocation of the least desirable dwellings to those with the most urgent housing needs. Clapham and Kintrea (1986) demonstrated this tendency clearly in their study of allocations in a part of Glasgow:

Although only 30 per cent of all households have per capita incomes of £18.00 a week or less, 55 per cent of those who accept a house in the least popular group of sub-areas fall into this category. Similarly, at the other end of the income scale, 16 per cent of households have per capita incomes of £52.50 a week or more, but 27 per cent of those in the most popular group of sub-areas have such an income. This makes it clear that poorer people are being allocated less popular housing than better-off people.

(Clapham and Kintrea 1986: 56)

Only a minority of local authorities have applied penalties to the refusal of an offer by waiting list applicants (Prescott-Clarke, Allen and Morrissey 1988) and thus those in less urgent housing need have been able to wait for a more acceptable offer. The financial penalties imposed on local authorities by the Department of the Environment for 'unacceptable' void rates and the desire of local authorities to maximise rent income have applied pressure on allocations officers. They have responded by attempting to cut down the number of refusals (and hence the time a property is vacant and subject to vandalism which, in turn, produces further delays in lettings) by offering 'difficult to let' property to people known to be disposed to accept them. Jones (1988) summarises the process:

The result of this process of complex bargaining is to establish a clear hierarchy wherein offers of good quality property are most often made to those most able to 'operate' the system whether by political influence, by possessing a bargaining counter, or by articulacy and social acceptability. Conversely, property perceived by the Allocations staff as poor quality will be offered to those least able to refuse, least articulate and least able to enlist effective support.

(Jones 1988: 96)

Homeless people have been particularly vulnerable in this system. Loveland comments:

. . . there was apparent unanimity within Midland's housing department that the city contained several particularly undesirable estates, of which Woodley Park had reputedly been the worst. Until 1990 this was where most Part III allocations had been made.

(Loveland 1995: 262)

By the early 1970s the geographical pattern of local authority accommodation had been set and people with low incomes were beginning to find it easier to gain access to council housing. Unfortunately, as the chances of obtaining a local authority home increased, the quality of dwellings on offer declined. The more desirable properties, heavily subsidised in terms of market rents, were occupied by the skilled and semi-skilled working class who, if they had started on the lowest rung of the local authority ladder, had progressed upwards through the internal transfer system (Williams, Sewel and Twine 1986). During the 1980s newly formed households with low incomes found that their housing opportunities outside the council sector were limited. The private landlord sector continued to decline as, with vacant possession, properties were sold to owner-occupation. The system of consumer subsidies to owner-occupation operated regressively with tax relief being worth more to higher than to lower earners. The numerous low cost housing schemes introduced during the 1980s existed more on paper than in reality and produced only 12,349 dwellings per year between 1979–80 and 1987–88 (Social Trends 1989).

Impetus was given to the polarisation process by the 1980 Housing Act. Its right-to-buy provisions were eagerly taken up by those living in the best quality estates, depriving waiting list applicants of the opportunity to move immediately into a desirable area and the chance to 'filter up' the local authority system in the future. Recent evidence on the resale of dwellings bought under the right to buy suggests that, on transfer, they have been occupied by existing owner-occupiers rather than by first-time buyers (Williams and Twine 1992). Mullins's comment (1992: 404) on the local authority housing system in the context of the issue of racial equality that 'equality targets can have little real impact when there is little left to allocate and an increasing proportion of lettings are of the least desirable homes', is applicable to all low income groups entering social housing since the middle 1980s.

Priority estates

There are sporadic references to 'problem' estates in the housing literature of earlier periods, mainly in the context of the location of former slum dwellers (LCC 1928 quoted in Power 1987a, White1937, Ministry of Health 1938, Wilson 1963, Kirby 1971), but they first received the systematic attention of the central state in the 1970s. In 1974 the Housing Development Directorate of the Department of the Environment carried out a national postal survey of post-war 'difficult to let' dwellings (Wilson and Burbidge 1978). Thirty-three per cent of local authorities who responded to the request for information reported at least one such 'difficult to let' estate and, although each authority was limited to only three example estates, 62,000 properties were identified. In July 1977, the Architectural Research Unit produced a report for the Lewisham Council on two high rise, high density estates and concluded that, although the original brief of the study had concentrated on design and the physical environment, 'it became apparent quite early on that the problems of these estates were by no means primarily physical and that in fact managerial and social difficulties contributed equally if not more to the general feeling of discontent of the tenants' (Heffernan 1977).

In October 1978 the Secretary of State for the Environment set out proposals to tackle the issue: a new category of housing – management priority estates – would be created, on which capital expenditure and labour would be concentrated. An investigation of the problems of 'difficult to let' dwellings was published in 1981 (DoE 1981). Glennerster and Turner comment:

The report was admirably forthright. Obviously shocked by the scale of physical neglect they observed and the concentration of poor social conditions on some estates, the team concluded that the 'hard to let' label was a misnomer. What they were really observing was merely the most unattractive end of the public housing market. They were the tip of a much larger problem of poor housing management. The surveys described in vivid detail, supported by photographs, the physical conditions and some of the social consequences for the tenants. They also described the steps the local authorities were taking to remedy the situation.

(Glennerster and Turner 1993: 3)

The Department of the Environment responded to the identified problem by setting up the Priority Estates Project with Anne Power as consultant. Three local authorities, Hackney, Bolton and Lambeth, were selected as areas for action research and 72 other local authorities benefited from the advice of the consultant. The Priority Estates Project had a similar emphasis to the original brief of the Community Development Projects established in the late 1960s to tackle the problem of urban deprivation (Lees and Smith 1975). The coordination of bureaucracies at the local level and the participation of people were given prominence, but as academic attention focused on the issue three major explanations of the existence of such unpopular estates became available: poor management, poor design and poor tenants. The Priority Estates Project focused on deficient management as the most important causal factor capable of being influenced by policy, and promoted local estate management as a solution (see Document 17, page 220). Existing housing management structures were deemed to be incapable of providing 'flexible, adaptable, renting styles and systems' due to:

lack of definition; it was no one's specific responsibility. It grew in layers of reaction to problems and the division of functions was never resolved. At the same time, the size of the local authority stock expanded far more rapidly than the systems could cope with. The reaction of local authorities was to 'streamline' their systems, leading to the further removal of direct services such as cutting rent collection, reducing caretaking responsibilities, cutting back on estate cleaning, withdrawing further into town halls. Estates deteriorated rapidly as a consequence of the remote, town-hall-based administrative system and the low level of direct services.

(Power 1993: 202)

Architectural determinism

In contrast to the management/participatory approach of Anne Power, Alice Coleman (1985) placed her emphasis on bad design. Using the basic premises of Oscar Newman (1973) concerning the lack of 'defensible space' (characterised by a dearth of surveillance and the presence of numerous escape routes), Coleman claimed that many of the problems of unpopular estates could be eradicated by amending their design features. She grounded her argument in a study of 4,099 blocks containing 106,520 dwellings and 4,172 houses. Five indicators of social malaise – litter, graffiti, excrement, vandalism and children in care – were correlated with 15 design features, and significant relationships were discovered: dwellings per entrance, dwellings per block, storeys per block, overhead walkways and spatial organisation registered the highest levels of relationship to social malaise. Coleman linked such design faults to the 'utopianism' of the Garden City of Ebenezer Howard and the Radiant City of Le Corbusier. Such 'utopian planners' had attempted to create a sense of community and social life through the imposition of an architectural style but had failed to recognise the 'territorial imperative' inbuilt through human evolution which 'has led us to produce a shelter with its adjoining piece of territory and to impress it with distinctive marks of identity' (Coleman 1985: 18).

Estate Action

Both the poor design and poor management hypotheses on the causes of 'problem' estates received official support in the 1980s and early 1990s. The Priority Estates Project claimed high levels of success in its early demonstration projects. Following some informal steering of resources for physical improvement to local authorities adopting the priority estates approach, the Estate Action initiative, introduced in 1986, 'top sliced' a part of the housing investment programme, earmarking it for spending in specific locations according to the needs of the area and the viability of the action proposed by the council. Decentralisation of management was an essential ingredient of a successful Estate Action bid but, in addition, some element of privatisation was necessary in order to satisfy the cabinet and Prime Minister (Pinto 1993). Compliance with central demands produced substantial capital resources for the physical refurbishment of an estate. The resources available for 'depressed' estates increased markedly after 1986 from £45 million in 1986–87 to £373 million in 1994–95 – and the application of Coleman's design ideas formed part of some of the successful bids. In addition £50 million were set aside for the Design Improvement Controlled Experiment (DICE) through which the number of flats with a common entrance was reduced, walkways demolished and cul-de-sacs converted into roads. Alice Coleman's work had impressed Mrs Thatcher.

... I went further than the DoE in believing that the design of estates was crucial to their success and to reducing the amount of crime. I was a great admirer of the work of Professor Alice Coleman and I had made her an adviser to the DoE, to their dismay.

(Thatcher 1993: 605)

City Challenge and the Single Regeneration Budget

During the late 1980s there were signs that the officials at the Department of the Environment were beginning to recognise that the fundamental cause of the 'problem' estates might be located in economic processes rather than in poor management and poor design. Guidance on Estate Action bids started to emphasise the inclusion of job creation measures, and Housing Action Trusts – with their initial emphasis on diversification of tenure – may be interpreted as a sign of the new approach. In 1991 a new initiative – City Challenge – was announced. Its title was significant because the allocation of funds, mainly 'top sliced' from other programmes, was to be based on competition between local authorities, the winners being those who submitted the programmes most acceptable to the government. Initially 21 of the urban programme authorities were asked to bid and there were 11 winners of additional funding. The scheme was not targeted at 'problem' estates but they could be included in a bid. A second round of City Challenge followed in 1992 and this time all 57 urban programme authorities were invited to take part; 20 were successful.

After a period when no new City Challenge funds were made available, the government announced another initiative: the Single Regeneration Budget. From April 1994 20 specific government programmes, including Estate Action and the HAT programme, were brought together in a single budget. Local authorities and other organisations were invited to bid for resources in a competition governed by rules similar to those used in City Challenge. The bids were assisted and assessed by the new regional offices of the Department of the Environment, which brought together civil servants from a variety of government departments.

One of the ideas behind the Single Regeneration Budget was to produce a comprehensive strategy including both economic and social measures that would revitalise an area and produce additional private investment. This emphasis on a comprehensive and integrated approach has provided a refreshing change from the dominance of the design and management approaches applied to 'problem' estates in the 1980s. Unfortunately the new form of urban aid was introduced at a time when resources for regeneration were cut by 11 per cent and it is difficult to avoid the conclusion that the new system was designed as a smokescreen for reducing expenditure; failure in a competition was to be used as the reason for the refusal to allocate resources to deprived areas. It is also possible that the share of the available funds allocated to 'problem' estates will diminish as some of the estates in need of resources will be in competition with deprived inner areas. It is much more difficult to generate *economic* initiatives on periphery estates than in the heart of a city.

Policies for 'problem' estates – an evaluation

Although the 'poor management' explanation of 'problem' estates was developed during a Labour government, its emphasis on the inflexibility of local state bureaucracies fitted neatly into the doctrine of economic liberalism. Alice Coleman gave her ideas political appeal by associating the social pathology of council housing with 'utopian socialist planning'. However it is evident that although the programmes that have applied the bad design and poor management theses have produced significant and worthwhile change, they have failed to solve the problem of 'problem' estates.

Poverty and 'problem' estates

Although inappropriate design and inadequate management have contributed to the production of 'problem' estates, a third factor has had a significant influence: the concentration of families with low incomes.

Power recognised poverty as the possible 'overriding factor' in the creation of depressed estates but declared the extent of its influence to be 'unclear' (Power 1987b). Her Priority Estates Project contained few initiatives designed to change the socio-economic composition of run-down estates or to improve the economic welfare of the existing inhabitants. Coleman made a specific attempt to assess the impact of poverty relative to her design thesis and came to the conclusion that because her indicators of pathology were not correlated with the percentage of the population in the three poorest social classes – skilled manual workers, semi-skilled and unskilled – then poverty must have a limited impact on social malaise. She developed her argument by 'singling out a special group that has, by definition, become poorer than it was previously' and went on to argue that 'if pensioner poverty is a cause of social breakdown, then the more pensioners there are among the population, the more common we should expect each form of abuse to be. This expectation, too, proves to be false' (Coleman 1985: 85). The limitation of this assessment – apart from the notion that pensioners might be prone to spraying graffiti – is its inadequate measurement of poverty. No direct income measure was used and the impact of each dimension of poverty was assessed separately, thus undermining the overall impact of the concept's explanatory power. Many factors associated with extreme concentrations of people with low income can impact on the area as a whole. Spicker (1987) lists some of these factors, to which may be added:

- Dogs: these involve low capital expenditure compared to other forms of security but are more prone to bark, bite and defecate.
- Lack of carpets and furnishing: this magnifies noise to neighbours.
- Old cars: the cannibalisation of old cars to keep not so old cars on the road is very unsightly.
- Absence of public telephones: not present in the first place even to be vandalised.
- The activities of the young children of the tiny number of 'problem families', a term now eradicated from the social welfare literature but who feature strongly in the minds of those who live and work in the affected areas.
- Groups of unemployed young people who congregate at certain meeting places and sometimes engage in unruly behaviour.

The local management approach advocated by Power and her associates can make a contribution to solving such problems but it cannot overcome them. Why should some council estates require intensive management whereas others do not? In the same way that Octavia Hill's benign social control of her tenants (praised by Power 1987a) failed to improve the housing conditions of the urban poor, so the new benevolent control and support of locally based management has failed to remedy the problems of the most unpopular council estates. A study of 20 estates that benefited from the priority estates package in the 1980s demonstrates this. Based on data compiled in 1988 and appropriately titled *Running To Stand Still*, it concluded that 'the malaise in council housing continues' (Power 1991: 10). Why did this malaise continue given that all but one of the estates examined benefited from substantial capital works as well as from local management? Power continued to attribute much of the problem to management issues, stating that 'local authority systems are generally complex and often cumbersome' and 'urban local authorities are still very large landlords', and her remedies were couched in terms of the managerial perspective. However *Running To Stand Still* acknowledged that 'wider social and economic problems impinge directly on the poorest areas'.

> There was no information to suggest that the estates were moving 'up-market'. Quite the opposite, on most estates both tenants and staff reported continuing problems of 'dumping', stigma and social difficulties. By far the most common difficulty uncovered in the survey was the bad reputation of the estate, affecting all but four estates. It was not surprising to find that the estates still suffered from their original stigma. None of the efforts to improve the estates involved moving out people who lived there . . . The lower the popularity of an estate, the more likely it was to house those in greatest need. The poverty of incoming tenants in turn reinforced the social reputation of the estate
>
> (Power 1991: 51)

Additional evidence on the connection between the concentration of low income families and social pathology has been provided by Page (1993) in relationship to the housing association sector. Page notes that in the late 1980s and early 1990s housing associations became the major providers of new social housing and were under pressure to house homeless families and to produce more dwelling units from each pound of housing subsidy. The result of these pressures was the production of larger housing estates (from consortia arrangements formed to take advantage of the economies of scale of volume builders) and the purchase of completed estates 'off the shelf' to let to people on low incomes. Signs of social malaise are beginning to appear in such estates and Page anticipates further problems in the future (see Document 18, page 221).

Filtering

An important element of government housing policy in the 1990s has been to rely on 'filtering' theory. 'Filtering' theory suggests that if families can be encouraged to use their own resources to move out of a local authority or housing association dwelling then this house becomes available for a homeless family. Cash inducements are available to persuade people to move, and although such initiatives offer hope for those in dire housing need they intensify the existing trend towards geographical segregation by income. A study of the same 20 estates scrutinised in 1988, based on 1994 data, noted that estate-based management (despite some dilution of the approach by local offices having to service larger areas) had produced useful gains: the volume of empty properties had fallen, population turnover had declined and services and facilities had 'greatly increased' (Power and Tunstall 1995: 4). However, 'polarisation was far more extreme in 1991 than in 1981' and 'concentrations of unemployment, lone parenthood, minority ethnic groups and young people remained far above the national or local levels and were significantly higher in 1991 than in 1981'.

The policy recommendations made by Power and Tunstall in 1995 reflect a more structural perspective than the recommendations of earlier reports from the Priority Estates Project. Noting that 'marginal social housing estates may symbolise a deep rift in Western societies between the dominant and the disadvantaged', they recommended 'breaking out from the "estate" concept and linking estates to cities' and that 'work . . . must be shared if more people are to move out of dependence.'

So, even the strongest advocate of the management approach to 'problem' estates has recognised that local estate management and refurbishment are necessary but not sufficient conditions for the revitalisation of unpopular estates. Measures need to be introduced to diversify the income profile in such estates. Housing Action Trusts introduced by Housing Act 1988 were partially motivated by an attempt to diversify the tenure (and hopefully the social composition) of the largest local authority estates. However, they were initially presented as acts of aggression against local authorities (Karn 1993) rather than as attempts to improve housing conditions, and tenants wondered whether or not they would be able to afford to live in the refurbished accommodation after it had been transferred to new ownership. It was only when Nicholas Ridley departed from the Department of the Environment that an attempt was made to enlist the support of tenants and local authorities for HATs. This support appears to have been successfully bought by the promise that the properties will be returned to local authority control when the work of the Trust is complete: an outcome which, if achieved, may defeat the objective of diversifying the tenure and social composition of the estates.

Policy for 'depressed' estates requires a new start based on the idea of partnership between central and local government and a firmer recognition that 'depressed' estates and the more affluent suburbia are two sides of the same coin. The idea, implicit in the notion of Housing Action Trusts, that certain estates require greater diversity of tenure and a greater diversity of income is a sound one for, as has been demonstrated above, it is the compounding impact of poverty that generates a significant element of the problem. The White Paper *Our Future Homes* (1995) recognised this in stating:

Over the next ten years, we will tackle the problems of the most deprived estates . . . Government Offices for the regions and local authorities will work together to identify the best way of tackling the estates with the worst social, economic and housing problems . . . One of our aims in doing this will be to encourage the development of mixed communities. We want to break down the barriers between the old estates and the rest of the community and help construct sustainable communities where a balanced mix of households, young and old, low income and better off, home owners and renters, live along side each other.

(Department of the Environment 1995: 35)

However, as the experience of slum clearance in the nineteenth century has demonstrated, it is insufficient to attract more affluent people to an area unless there is also somewhere for poor people to live. Over time investment in an estate will enhance values which can be realised by sale to owner-occupation. The returns from these enhanced values need to be retained in the social housing pool so as to provide the resources for the producer subsidies necessary to assist low income households to move into more affluent areas via small-scale housing developments. Such an objective appears to be at the heart of the existing Department of the Environment policies but the mechanisms for achieving the objective have either been discredited and changed (Housing Action Trusts) or are too prone to leakage (the Treasury claiming a cut of the right to buy proceeds to reduce the public sector borrowing requirement and local authorities creaming part of the receipts for other capital purposes) to be successful.

Solutions to the problem of 'depressed' estates depend on a settlement as to how the maturing asset of local authority housing can be used either through local housing companies or by changes in the definition of the public sector borrowing requirement (see Chapter 10). The planning system also offers a glimmer of hope. In the nineteenth and early twentieth centuries local authority housing provision received considerable support from those who wished to see the gain produced by land development retained by the community. State housing was seen as a method (in the absence of other instruments such as a tax on development gain) of retaining community-created values to promote social purposes. The attempt to tap this development gain by requiring developers of private housing schemes to include a proportion of affordable homes (Planning Guidance Note 3, 1992) might result in a reduction in the cost of 'affordable' houses and allow some low-income households to move into more affluent areas. Nonetheless, if such a policy is to produce a significant impact it will require considerable amendment and a revival in the housing market. The notion of creating a social mix in an area as close to the wider community as possible has not featured in the guidance issued to local authorities by the Department of the Environment in the preparation of local development plans or housing investment strategies. Also the specification of tenure is not allowed in any planning agreement between local authority and developer despite the fact that renting is the most effective way of ensuring that subsidised housing remains available to people with low incomes.

The 'problem' tenant

Surveys of tenants and housing managers on what makes certain estates difficult to let and difficult to live in demonstrate a strong consensus on an important factor: the presence of anti-social tenants in the area. In 1974 a Housing Development Directorate survey revealed that 'the presence of families with problems on the estate' was cited by managers and tenants as a factor in it being 'difficult to let' more often than any other. In Power's 1991 survey of 20 unpopular estates, 'social conditions, weak social relations and anti-social behaviour was mentioned most frequently by housing staff as the outstanding problem of the estate on which they worked'. This was followed by the related reason of 'crime, security and enforcement of tenancy conditions'. Tenants placed such issues as third and fourth on their list behind physical problems and repairs (Power 1991). The evidence suggests that such crime and related 'incivilities' are internally generated, with certain council estates having high rates of both victimisation and offenders (Department of the Environment 1993) and with council tenants in council areas facing a much higher risk of burglary than council tenants in non-council areas (Hope and Hough 1988). Further evidence on the impact of the presence of difficult tenants on an estate is provided by an evaluation of estate-based housing management carried out by Glennerster and Turner between 1987 and 1990. Discussing the fortunes of one experimental priority estate they comment:

The significant worsening took place in and around one block of flats. From mid 1989 these began to show marked worsening in rubbish and internal damage scores and a lesser increase in the graffiti levels. The average score rose from 6.6 in July 1988 to 14.0 in June 1990 with most of the rise occurring after the summer of 1989. Certainly building work began on the flats in November 1989 but the main factor seems to have been the changing social composition. It was the combined effect of the local authority's intention to keep families out of flats and a desire to increase the number of homeless and at risk people the authority would house. The flats had always housed some formerly single homeless people (their first accommodation) but the numbers began to rise. Local managers had to find places for these new tenants in the one part of the estate where they had vacancies. With a small but growing group of more demanding tenants giving rise to nuisances and damage, the caretaking service and informal social controls in the block seem to have become unable to cope or contain the situation. The situation deteriorated suddenly and sharply. Once that happened tenants and caretakers alike gave up or lost heart, conditions in the flats degenerated. A fire made one floor uninhabitable and serious damage to public areas led to the closure of another whole floor. Our survey shows the effect spread beyond the flats to the surrounding areas.

(Glennerster and Turner 1993: 69)

In the 1990s local authorities have taken firmer action against the 'problem' tenants whose malign influence on the quality of life in an area is disproportionate to their number. The introduction of probationary tenancies in some authorities and the eviction of troublesome tenants, are severe measures but it is reasonable to ask whether or not the interests of difficult tenants should take precedence over the good of an estate. 'Problem' tenants do have recourse to housing associations but, as the authors of a study of local authority nominations to housing associations have commented:

It might be expected that local authorities would have the right to nominate whosoever they choose and to ask the association to house that person, but this is not so. Often the associations ask for several names to be put forward for a particular vacancy and expect to make the choice themselves.

(Parker, Smith and Williams 1992: 40)

The reasons for this practice are obscure but it allows housing associations the opportunity to select particular types of tenants. In order to ensure that vetting of prospective tenants does not take place, housing associations might be obliged to accept a specific, named applicant from a local authority. Although, as Page has demonstrated, the social polarisation of the housing association sector is a looming spectre, the future development programme of the housing association movement is sufficient to avert such a consequence and housing associations have the resources to cope with difficult tenants. Page makes some illuminating comments on this issue:

Almost every association visited in the course of the study had a story to tell about local authorities using nomination rights for management transfers in order to rid themselves of problem tenants who included perpetrators of racial harassment and with a history of violence and disruptive behaviour against their neighbours. There is no reason why housing associations should accept nominations of this kind from a local authority if the history is known.

(Page 1993: 35–36)

However, if housing associations with a dwelling/staff ratio of 15/1 (Lomas 1993) cannot cope with such tenants, can local authorities with a dwelling/staff ratio of 67/1 be expected to deal with the problem?

Conclusion

The phrase 'for the working class' – included in all prior legislation relating to local authority house building – was struck from the statute book by Aneurin Bevan in 1947. In removing the phrase Bevan expressed the view that 'we should try to introduce in our modern villages and towns what was always the lovely feature of English and Welsh villages, where the doctor, the grocer, the butcher and the farm labourer all lived in the same street'. Bevan believed that social segregation produced 'castrated communities' but his ideal of balanced communities was not achieved. Indeed the geographical pattern of local authority building – at least until the late 1970s – produced the opposite result. Fortunately, despite the asset-stripping of the local authority sector in the 1980s, one of the original ideas underlying council housing (the retention of development value by the community) has remained powerful enough to provide the resources to rectify some of the damage. The failure to use the remaining resources generated through the increase in the asset value of the local authority housing to create more balanced local communities, would be an act of injustice against those who have yet to benefit from these community-created assets and will produce a geographically segregated underclass.

References

Bentham, M. (1986) 'Socio-tenurial Polarisation in the United Kingdom, 1953–1983: the income evidence', *Urban Studies*, 23 (2), pp. 157–62.

Boleat, M. (1989) *Housing in Britain*, The Building Societies Association, London.

Central Statistical Office (1989) *Social Trends*, HMSO, London.

Clapham, D. and Kintrea, K. (1986) 'Rationing, Choice and Constraint: the allocation of public housing in Glasgow', *Journal of Social Policy*, 1 (15), pp. 51–67.

Cole, I. and Furbey, R. (1994) *The Eclipse of Council Housing*, Routledge, London.

Coleman, A. (1985) *Utopia on Trial*, Hilary Shipman Limited, London.

Coles, A. (1991) 'Changing Attitudes To Owner Occupation', *Housing Finance* No. 11.

Department of the Environment (1981) *An investigation into hard to let housing*, Vols. 1–3, HMSO, London.

Department of the Environment (1992) *Planning Policy Guidance: PPG3 (revised)*, Department of the Environment, London.

Department of the Environment (1993) *Crime Prevention on Council Estates*, HMSO, London.

Department of the Environment and the Welsh Office (1995) *Our Future Homes: opportunity, choice, responsibility*, CM 2901, HMSO, London.

Duncan, S. and Evans, A. (1988) *Responding To Homelessness: local authority policy and practice*, HMSO, London.

English, J. (1979) 'Access and Deprivation in Local Authority Housing' in Jones, C. (ed.) *Urban Deprivation and the Inner City*, Croom Helm, London.

Forrest, R. and Murie, A. (1983) 'Residualisation and Council Housing: aspects of the changing relationships of housing tenure', *Journal of Social Policy*, 12 (4) pp. 453–468.

Forrest, R. and Murie, A. (1990) *Residualisation and Council Housing: a statistical update*, SAUS, Bristol.

Forrest, R. and Murie, A. (1991) *Selling The Welfare State*, Routledge, London.

Glennerster, H. and Turner, T. (1993) *Estate Based Housing Management: an evaluation*, Department of the Environment, HMSO, London.

Hamnett, C. (1984) 'Housing the Two Nations: socio-tenurial polarisation in England and Wales, 1961–81', *Urban Studies*, 21 (4), pp. 389–405.

Hamnett, C. and Randolph, B. (1987) 'The Residualisation of Council Housing in Inner London 1971–1981' in Clapham, D. and English, J. (eds) *Public Housing: Current Trends and Future Developments*, Croom Helm, London

Heffernan, D. (1977) *Difficult-to-Let*, Architectural Research Unit, Edinburgh.

Hills, J. (1991) *Unravelling Housing Finance*, Clarendon Press, Oxford.

Holmans, A. (1987) *Housing Policy in Britain: a history*, Croom Helm, London.

Hope, T. and Hough, M. (1988) 'Area, Crime and Incivilities – a profile from the British Crime Survey', in Hope, T. and Shaw, M. (eds) *Communities and Crime Reduction*, HMSO, London.

Jones, M. (1988) 'Utopia and Reality: the utopia of public housing and its reality at Broadwater Farm', in Teymour, M., Marcus, T. A. and Woolley, T. (eds) *Rehumanizing Housing*, Butterworths, London.

Karn, V. (1993) 'Remodelling a HAT: the implementation of the Housing Action Trust legislation 1987–92', in Malpass, P. and Means, R. (eds) *Implementing Housing Policy*, Open University Press, Buckingham.

Kirby, D. A. (1971) 'The Inter-war Council Dwellings. A study of residential obsolescence and decay', *Town Planning Review*, 42.

Lees, R. and Smith, G. (1975) *Action – Research in Community Development*, Routledge and Kegan Paul, London.

Lomas, G. (1993) *Item in Inside Housing*, 2 April.

Loveland, I. (1995) *Housing Homeless Persons*, Clarendon Press, Oxford.

Malpass, P. and Murie, A. (1982) *Housing Policy and Practice*, Macmillan, London.

Ministry of Health (1938) *The Management of Municipal Housing Estates*, HMSO, London.

Mullins, D. (1992) 'From Local Politics to State Regulation: The legislation and policy on race equality in housing'. *New Community*, 18 (3), pp. 401–25.

Newman, O. (1973) *Defensible Space*, Architectural Press, London.

Opinion Research Centre (1967) *Housing Problems, Priorities and Preferences*, Opinion Research Centre, London.

Parker, J., Smith, R. and Williams, P. (1992) Access, Allocations and Nominations: the role of housing associations, HMSO, London.

Page, D. (1993) *Building for Communities: A study of new housing association estates*, Joseph Rowntree Foundation, York.

Parker, J., Smith, R. and Williams, P. (1992) *Access, Allocations and Nominations: the role of housing associations*, HMSO, London.

Pinto, R. (1993) *The Estate Action Initiative*, Avebury, Aldershot.

Power, A. (1987a) *Property Before People: the management of twentieth-century council housing*, Allen and Unwin, London.

Power, A. (1987b) 'The Crisis in Council Housing – is public housing manageable?' *Political Quarterly*, July–September, pp. 283–96.

Power, A. (1991) *Running To Stand Still : progress in local management on twenty unpopular housing estates*, a PEP survey, Priority Estates Project, London.

Power, A. (1993) *Hovels to High Rise: state housing in Europe since 1850*, Routledge, London.

Power, A. and Tunstall, R.(1995) *Swimming Against the Tide: polarisation or progress on 20 unpopular council estates*, Joseph Rowntree Foundation, York.

Prescott-Clarke, P., Allen, P. and Morrissey, C. (1988) *Queuing for Housing: A Study of Council Housing Waiting Lists*, HMSO, London.

Spicker, P. (1987) 'Poverty and Depressed Estates: A Critique of "Utopia On Trial"', *Housing Studies*, 4 (2), pp. 283–91.

Thatcher, M. (1993) *The Downing Street Years*, HarperCollins, London.

White, L. E. (1937) *Community or Chaos*, National Council of Social Service, London.

Williams, N. J., Sewel, J. and Twine, F. (1986) 'Council House Allocation and Tenant Incomes', *Area*, 18 (2), pp. 131–40.

Williams, N. J. and Twine, T. (1992) 'Increasing Access or Widening Choice: the role of resold public-sector dwellings in the housing market', *Environment and Planning*, 24, pp. 1585–98.

Willmott, P. and Murie, A. (1988) *Polarisation and Social Housing*, Policy Studies Institute, London.

Wilson, R. (1963) *Difficult Housing Estates*, Tavistock, London.

Wilson, S. and Burbidge, M. (1978) 'An Investigation of Difficult to Let Housing', *Housing Review*, July–August.

CHAPTER 8

Inequality and housing

Unfairly structured inequality in access to good accommodation exposes some people to greater risk of housing hardship than others. It also helps to perpetuate divisions in economic power and, through the impact of the poor housing conditions on health and education, impairs the ability of some groups to compete in a market economy.

Social class

Analysis of the relationship between social class and housing is complicated by different interpretations of the concept of class. Marx thought in terms of a two-class model: a bourgeoisie that owned the means of production and a proletariat without access to capital. Contemporary Marxists attempt to explain the operations of the housing system by exploring housing as a commodity produced and distributed in the interests of the capitalist class. This perspective has been discussed in Chapter 1.

Max Weber (1864–1920) introduced a different construction of the concept of social class. He claimed that class referred to a number of people 'who have in common a specific causal component of their life chances' – their 'typical probabilities' of 'procuring goods', 'gaining possessions in life' and 'finding inner satisfaction' (Weber 1970). In not designating ownership of the means of production as the decisive factor in social stratification, Weber opened the way to the identification of a more differentiated stratification system. Weber's notion of class was widely adopted in the 1960s and became the basis for the compilation of the limited official statistics on the subject. Classification into five or six categories based on occupation became the norm and it was commonplace to find tables in housing textbooks linking housing conditions to class accompanied by commentaries based on the assumption that, because class was a determining force created by the structure of society, then any link between housing standards and class was unjustified. However it is not sufficient to assume that the operations of the capitalist system are unfair. This unfairness has to be demonstrated by exploring, on a historical basis, the ways in which the operations of the housing market have perpetuated unjustifiable inequalities.

Tenure

Information on the tenure structure of the nineteenth century is sparse and the available data is difficult to interpret because of the complex system of land ownership. The evidence suggests that by the end of the century the percentage of home owners varied from 60 per cent in some parts of South Wales to 5.9 per cent in York (Dennis 1984, Daunton 1983). These figures indicate that the owner-occupation/renting division did not totally replicate social class; difference in tenure between the 'artisan elite' and the middle class seems to have been as much a response to individual choice and local factors such as support for self-help movements and industrial prosperity as to differences in social position.

By the late 1930s tenure had acquired an identifiable if tenuous relationship to class. Suburban home ownership was led by social classes one and two; the estates constructed by local authorities 'for the working class' became the residential areas of social classes three and four and private landlordism began to evolve into the 'residual' domain of classes five and six. These tendencies grew stronger in the post-war years. Local authority housing came to be occupied by skilled and semi-skilled workers as a consequence of the dominance of building for 'general needs' and the reluctance of people with low incomes to occupy new council houses because they could not afford to pay the rent.

A metamorphosis in the class composition of the various housing tenures began in the 1960s, gathered momentum throughout the 1970s and snowballed in the 1980s. The composition of the owner-occupied sector diversified through the inclusion of more people from classes three and four, whereas local authority estates became the territory of classes five and six and the economically inactive. Private renting continued to decline, becoming the tenure of young, geographically mobile groups and elderly people. Table 8.1 sets out the tenure pattern in 1991 according to social-economic groupings. Some of the implications of these figures have been discussed in Chapter 7; the focus here is on the impact of tenure on the distribution of wealth.

Positive equity

Between 1954 and 1989 – despite a downturn in real terms in the middle 1970s – house prices increased at twice the rate of inflation (Nationwide 1985, Newton 1994). This real price increase prompted Saunders to comment:

... millions of people have accumulated a substantial amount of wealth from their participation in the housing market. Since I left home my parents have moved between a number of different houses and they now own a detached bungalow on the outskirts of London valued at £130,000. My wife's parents also live in the south-east and own a house worth well over £200,000. As an

Table 8.1 **Tenure by socio-economic group: heads in employment, 1991 (percentages: figures rounded)**

	Profes- sional	Employers/ Managers	Other non- manual	Skilled manual	Semi- skilled manual	Unskilled
Owners	89	88	80	79	61	48
Rented privately	9.6	9	10	7	14	10
Rented from council	1	2	8	12	22	38
Rented from housing association	0.4	0.6	2	2	3	3

Source: Adapted from DoE (1993)

only child I expect eventually to inherit most of my parents' wealth, although they may be well advised to cash in on some of it to supplement their pensions.

(Saunders 1990: 3)

Although prices declined after 1989 producing 'negative equity' for 1.5 million households, these losses have to be balanced by a consideration of the 'positive equity' of those who bought before the recession. Real net residential wealth (asset value minus mortgages) increased from £347 billion in 1977 to £755 billion in 1992 (Hills 1995). Although net equity has declined in recent years it was nearly £40,000 per dwelling in 1994 (Wilcox 1995). Three questions need to be asked about this 'positive equity'.

Is it real?   It can be argued that the positive equity arising from inflation in house prices is illusionary; the capital gain made from a rise in house prices above general inflation cannot be spent because when a house is sold then the owner must buy a replacement property at the new, higher level of price. However, the capital gains from home ownership can be realised in four ways: by using the enhanced equity of a house to raise income, by selling the house and renting for the remainder of a life span (the income from the realised capital can be higher than the rent that has to be paid), by moving downmarket and by inheritance (which either provides the donee with a home or a capital sum raised from the sale of the dwelling). These avenues of gain have been modified in recent years by the increased use of capital tests to determine eligibility for social care: the value of a house is taken into account in assessing residential and nursing home charges and this can result in the rapid erosion of housing wealth.

Who has gained most from positive equity?   Some theorists assume that home ownership constitutes a distinct 'consumption cleavage' with owners sharing common life chances (Saunders 1984). In fact there is great diversity within home ownership (Morris and Winn 1990, Forrest, Murie and Williams 1990) and thus the size of the capital gain produced by home ownership depends on a number of variables: when the house was purchased, its location and the quality of the dwelling. All these factors are related to social class but the relationship is difficult to investigate because of the dearth of information on the variables involved; we lack periodic wealth surveys from which data can be obtained on the value of property over time. Holmans and Frosztega (1994) have demonstrated that the inheritance of wealth from housing property is more equally shared than wealth from other sources such as company shares, but it still reinforces rather than reduces inequality. Housing wealth increases with income for outright owners and for people with mortgages who have a gross family income of over £11,000 (Hills 1995). Saunders (1990) attempted to assess the overall impact of the capital gains derived from home ownership through a survey of home owners in Burnley, Slough and Derby carried out in 1986. Using a three category division – service, intermediate and working class – he concluded:

> ... it is clear that total gains are greatest for the service class and lowest for the working class. Whether we take the mean, the median, or the range, the service class comes out best, and the working class trails behind on all four measures of total gain ... The differences are particularly striking as regards the real net capital gain figures where the working class median is around half that of the service class while the mean is only a quarter as large.
>
> (Saunders 1990: 172)

The length of time as a home owner (the service class entered the tenure earlier than the working class), and the location of the home (inner areas doing less well than suburbia in terms of absolute gains), helps to account for this relationship but regional location modifies the link between class and capital appreciation; working class people in Slough made larger real gains than the service class in Burnley.

Do the beneficiaries deserve their gains?   Home ownership involves a number of sacrifices: most mortgage applicants have been obliged to make a downpayment on their homes involving some reduction in living standards whilst the deposit is saved; in the early years of a mortgage repayments are high relative to earnings and the mortgagee is responsible for the maintenance of the dwelling. Nevertheless, in the past the gains from owner-occupation have been considerable and a percentage of this yield has been created by the actions of the state rather than through the workings of the free market. Exemption from capital taxation and tax relief on mortgage interest has provided high levels of subsidy to home owners.

Hills (1991), making the assumption that owner-occupiers should be taxed on the imputed net rental value of their dwellings (deducting real interest) and the capital gains that home ownership produces, estimated that in 1989–90 owner-occupiers obtained £13.95 per week each in subsidies. He concluded that 'the value of tax allowances is low at the bottom of the income distribution, rises slowly for most of the income range, but rises sharply for the highest income group'. Hills also provided an estimate of the value of subsidies to council tenants. Employing capital value rents (rent levels sufficient to give a reasonable rate of interest to the owner) rather than market rents as a benchmark, he calculated that in 1989–90 the subsidy per tenant was £9.30 per week with higher income tenants receiving the most subsidy because they lived in the best property. Walker and Marsh (1993) applied the difference between actual rents in the local authority sector and a rate of return that could be achieved by investing the value of a local authority dwelling elsewhere in order to produce a measure of the subsidy granted to each local authority tenant. They compared this to a measure of subsidy to home owners derived from the real rate of return on investment and the taxation that owner-occupiers paid. Based on data gathered in the Birmingham travel-to-work area in 1988–89 they concluded:

The way in which the current UK subsidy system treats the two major housing tenures – owner-occupation and public renting – fails to achieve equity both in respect of subsidy receipt in the two tenures as a whole and between households with similar incomes residing in different sectors. The full definition of subsidy employed – incorporating capital gains tax – suggests that in 1988–89 owner-occupiers received on average nine times the financial benefit from the system than local authority tenants.

(Walker and Marsh 1993: 1557)

During the 1990s the value of mortgage tax relief has been reduced from an average of £820 per beneficiary in 1990–91 to £270 in 1995–96 (Wilcox 1995).

Land

Although the Labour Party Manifesto of 1945 stated that 'Labour believes in land nationalisation and will work towards it', when in government the Party concentrated on the taxation of development gain arising from the granting of planning permission. Labour made an attempt to tax 'betterment' value (the difference between the value of land with an existing use and its value with planning permission) in each of its periods of office. The last attempt was contained in the Development Land Tax Act of 1976 which imposed a tax of 80 per cent on development gain after the first £160,000. Each Labour measure was repealed by a subsequent Conservative government and so the community received meagre benefit from the substantial increases in the value of the land granted planning permission. A study by the Department of Land Economy at Cambridge University revealed that between 1968 and 1988 '. . . housing land prices rose by more than double the rate of increase in house prices. Furthermore the land price data are in terms of plots which tended to reduce in size so the price per unit of land has increased even faster' (Eve 1992: 23). In 1989 private sector house building land was sold for a median price of over £3 million pounds per hectare in Greater London compared to £533,000 in 1982. The price of housing land declined in the early 1990s but in 1992 was still almost three times higher than in 1982 (GSO 1994).

Gender differences in housing

Gender inequality in housing now forms a part of the political and academic agenda but in the mid-1960s almost all discussions of housing assumed that the 'patriarchal family' was the household form to which policy should be directed and gender difference in housing provision was not a public issue.

The term 'patriarchal family' was devised by a branch of the feminism movement to conceptualise the relationships involved in an 'ideal' family form which was promoted in the nineteenth and twentieth centuries and regarded today by many people as the most desirable form of household structure. The patriarchal family consists of a male breadwinner regarded as the source of authority and a female carer who relies on the male to obtain the resources for her to perform a care and nurturing role: raising children and tending to the physical and emotional needs of relatives. Feminists insist that, rather than accepting the patriarchal family form as the basic building block of society, it is necessary to disaggregate its structure and assess its impact on the status and life chances of women. Unfortunately such disaggregation is a laborious task because in the past the compilation of data seldom incorporated a gender dimension and, even today, the dominant ideology regards the family as a private area in which relationships are negotiated on a voluntary basis. What goes on within the family is not thought to be a matter for public or state concern unless significant harm is done to one of its members. Thus the gender divisions in the consumption of housing, such as a study or workroom for many men but for few women, receive scant attention (Little 1994).

One way into the issue of gender inequality and housing is to consider the position of women who form separate households. Morris and Winn (1990) argue:

it should be recognised that one in four households is headed by a woman and the housing opportunities of such households are also of crucial importance to women living in male headed households. Most women will go through stages in their lives when they either wish to, or are forced to, be part of a household where there is not a man present – such as younger single women, women experiencing relationship breakdown, and older women. The opportunities and constraints for all women are therefore indicated by the housing experiences of the 25% of households which, at any one point in time, are headed by a woman.

(Morris and Winn 1990: 180)

Single women without children

Owner-occupation, despite the difficulties experienced since 1989, is still regarded by the majority of people as the most desirable form of tenure. Table 8.2 sets out the pattern of tenure according to gender. Fewer single women than single men are owner-occupiers, mainly because women receive lower pay than men. In 1994 33 per cent of women earned less than £190 per week compared to 13 per cent of men (Whitmarch 1995). As Gilroy and Woods (1994: 34) have pointed out, 'the British form of home ownership with mortgages which bear down heavily in the early years, favours high or dual earners and therefore generally not women'. The absence of a high quality rental sector with rents determined by the historic costs of the dwellings rather than by current market value is an important obstacle to independent living (Kemeny 1995).

Single women appear to have a lower risk of homelessness than single men. A survey of single homeless people carried out by the University of York found that 'the great majority of single homeless people interviewed were men ... 23% of people in hostels and Bed and Breakfasts were women as were only 7% in day centres and 13% on soup runs' (Anderson, Kemp and Quilgars 1993: ix). However Watson and Austerberry (1986) have argued that female homelessness is not less common than male homelessness, it is simply less conspicuous. Women are more likely to experience homelessness in private than in public. The NFHA (1993) has pointed out that single women 'will avoid at all costs becoming *street* homeless due to the attendant fear risks of rape, harassment and violence' (emphasis added).

Single women with children (never married)

Many feminists would defend the right of a woman – whatever her financial circumstances – to rear a child without having to rely on a

Table 8.2 **Tenure by gender of household: single males and single females (per cent): 1992**

Kind of tenure	Single males	Single females
Owned outright	15	16
With mortgage	35	26
Local authority	20	32
Housing association	6	8
Rented with job	2	2
Private rented – unfurnished	6	6
Private rented – furnished	16	10

Source: General Household Survey 1992

male breadwinner, and there are some who think that a social structure that allows such a choice is an essential condition for women's emancipation. In 1974 a government committee set up to examine the circumstances of lone parents (Finer 1974) made no distinctions between one-parent families on the basis of the cause of their status but it noted that fatherless families were seriously disadvantaged in the housing market when compared to two-parent families. Fatherless families were more likely to be sharing accommodation, compelled to move home, to be living in furnished accommodation rented from a private landlord and 'at special risk of becoming homeless'. The Finer report also stated that 'much of the evidence received on the subject of local authority housing was concerned with discrimination in the allocation of council tenancies, either against one-parent families in general, or against unmarried mothers'.

Viewed in the light of the findings of the Finer report, the Housing (Homeless Persons) Act 1977 was a step forward in improving the status of women. By placing an obligation on local authorities to provide accommodation for all homeless people with a child or expecting a child the Act prevented the practice, common to many authorities before the Act, of giving preference to married, two-parent families with less pressing needs than homeless single parents. The Housing (Homeless Persons) Act and the Housing Finance Act (which introduced a national rent rebate scheme related to income) made parenthood a more tolerable status for single women. However, as explained in Chapter 5, this observation should not be interpreted to mean that the legislation has been a significant cause of the substantial growth of single parenthood in the 1980s. Whereas there is obvious equity in ensuring that single parents do not have absolute priority over couples with children, single parenthood should not be regarded as a product of the 'perverse incentives' of the operations of the housing and benefits systems.

Single women with children (separated/divorced)

The housing consequences of relationship breakdown are diverse and complicated. The divorce courts have comprehensive powers to divide the assets of the family home between married couples. In deciding who should keep the matrimonial home, the courts are required to give first consideration to the interests of the children of the marriage (Matrimonial Homes Act 1983, Matrimonial Family Proceedings Act 1984). However, the legislative provisions do not apply to cohabiting couples and, in the case of married couples, the process of marriage breakdown can cause severe housing problems. A full account of such problems is given by Bull (1993) and only a few examples of the difficulties that can occur are presented here.

A woman may be forced to leave the marital home because of domestic violence. Legal remedies are available to inhibit such violence and enable a woman to remain at home, but according to Bull (1993: 48), 'where violence was involved, it was apparent that the ability of the applicant to return home by pursuing legal remedies in the short or long term was still an important factor in determining whether or not an applicant would be considered by a local authority as homeless following relationship breakdown'. Local authority officers may have thought that such practices were necessary to prevent false claims of domestic violence but legal remedies such as injunctions can be ineffective in preventing future attacks and may result in the abused woman having to live with friends and relatives or continue to suffer for want of assistance from her local authority. Some local authorities have helped to establish special refuges to enable women to escape from domestic violence and to receive support in returning home or finding new accommodation but a study by the London Research Unit (1994) estimated that the 1,700 places in England did not match a potential need for over 8,000 places.

In 1993–94 41 per cent of formerly married lone mothers were owner-occupiers but a comparison between lone mothers and two-parent home owners reveals that lone mothers were less likely to live in a detached house and more likely to live in a flat, indicating 'down market' moves following the breakdown of a relationship; 13 per cent of lone mothers were in mortgage arrears, double the proportion for all owner-occupiers (Green and Hansbro 1995). Research by McCarthy and Simpson (1991) has revealed that fathers granted custody are more likely than custodial women to retain their status as owner-occupiers; income was the major explanation of this difference.

Women, housing design and planning

Feminists have started to explore the implications of the male dominance of architecture and planning for the everyday lives of women who have to live in the dwellings created by male architects and planners. Roberts (1991) provides an account of the history of housing design from a feminist perspective. She notes the low incidence of female representation on the committees that have determined the design of working-class housing (the Tudor Walters Committee 1919, the Dudley Committee 1944) and the ways that patriarchal family forms have been reflected in housing layouts: the absence of adequate space in which children can play and the reluctance to include labour-saving amenities in working-class housing. She quotes Beveridge to illustrate the influence of pro-natalism in housing policy after the Second World War: 'It is important also that those who design homes today should realise that they must be the birthplaces of the Britons of the future – of more Britons than are being born today. If the British race is to continue there must be many families of four or more children' (Roberts 1991: 45).

A limitation of the feminist analysis of housing is its reluctance to specify the forms of housing design that might have been preferred by the majority of women. The experiments that have been made in providing alternative living arrangements have not been successful. Colonies established by Robert Owen between 1821 and 1845 (Pearson 1988), based on 'free union', cooking rotas and communal nurseries, were short-lived, although this may have been due to the rigid gender division of labour which was practised in the colonies: domestic labour was collectivised but not divided equally between men and women. Unwin and Parker, two pioneers of the garden city, included communal kitchens in two areas of Letchworth, but proposals to include such facilities in working-class estates – when investigated by the Women's Sub-Committee of the Tudor Walters Committee – were found not to have enthusiastic support. All the available evidence suggests that the homes built by speculative developers in the period between the wars – with their parlours, gardens and provision for the installation of labour-saving devices according to personal preference – were what women wanted. Flats with communal facilities and pre-installed labour-saving devices – rejected by the pro-natalists such as Beveridge – were promoted by socialist architects sympathetic to feminism.

Greed (1994) has placed planning under the spotlight of feminist analysis. She draws attention to the ways in which the needs of women have been ignored in the past. The reluctance to build houses with parlours in the local authority sector has deprived women of the opportunity for private space away from the family. The zoning of areas for different purposes (e.g. residential/industrial) has emphasised the division between work and home and created 'great inconvenience for many women, especially those without cars', and the neglect of the personal safety of women in making decisions about public space.

Women and 'social' housing

The concentration of women, especially lone parents, in the 'social' housing sector (see Table 8.3) has important implications for gender inequality: local authority provision – still the dominant form of 'social' housing – now contains a disproportionate share of badly designed dwellings, gives no opportunity for capital gains unless the right to buy is exercised and, in a few areas, is the locale of high rates of crime and harassment. In part this 'feminisation' of public housing is related to the number of women over 75 who are more likely to be living in the 'special' housing constructed with the assistance of the state. It is also a reflection of interacting influences in the labour market, the sexual division of labour within the home that limits the employment opportunities of women, and the ways in which the system of maintenance has operated to restrict the incomes of women separated from their spouses (CPAG 1993). In addition, although it has been argued that differences in wages are the product of the current value of women in the labour market (Conway 1992), the influence of the notion that 'male' employment should bring with it a 'family wage' is still strong.

Table 8.3 **Tenure of lone parents/couples (percentages): England 1991**

	Lone parents[1]	Couples
Owner-occupation	36.3	78
Rented from council	49.2	13.4
Rented from housing association	6	1.7
Rented from private landlord	8.5	6.6

[1] with dependent children

Source: Adapted from DoE (1993)

Ethnic differences in housing

Useful statistical information is now available on the differences in tenure, location and standards of accommodation that exist between ethnic minorities and the majority community. A selection from this information is given in Document 19, page 222. Several explanations of these differences are available.

Patterns of settlement

Daniel (1968: 9) estimated that in 1950 'there were in the whole of Britain probably no more than 100,000 coloured people, i.e. people with non-white skins with their origins in the Caribbean, Africa, Asia and the Middle East'. Immigration from the New Commonwealth countries during the 1950s and 1960s was mainly a response to the availability of work in Britain, and in some cases it was the direct result of recruitment campaigns by employers experiencing a labour shortage. The jobs available were restricted mainly to specific sectors of the economy: textiles, the metal industries of the Midlands, public transport, catering and manual tasks in the public services. The available work was concentrated in particular areas and this, combined with a form of settlement whereby established immigrants sponsored friends and relatives, and the constraints placed on the availability of housing, produced a distinctive residential pattern.

Initially local authority housing was difficult to obtain as many local councils insisted on a period of residence in the area (up to five years) as a condition of acceptance to the waiting list or they produced the same discriminatory result by awarding extra points for length of residence. Although a number of people from the West Indies became owner-occupiers, most found accommodation in the private landlord sector, often paying a high price for their living space. People from South Asia were more likely to find ways of purchasing their homes but their low incomes, restrictions on the availability of mortgages, the unwillingness of white vendors to sell to Asians and the 'steering' practices of certain estate agents pushed them towards the poorer quality properties located mainly in the inner-city areas.

In the late 1960s and throughout the 1970s local authority homes became more accessible. The slum clearance drive began to include some members of ethnic minority groups (mainly Afro-Caribbeans who had managed to become the mortgage holders of structurally deficient homes in the 1950s), but clearance was scaled down as it was about to encompass large numbers of black and Asian people. The residential qualifications of local authorities were modified in response to the guidance contained in the Cullingworth Report (1969) and more people with Afro-Caribbean origins entered the local authority sector, to be joined by the Bangladeshi community whose settlement was more recent than the other groups from South Asia. Few people with origins in Pakistan or India became local authority tenants, a fact that has been explained partially by a positive preference for owner-occupation due to cultural factors, and partially by institutional constraints on access to other forms of tenure. The 'choice' explanation is favoured by Davies (1985) who stated that in the course of his research in Newcastle he could not find one Indian or Pakistani who had applied for a council house and is supported by Karn, Kemeny and Williams (1985) who found a strong commitment to the independence and autonomy associated with ownership. In contrast Rex and Moore (1967), Gray (1982) and Luthera (1988) locate the cause of Indian and Pakistani home ownership in institutional racism.

Whatever may have been the exact cause of the tenure pattern of ethnic minorities their homes tended to become concentrated in the inner areas of a number of cities and towns. The economic decline of these inner areas had started before the newcomers arrived (which partially accounts for the pattern of initial settlement) but structural change in the economy accelerated the decline during the 1960s and 1970s. It was only in 1977 that the economic causes of inner-area decay were fully recognised by central government. The White Paper *Policy for the Inner Cities* (Secretary of State 1977: 2) stated that 'the decline in the economic fortunes of the inner area often lies at the heart of the problem. Compared with their own conurbations, the inner areas of the big cities suffer from higher unemployment at all stages of their economic cycle'.

Since 1977 inner areas have been subject to a large variety of social and economic initiatives developed by different central government departments competing for influence and control. These policies have had only a marginal impact on the economic and the associated housing problems of inner areas and a disproportionate number of people from ethnic minorities remain in areas with extremely limited employment opportunities and where rates of pay are low. A significant percentage of the people who have managed to become home owners have only modest levels of equity in their property, which places real constraints on their ability to move within the owner-occupied sector (Smith 1989). Those with local authority homes find restrictions on their opportunity to transfer to new locations because so many houses have been lost to the local authority sector under the right to buy provisions of the 1980

Housing Act. These restraints on movement have contributed to the creation, over time, of areas where many members of ethnic minorities feel secure, at ease, at home and hence reluctant to leave. A study of the Asian community in Rochdale concluded that:

With the exception of access to town, those features of the neighbourhood which we tested for were regarded as either very important or important by totals in the range of 60% to 90% of applicants. Those which were given the greatest importance were the presence of family in the area (89.8%) and the security of living in the area (91.8%). These were prioritised even above the proximity of the mosque (82%).

(Habeebullah and Slater 1990: 21)

Subjective racism

Ginsberg (1992), although careful to point out the interactions between his categories, makes a useful distinction between subjective racism, institutional racism and structural racism. Subjective racism refers to overt racial prejudice and discrimination by individual landlords, estate agents, local authority officials, housing association workers, home owners and tenants. It can take a variety of forms such as racially motivated attacks, harassment, the steering of minorities to certain geographical areas and the refusal to sell a property to a member of a particular ethnic group. The extent of such behaviour is difficult to quantify as there is no national mechanism for recording its reported incidence. In 1989 the Commission for Racial Equality examined the practices of accommodation agencies, landlords and landladies, small hotels and guest houses. Testers differing only in their ethnic origin visited agencies asking for details of accommodation, and testers with pronounced Afro-Caribbean or Asian accents telephoned to request details of a property and, if told none was available, a white tester phoned ten minutes later. They found that 20.5 per cent of accommodation agencies, 5.5 per cent of landlords and landladies and 5 per cent of small hotels and guest houses discriminated against black and Asian people (CRE 1990).

Institutional racism

The concept of institutional racism rests on the assumption that if the outcome of established bureaucratic and administrative processes is unequal then the agency is responsible for this outcome; there must be a deeply entrenched racism operating through its power structure and everyday practices. A large number of research studies exist of what, according to Ginsberg (1992: 111), 'can only be described as institutionally racist processes in housing'.

Simpson (1981) examined the outcomes of Nottingham's process of rehousing applicants and found that, because black families had a greater need for more dwelling space than white families and the authority had a restricted supply of larger accommodation concentrated in the rundown inner-city areas, then black families had to wait longer for housing and had to accept poorer quality property. In addition black people were more likely to be allocated flats than white people.

Henderson and Karn (1987) investigated the procedures and policies of Birmingham in the 1970s and discovered a number of discriminatory practices. Some of these practices – housing visitors commenting negatively on the cooking smells of Asian applicants, for instance – might be construed as subjective racism but they can also be thought of as institutional racism because of the failure of the local authority to eradicate the practice. Other procedures, including the application of residence qualifications, the disqualification of owner-occupied applicants and a dispersal policy that meant that black applicants had to wait longer for housing than white applicants, are clearer examples of institutional racism.

The Commission for Racial Equality has carried out a number of formal investigations into the allocation procedures used by local authority housing departments. The methods of allocation adopted by Hackney in 1978–79 were found to be discriminatory in that, with reference to three of the four 'access channels' under examination – waiting list, homeless and 'decants' (rehousing to facilitate rehabilitation) – black people were more likely to receive inferior quality accommodation (CRE 1984). The major explanatory factor in this outcome was the grading system applied by housing visitors (see Document 20, page 224). An examination of the procedures of Liverpool City Council (CRE 1989) discovered that access to advocates such as councillors and social workers was a factor in the quality of accommodation offered: 13 per cent of black applicants as compared to 35 per cent of whites had managed to obtain such assistance. The Commission found that the London Borough of Tower Hamlets had directly discriminated against a homeless Bangladeshi by procrastination in finding him an acceptable home in contrast to the prompt attention given to the needs of white applicants; had directly discriminated against Bangladeshi homeless families in the way that they had been treated compared with white families in respect of waiting times for offers of accommodation; had indirectly discriminated against Bangladeshi families in respect of the treatment of separated families where part of the family was resident outside the UK; and had directly discriminated against Bangladeshi and other ethnic minority applicants for housing in that it had allocated them disproportionately to a poor estate (CRE 1988). An investigation of the procedures used to allocate local authority dwellings in Oldham between 1988 and 1990 (CRE 1993) found evidence of stereotyping and steering by housing officers and came to the conclusion that the policy adopted by the council in 1983 of allowing members of ethnic minorities with children to occupy flats above the first floor on one estate (contrary to its policy on other estates) in order to alleviate overcrowding amongst ethnic minorities was discriminatory in its impact.

Niner (1985) examined the operations of two housing associations in Birmingham. She found that a number of the procedures used by these associations contained the potential for discriminatory outcomes: the extensive discretion of members of staff in allocating homes, the reliance on informal contacts for the receipt of applications and the connections that one of the associations had with a religious organisation. However, she found it difficult to arrive at firm conclusions on the overall impact of these procedures. Black and Asian applicants were less likely to be offered a house but this difference could be partially explained by area preferences. Newly improved properties were more likely to be occupied by European households whereas new dwellings were more likely to be offered to black and Asian applicants.

There is no incidence of the housing practices of a housing agency being investigated either by academics or the Commission for Racial Equality without the discovery of some evidence of institutional racism. This raises the question as to why such practices persist. One reason is that some of the findings can be questioned (and hence ignored) because of the inadequate research methods by which they were generated. Before attributing causation to institutional racism it is important to ensure that other explanatory variables are identified and taken into account. Area preference can be an important influence on the outcome of allocative systems but neither the Oldham nor the Tower Hamlets study gave sufficient attention to this variable. The economic situation of the applicants is also significant. Several studies of the local authority housing process have demonstrated that those with limited alternatives and in the most desperate circumstances have to accept the homes in least demand: they trade shorter waiting times for inferior accommodation (Clapham and Kintrea 1986). Thus one possible explanation for ethnic differences in the quality of local authority homes allocated might be that the economic circumstances of black and Asian British people are more limited than the 'average' white applicant (but not whites who share the same class position), thus indicating an 'economic' rather than a 'housing' cause of racial inequality. None of the studies listed above controls adequately for this factor although nearly all the applicants studied in the Hackney enquiry accepted their first offer, and hence 'bargaining power' is unlikely to have played a part in this outcome. In the Oldham study evidence that waiting time might be a cause of the differential allocation between particular estates was ignored.

A further reason for the continuance of racial inequality has been the failure of the Commission for Racial Equality to give firm guidance on the acceptability of rules and practices that result in discriminatory outcomes. Rather than state specifically that certain practices are discriminatory and ought to be ended, the Commission has issued non-discrimination notices requiring ethnic monitoring, training programmes and reviews of allocation procedures without specifying – as a matter of the Commission's interpretation of the law – what the content of a fair allocation system ought to be.

Structural racism

This refers to the overall context of housing policy set by the government, that results in racial inequality. Although academics and the CRE have concentrated their attention on local authorities, 'national legislation has been influential in determining the location and quality of black people's housing opportunities . . .' (Smith 1989: 49). A number of recent examples of structural racism can be presented:

- The right to buy has resulted in many of the most desirable council homes being sold on those estates 'populated mostly by white working-class households who benefited from the racialised allocation policies of previous decades' (Ginsberg 1992: 121).
- Central government cutbacks in the allocation of borrowing approvals to local authorities in the 1980s have prevented them from meeting the housing needs of ethnic minorities. A stark example of this relates to the system of means-tested mandatory improvement grants set up in 1989. Ethnic minorities tend to have low incomes and to live in dwellings requiring major repair to bring them up to the fitness standard. The allocation of finance to local government to meet the demand for grants has been well below the amount necessary and it has not been distributed to the areas in greatest need of the available resources.
- Financial penalties have been applied to local authorities with an unacceptable number of empty properties, thus contributing to the pressure on local housing officials to find tenants for 'difficult to let' properties rather than attempting to find properties in which potential tenants want to live.

None of these policies have been challenged by the Commission for Racial Equality and therefore it is difficult to determine whether or not such policies contravene the 1976 Race Relations Act.

Policies for the promotion of racial equality in housing

The legal framework: The Race Relations Act 1976 provides the statutory basis for the elimination of racial discrimination. Under the terms of the Act it is unlawful to discriminate, both directly and indirectly, on racial grounds. Racial grounds are defined as those of race, colour, nationality and ethnic or national origins. Direct discrimination means treating a person less favourably than another on the grounds of race and includes segregation on racial grounds. Indirect racial discrimination consists of applying a condition such that the proportion of persons of the victim's racial group who can comply with it is considerably smaller than the proportion of persons not of that group who can comply. The condition must be to the detriment of the victim and the discriminator must fail to demonstrate that the practice is justifiable irrespective of race, colour, nationality or the ethnic or national origins of the person to whom it applies. If, for example, 'a housing cooperative fills its vacancies via friendship networks, i.e. by word of mouth, rather than by a more formal system of allocation' then 'where members of a housing cooperative are predominantly white, such a rule will disadvantage members of ethnic minorities' (CRE 1991: 2.7).

Any individual who thinks that he or she is a victim of discrimination can bring civil proceedings against the alleged discriminator through the courts. In addition the Commission for Racial Equality can organise a formal investigation into an organisation in which it has a reasonable belief that discriminatory procedures are being practised. On completion of the formal investigation the Commission is obliged to prepare a report on its findings and, if it concludes that an act of unlawful discrimination has been committed, it can issue a non-discrimination notice. This notice may require the organisation to change its practices and gives the Commission the power to monitor these changes over a period of time. Appeals against non-discrimination notices may be lodged to a county or sheriff court. If an organisation does not comply with the terms of a confirmed notice then the Commission can start proceedings for an injunction prohibiting the respondent from continuing to breach the terms of the notice.

Welfare pluralism: In the 1950s some members of ethnic minority communities started to develop schemes aimed at helping to alleviate the general housing problem and to meet the particular needs of the communities to which they belonged (Deacon 1970). In 1986 the Housing Corporation started a five-year programme for ethnic housing associations which, according to Harrison, 'was part of a broader stance on "race" equality which arose from external pressures and internal commitment by key officers' (Harrison 1993). During the period 1986 to 1991, 44 new minority ethnic housing associations were registered, adding to the 19 such associations registered before 1986. Although these housing associations manage very few properties they have targeted particular communities – often identifying needs that have been neglected by mainstream organisations – and they offer the foundation for growth. Unfortunately their potential has been undermined by the financial regime imposed by the 1988 Housing Act which requires associations involved in development to have a secure asset base. Most ethnic minority associations, being relatively new, do not possess properties built at low cost to use as security on loans and are therefore at a disadvantage in the development process. The Housing Corporation has encouraged established associations to transfer stock to associations controlled by ethnic minorities and has stimulated ethnic minority associations to form partnerships with larger white-led associations. This may promote new development but will result in a loss of diversity and autonomy.

Positive action: Section 56 of the Housing Act 1988 extended to the Housing Corporation, Scottish Homes, Tai Cymru and any new Housing Action Trusts the duties that applied to local authorities under Section 71 of the Race Relations Act 1976. They were required to 'make appropriate arrangements with a view to securing that their various functions are carried out with due regard to the need to eliminate unlawful racial discrimination and to promote equality of opportunity and good relations between persons of different racial groups'.

Promoting equal opportunities, as distinct from avoiding discrimination, often begins with the setting of equality targets which, on the grounds that a workforce that is representative of the community can offer a better service, often includes staff as well as service targets. A target has been defined by the Commission for Racial Equality in the following terms:

This measurement or target, will be the yardstick by which the data are analysed to check whether ethnic minorities have received a fair share of the properties and services available. It is emphasised that a target is a system of measurement and should not be confused with a predetermined quota, which is unlawful under the Race Relations Act. A quota is a fixed number or percentage which is imposed for a particular area, and there is an obligation to achieve it. A target on the other hand is not an absolute minimum or maximum, as it may be over or underachieved. It is a yardstick for measuring success or failure. Achievement of a target does not lead to the exclusion of any particular applicant.

(CRE 1991: 21–22)

Having established targets an organisation concerned to promote equal opportunities may take positive measures to ensure that such targets are met. These may include the use of Section 11 of the Local Government Act 1966 to employ people to ensure that the specific needs of ethnic minorities are met, and the use of Section 37 of the Race Relations Act 1976 which allows the provision of access by members of a particular racial group to facilities for training for particular work, or encouragement to 'take advantage of opportunities for doing that work when they have been underrepresented in that work at any time within the previous twelve months'. The 1976 Race Relations Act specifically forbids the use of fixed quotas to promote equal opportunities.

Conclusion

The structure of the housing system in Britain has not only contributed to inequalities in life chances but has also influenced the ability of certain people to compete in a market economy. As Smith succinctly summarises the issue in the context of racial equality: '*where* people live, within cities and regions, has a bearing on their access to services and employment; ·and the quality, condition, tenure and location of dwellings can prevent people moving to take advantage of new jobs and benefits in a spatially restructuring economy and in a shrinking welfare state' (Smith 1993: 128). The aim – proclaimed by all parties in the 1970s – of ensuring the provision of a decent home for everyone at an affordable price, has not been achieved, with the result that a significant number of people are homeless or are forced to live in housing conditions that fail to meet minimum standards. Living in these conditions reduces the ability of adults and their children to compete in markets and therefore perpetuates inequality and disadvantage.

References

Anderson, I., Kemp, P. and Quilgars, D. (1993) *Single Homeless People*, HMSO, London.

Bull, J. (1993) *Housing Consequences of Relationship Breakdown*, HMSO, London.

Child Poverty Action Group (1993) *Child Support Handbook*, CPAG, London.

Clapham, D. and Kintrea, K. (1986) 'Rationing, Choice and Constraint: The allocation of public housing in Glasgow', *Journal of Social Policy* (15), pp. 51–67.

Commission for Racial Equality (1984) *Race and Council Housing in Hackney: report of a formal investigation*, Commission for Racial Equality, London.

Commission for Racial Equality (1988) *Homelessness and Discrimination: Report of a formal investigation into the London Borough of Tower Hamlets*, Commission for Racial Equality, London.

Commission for Racial Equality (1989) *Racial Discrimination in Liverpool City Council; report of formal investigation*, Commission for Racial Equality, London.

Commission for Racial Equality (1990) *Sorry, Its Gone: Testing for racial discrimination in the private sector*, Commission for Racial Equality, London.

Commission for Racial Equality (1991) *Code of Practice in Rented Housing*, Commission for Racial Equality, London.

Commission for Racial Equality (1993) *Housing Allocation in Oldham: Report of a formal investigation*, Commission for Racial Equality, London.

Conway, D. (1992) 'Do Women Benefit From Equal Opportunities Legislation?' in Quest, C. (ed.) *Equal Opportunities: A Feminist Fallacy*, IEA Health and Welfare Unit, London.

Daniel, W. W. (1968) *Racial Discrimination in Britain*, Penguin, London.

Daunton, M. J. (1983) *House and Home in the Victorian City: working class housing 1850–1914*, Edward Arnold, London.

Davies, J. (1985) *Asian Housing in Britain*, Social Affairs Unit, London.

Deacon, N. (1970) *Colour, Citizenship and British Society*, Panther, London.

Dennis, R. (1984) *English Industrial Cities of the Nineteenth Century: a social geography*, Cambridge University Press, Cambridge.

Department of the Environment (1993) *Housing in England: housing trailers to the 1988 and 1991 labour force surveys*, HMSO, London.

Eve, G. (1992) *The Relationship between House Prices and Land Supply*, Department of the Environment, HMSO, London.

Finer, M. (1974) *Report of the Committee on One-parent Families*, Cmnd 5629, HMSO, London.

Forrest, R., Murie, A. and Williams, P. (1990) *Home Ownership: differentiation and fragmentation*, Unwin Hyman, London.

Gilroy, R. and Woods R. (eds) (1994) *Housing Women*, Routledge, London.
Ginsberg, N. (1992) 'Racism and Housing: concepts and reality', in Braham, P., Rattans, A. and Skellington R. (eds) *Racism and Antiracism*, Sage, London.
Government Statistical Office (1994) *Housing and Construction Statistics 1983–1993*, HMSO, London.
Gray, F. (1982) 'Owner-occupation and Social Relations', in Merrett, S. with Gray, F. *Owner Occupation in Britain*, Routledge and Kegan Paul, Oxford.
Greed, C. H. (1994) *Women and Planning*, Routledge, London.
Green, H. and Hansbro, J. (1995) *Housing in England 1993/4*, Office of Population Censuses and Surveys, HMSO, London.
Habeebullah, M. and Slater, D. (1990) *Equal Access: Asian access to council housing in Rochdale*, Community Development Foundation, London.
Harrison, M. (1993) 'The Black Voluntary Housing Movement: pioneering pluralistic social policy in a difficult climate', *Critical Social Policy*, 13 (3), pp. 21–36.
Henderson, J. and Karn, V. (1987) *Race, Class and State Housing: inequality and the allocation of public housing in Britain*, CURS, Birmingham.
Holmans, A. E. and Frosztega, M. (1994) *House Property and Inheritance in the UK*, Department of the Environment, HMSO, London.
Hills, J. (1991) *Unravelling Housing Finance*, Oxford University Press, Oxford.
Hills, J. (1995) *Joseph Rowntree Foundation Inquiry into Income and Wealth*, Vol. 2, Joseph Rowntree Foundation, York.
Karn, V., Kemeny, J. and Williams, P. (1985) *Home Ownership in the Inner City*, Gower, Aldershot.
Kemeny, J. (1995) *Understanding European Rental Systems*, SAUS, Bristol.
Little, J. (1994) *Gender, Planning and the Policy Process*, Pergamon, London.
London Research Unit (1994) *Nowhere To Run: underfunding of women's refuges and the case for reform*, London Research Unit, London.
Luthera, M. S. (1988) 'Race, Community, Housing and the State – a historical overview' in Bhat, A., Carr-Hill, R. and Ohri, S. (eds) *Britain's Black Population*, Gower, Aldershot.
McCarthy P. and Simpson, B. (1991) *Issues in Post Divorce Housing*, Gower, Aldershot.
Morris, J. and Winn, M. (1990) *Housing and Social Inequality*, Hilary Shipman, London.
Munro, M. and Smith S. (1989) Gender and Housing: Broadening the Debate, *Housing Studies* (4) 1 pp. 3–18.
National Federation of Housing Associations (1993) *Single Women in Housing Need: improving access to housing association homes*, NFHA, London.
Nationwide Building Society (1985) *House Prices Over the Past Thirty Years*, Nationwide Building Society, London.
Newton, J. (1994) *All in One Place: the British Housing Story 1973–1993*, Catholic Housing Aid Society, London.
Niner, P. (1985) *Housing Association Allocations. Achieving racial equality*, Runneymede Trust, London.
Pearson, L. (1988) *The Architectural and Social History of Cooperative Living*, Macmillan Press, London.
Rex, J and Moore, R. (1967) *Race, Community and Conflict*, Oxford University Press, Oxford.
Roberts, M. (1991) *Living In A Man-made World*, Routledge, London.
Saunders, P. (1984) '"Beyond Housing Classes", the sociological significance of private property rights in the means of consumption', *International Journal of Urban and Regional Research*, 8 (2), pp. 202–27.

Saunders, P. (1990) *A Nation of Home Owners*, Unwin Hyman, London.

Secretary of State for the Environment (1977) *Policy for the Inner Cities*, HMSO, London.

Simpson, A. (1981) *Stacking the Decks: a study of race, inequality and council housing in Nottingham*, Nottingham Community Relations Council, Nottingham.

Smith, S. (1989) *The Politics of 'Race' and Residence*, Polity Press, London.

Smith, S. (1993) 'Residential Segregation and the Politics of Racialisation', in Cross, M. and Kieth, M. (eds) *Racism, the City and the State*, Routledge, London.

Walker, B. and Marsh, A. (1993) 'The Distribution of Housing Tax-expenditures and Subsidies in an Urban Area', *Urban Studies*, 30 (9), pp. 1543–59.

Watson, S. with Austerberry, H. (1986) *Housing and Homelessness: A Feminist Perspective*, Routledge, London.

Weber, M. (1970) in Gerth, H. and Mills, C. W. *Essays from Max Weber*, Routledge and Kegan Paul, London.

Whitmarch, A. (1995) *Social Focus On Women*, CSO, London.

Wilcox, S. (1995) *Housing Finance Review, 1995/6*, Joseph Rowntree Foundation, York.

CHAPTER 9

Housing and community care

The workhouse and the asylum

The present pattern of housing, health and social care for older people, people with a learning disability, those experiencing a psychiatric illness, people with a physical disability and other groups now deemed to have 'special' housing needs evolved from the Poor Law. During the nineteenth century the general mixed workhouse provided accommodation for people with insufficient resources for survival. Attempts were made to place different categories of workhouse inmate into separate buildings, but even at the turn of the century the use of the general mixed workhouse as a form of 'indoor relief' was common. Conditions in the workhouse were designed to be 'less eligible' than those of the 'lowest independent labourer' to prevent unnecessary reliance on the state and to encourage provision by formal voluntary organisations and informal care by friends, neighbours and family. As Checkland and Checkland (1973) have commented:

The Commissioners believed that, for the most part, the families of the impotent, though enjoined by the 43 of Elizabeth [the Poor Law legislation of 1601] to care for their natural dependants, were not being made by the overseers to do so; rather such persons, contrary to the 'natural affections' were put upon the parish. The Commissioners favoured a policy of encouraging or even forcing labouring families to take care of their own.

(Checkland and Checkland 1973: 36)

The sufficiency of informal care in the nineteenth century is unknown, but formal voluntary organisations developed residential care for some categories of disabled and elderly people and in a few areas the tradition of providing almshouses for 'respectable' older people continued. These facilities made little impact on the workhouse population and by 1906 there remained 114,564 people aged over 60 receiving 'indoor relief' from the state. The 1929 Local Government Act abolished the Boards of Guardians and allocated their responsibilities to the mainstream local authorities. One objective of this legislation was to enable local government to develop general medical services without the stigma of the Poor Law, but the administrative division adopted – health committees for those people with 'curable', acute illnesses and public assistance committees for those who were likely to be dependent for long periods – was not helpful in the development of appropriate forms of care. The regime in which elderly and disabled people were assisted became detached from mainstream medical treatment and a 'warehousing' rather than 'rehabilitative' paradigm of help prevailed.

People suffering from psychiatric illness and those with a learning disability were gradually removed from the responsibility of the Boards of Guardians and housed in special hospitals. The County Asylums Act 1808 enabled state institutions for mentally ill people to be established. Provision gathered momentum after 1850 and by 1900 77 such institutions had been built (Jones 1994). The 1886 Idiots Act made it possible for local authorities to set up separate establishments for people with a learning disability but it was the 1913 Mental Deficiency Act that accelerated the building of large institutions. This Act, although making some provision 'for training, occupation and supervision' for those 'mental defectives' (to use the terminology of the Act) who lived with their families, placed emphasis on the care of people with learning disabilities out of the community. It was thought that those who could not be cared for at home should be set apart from the rest of society in institutions or 'colonies' in order to ensure that they received training and were protected from exploitation.

Care in the community

The pattern of institutional care for people with 'special' needs established in the nineteenth and early twentieth centuries continued into the 1950s. Progress was made by local government in opening residential homes for elderly people with a maximum of 30–35 beds, and by 1960 the local authorities in England and Wales had built 1,100 such homes. However, despite Bevan's statement – made in 1947 – that 'the workhouse is to go', in the early 1960s places in former workhouses comprised over 50 per cent of the accommodation used by local government. An extract from Peter Townsend's graphic and moving description of these institutions is presented in Document 21, page 226.

In 1954 there were 148,000 mentally disturbed patients in hospitals for mentally ill people and in institutions for mentally handicapped people but towards the end of the 1950s a movement in favour of community care began to evolve which gathered momentum in the 1960s. Initially emphasis was placed on care *in* the community as an alternative to institutional care. Care in the community meant the provision of state services either in residential care establishments – smaller and more 'homelike' than the traditional institutions – or in the person's own home. The expectation was that care in the community would generate more care *by* the community: family, friends and neighbours would be able and willing to assume a greater role in tending to the needs of their loved ones because people with 'special' needs would be housed in closer proximity to informal caring networks.

Progress in developing the administrative mechanisms for community care was made in the 1970s. Joint planning machinery between local authorities and health authorities was established, national targets for the amount of provision were fixed and a system of joint finance was set up. However, these initiatives proved to be inadequate; the pace of closure of the large institutions varied in different parts of the country and in many areas the reduction in institutional provision was not matched by the development of services in the community.

Care by the community

In the early 1980s, the emphasis of policy statements began to shift to care *by* the community as an end in itself: family, friends and neighbours should take a greater share of the caring role. A government White Paper on elderly people stated that 'care in the community must increasingly mean care by the community' (Department of Health and Social Security 1981). As Clapham, Kemp and Smith have pointed out in the context of services for people with learning disabilities, this shift in the orientation of policy can be interpreted in two ways:

that the state should interfere only as a last resort and that family and friends should bear primary responsibility for care or ... that the state should bear the primary responsibility for ensuring the well-being of people with learning difficulties but it should discharge this responsibility through family and friends by ensuring that they have the means to provide care without undue burden.

(Clapham, Kemp and Smith 1990: 143)

Some critics of the policy have insisted that the implementation of care by the community has followed the first interpretation with women having to undertake an unfair share of the new obligations (Lloyd 1991).

The privatisation of care

In the 1980s a new element was added to the policy mix: the privatisation of residential care. It is not certain whether this occurred by accident or design but in the early 1980s people with a low income living in private and voluntary residential and nursing homes had their eligibility to claim their care fees from the social security system clearly established. Despite the capping of the residential care costs payable by the state, the changes in the social security rules coincided with a rapid expansion of beds in the 'independent' residential and nursing home sector. Nursing home provision grew by 400 per cent and residential homes increased by 334 per cent between 1980 and 1991 (Wistow *et al.* 1994). The development of such forms of care helped to relieve the pressure of an ageing population on the National Health Service – the average length of stay of geriatric patients fell from 62.3 days in 1982–83 to 23.3 days in 1992–93 (House of Commons Health Committee Report 1994) – but the overall growth in private sector care was greater than the rise in the number of elderly people. Darton and Wright (1993) have calculated that whereas the growth in the number of elderly people in residential care approximately matched the growth in the number of elderly people over 75 in the population during the period 1971 to 1981, between 1981 and 1986 the growth in residents was double the increase in the number of elderly people over 75.

This privatisation of residential care for elderly people was accompanied by a similar process for other groups deemed to be in need of 'special' provision. The growth in private sector residential places for people with a learning disability increased sevenfold between 1978 and 1990 and private home places for people with a mental illness increased from 593 new places in 1977 to 2,660 new places in 1990 (House of Commons Health Committee Report 1994).

Pressures for change

The progress made towards the achievement of community care was reviewed by the Audit Commission in 1985 and 1986. The 1985 report covered services for elderly people and concentrated on the residential care provided by local authorities. It maintained that some people were inappropriately placed in residential homes due to lack of effective management, that community services were not directed to those who needed them most and that there was 'inadequate co-ordination of health, housing and social services' with 'arrangements for the provision of sheltered housing and the selection and training of wardens, as well as for the provision of community nursing support and medical treatment for disabled elderly clients of social services departments . . . rarely as effective as they can, and should be' (Audit Commission 1985).

The 1986 report examined the whole range of services involved in the care of people with 'special' needs. The Commission produced statistics to demonstrate that the advance towards the targets set in 1971 for services for people with learning disabilities had been slow (only 56 per cent of the anticipated residential places and 52 per cent of adult training centre places had been provided), that progress in reducing NHS provision for mentally ill people had been more rapid than the build-up of community resources and that there had been no increase per person aged 75 or over in community services such as home helps and meals on wheels.

National figures concealed considerable variations in community care provision in different parts of the country: spending by local authorities on services for mentally handicapped adults varied by a factor of six to one, expenditure per resident on services for mentally ill people varied from less than £1 to more than £7 and local authority gross expenditure on services for elderly people per person over 75 varied from less than £200 to more than £1,000. The Commission identified a number of causes of this slow and uneven progress towards community care: the methods for distributing the available finance did not match the requirements for community care policies, the social security system had undermined any switch from residential to community care, a fragmented organisational structure had caused delays and difficulties and there had been a failure to provide sufficient retraining for existing staff in hospitals and to recruit the additional staff required in the community.

The National Health Service and Community Care Act 1990

In response to the trenchant criticisms of the Audit Commission which pointed out that 'too many people are cared for in settings costing over £700 per week when they could receive a more appropriate care in the community at a total cost to public funds of £100 to £130 per week', the Secretary of State for Social Services appointed Sir Roy Griffiths 'to review the way in which public funds are used to support community care policy and to advise me on options which would improve the use of these funds as a contribution to more effective community care'.

The Griffiths Report (1988: iv) arrived at the conclusion that 'in few areas can the gap between political rhetoric and policy on the one hand, or between policy and reality in the field have been so great'. To cure the problem Griffiths proposed that 'one authority should be responsible for assessing needs and organising suitable care' and that local government was 'best placed to assess local needs, set local priorities and monitor performance'. In future central government assistance to local authorities, including part of the social security budget spent on residential and nursing home care, should be reserved for spending on community care. Each local authority should draw up a plan demonstrating how it would cooperate with health and housing authorities and the private and voluntary sector, and in implementing the plan it should act as an enabler rather than a provider of services. People with the necessary resources should pay the full cost of their services and people receiving assistance must have a greater say in what is done to help them.

The Government pondered for 20 months on the proposals in the Griffiths Report. The appeal of a new dimension to the enabling role of local government, the emphasis on guided consumer choice and the potential to substitute a national cash limited system – with local authorities responsible for any shortfall – for the existing open and disorderly method of financing care, needed to be balanced by the implications of a major transfer of the funds from central to local control. Eventually a White Paper *Caring For People* was published in 1989. It listed a number of key objectives:

- to promote the development of domiciliary, day and respite services to enable people to live in their own homes wherever feasible and sensible;
- to ensure that service providers make practical support for carers a high priority;
- to make proper assessment of need and good case management a

cornerstone of high quality care with packages of care designed in line with individual needs and preferences;
- to promote the development of a flourishing independent sector alongside good quality public services: social services authorities should be 'enabling' agencies;
- to clarify the responsibilities of agencies, thus making it easier to hold them to account for their performance;
- to secure better value for taxpayers' money by introducing a new funding structure for social care: social security provisions should not provide any incentive in favour of residential and nursing home care.

Several changes in policy were identified as necessary to achieve these objectives. A new funding structure for those seeking public support for residential and nursing home care would be established and local authorities would take responsibility for the financial support of people in private and voluntary homes. Local government was to become responsible, in collaboration with medical, nursing and other interests, for assessing individual need, designing care arrangements and securing their delivery within available resources. They would be expected to produce and publish clear plans for the development of community care services, consistent with the plans of health authorities and other interested agencies and to make maximum use of the independent sector. The policies set out in the White Paper were given legislative authority in the National Health Service and Community Care Act 1990.

The implementation of the Act was phased over three years. The most significant phase was introduced in April 1993 when funds – the anticipated costs of new demands on residential and nursing home care – were transferred from the central social security budget to local government. In order to ensure that local authorities moved from a provider to an 'enabling' role, 85 per cent of the transferred revenue had to be spent on services bought from the independent sector. Thus, if local authorities wanted to divert people from residential care, where a significant number of independent suppliers had been created by the social security policies of the 1980s, they would have to stimulate a local private sector in domiciliary care.

Housing and community care

Institutional care developed because it was deemed necessary to control the behaviour of deviants, to segregate the 'unproductive' from society so as not to offend or contaminate the 'productive' and to offer sanctuary to people likely to be vulnerable to exploitation: accommodation, care and control usually came as a package. When the National Health Service was established in 1948, the medical profession consolidated its dominance over the care provided in the large institutions. The mainstream health service operated outside the domain of

local government and this administrative division offered an opportunity for social work to establish a professional identity distinct
from that of medical care. In the 1970s and 1980s the social services
departments – established as a result of the recommendations of the
Seebohm Committee (1968) – became the main local government
agencies involved in the implementation of the policy of community
care. However, during the 1960s housing departments had established
a strong foothold in the support of elderly people through the provision of sheltered housing. How younger people with specific needs
fared in access to 'ordinary' council housing is unknown: statistics
on access were not kept. The Seebohm Committee recommended
that housing departments should extend their responsibilities to 'cover
households containing mentally or physically handicapped members
as well as old people'. In the 1970s housing departments responded
to Seebohm's recommendations on physical disability and by 1979
were producing 5,953 mobility and 589 wheelchair homes per year.
Accommodation for other groups with specific needs increasingly
came under the influence of social services departments. The type of
accommodation they provided reflected the creed of the 'caring professions'; care and accommodation were delivered as a single package
with social service workers in control of both care and accommodation. In the 1980s health authorities entered the arena of community
care through the use of private sector accommodation, and housing
associations penetrated the community care marketplace by developing accommodation and associated care and support, often in partnership with a charitable organisation.

Many housing departments became detached from community care
in the 1980s. In part this was a consequence of division in county areas
between county districts with responsibility for housing and county
councils with responsibility for social services, but it also reflected the
growing preoccupation of housing departments with family homelessness (their main statutory responsibility under the 1977 Homeless Persons
Act), the need to reform their systems of housing management, the
problem of 'difficult to let' estates and the disengagement from building new homes imposed by central government: new local authority
wheelchair accommodation declined to 188 in 1989 and new mobility
housing to 525. There is evidence that housing and social services
departments were finding it difficult to cooperate. The Institute of Housing, in its submission to the Barclay Committee (1982) stated that
'unfortunately in many cases the working relationship between housing
officers and social workers are not good ... generally speaking they
view each other with considerable scepticism' (quoted in BASW 1985).
A 1987 survey of 21 local authorities produced some depressing conclusions among them that 'only three of the 21 housing departments in the
survey actually had a written policy on meeting the needs of disabled
people' and only 'two local authorities reported that they had a formal
liaison structure involving housing and social services departments'
(Morris 1990). A study of ten county districts concluded that the reason

for 'housing's under-developed contribution as the key to effective community care' was to be found in 'the marginal role of housing authorities in formal joint planning structures, and the competing pressures of rising homelessness, lengthening waiting lists and backlogs of repairs' (Arnold and Page 1992: 52).

A 'bricks and mortar'/care distinction?

The Griffiths report made a firm distinction between housing and care:

> The responsibility of public housing authorities (the Housing Corporation, etc.) should be limited to arranging and sometimes financing and managing the 'bricks and mortar' of housing needed for community care purposes. Social services authorities should be responsible for arranging the provision of social, personal and domestic services in sheltered housing and the finance of those services should be provided through social services, not housing budgets.
>
> (Griffiths 1988: 6.10)

This 'bricks and mortar'/care division received support from the Wagner Committee set up to provide an independent review of residential care. The Wagner Report stressed the function of residential care as an *accommodation* resource within which a variety of support and care systems could be established. It went on to urge that 'all service providers should begin to look at people's requirements in a new way by distinguishing between need for accommodation and need for support services' (Wagner 1988).

In the early 1990s there were indications that the Department of the Environment had accepted the 'bricks and mortar'/care divide as a way of partitioning responsibilities between housing and care agencies and ensuring that the costs of care were met by the Department of Health. Consultation papers were issued suggesting that the cost of the welfare elements of local authority housing should be taken out of the housing revenue account; 'wet' hostels for alcoholics were not permitted under the Rough Sleepers Initiative unless care costs were guaranteed; hostel deficit grant paid to housing associations, and often used to cover some care expenses, was remodelled into a more restricted special needs management allowance; and the Department of the Environment refused to acknowledge that the new emphasis on home care required additional housing resources or produced any new entitlement to housing provision. The NHS and Community Care Act imposed a duty on social services to notify the local housing authority and invite it to assist in assessment where a potential housing need is identified, but no obligation was imposed on housing authorities to give assistance (Mandelstam and Schwehr 1995).

This 'bricks and mortar'/care distinction was not supported by local government or by housing associations, who argued that such a division was unrealistic and damaging because housing workers were well positioned to *support* people with 'special' needs. As a result of such concerns the advance towards enforcing the 'bricks and mortar'/care division was modified in favour of a more gradual approach with emphasis placed on improving the mechanisms for joint coordination at the local level (Department of Health 1994).

Renovation and adaptation

It is difficult to deliver effective domiciliary services to people living in unfit dwellings, and the adaptation of homes to meet the needs of disabled people may help to prevent the use of residential care. Between 1986 and 1991 the conditions of elderly people living in older homes improved, mainly because the buoyancy in the housing market up to 1990 allowed some elderly home owners to use their housing equity to finance repair and improvement. The number of unfit dwellings declined, the proportion of 'lone older' households in the worst dwellings fell from 18.2 per cent in 1986 to 12.4 per cent in 1991 and the proportion of 'two older' households in the worst dwellings dropped from 11.4 per cent to 7.6 per cent (DoE 1993). The reform of the system of renovation grants, introduced in 1990, promised a further improvement for those elderly and disabled people with low incomes whose homes needed to be improved, repaired or adapted. The White Paper *Caring For People* (1989) placed great emphasis on the potential of the new grant system in developing community care. A number of grants became available which replaced the system operated under the Housing Act 1985.

Mandatory renovation grants were discussed in Chapter 6. Disabled facilities grant are available to anyone registered as disabled, or who could be registered as disabled, or to anyone who has a disabled person living with them. They are mandatory for certain basic works but subject to an income and capital test, harsh on those people who have received compensatory payments for their impairment that they expected to produce an income sufficient to live on in the future. Payment is made from the same budget as mandatory renovation grants and the pressure on this budget has resulted in considerable delays in the payment of disabled facilities grant in many areas. If implemented, the proposals contained in the consultation document *The Future of Private Housing Renewal Programmes* (DoE 1995) will ease the situation in the long term. Mandatory renovation grants are to be replaced by discretionary grants but mandatory disabled facilities grant will be retained. When the backlog of mandatory renovation grant applications is cleared, more resources should be available for adaptations.

Adaptations cannot meet the requirements of all disabled people and hence a supply of purpose-built accommodation is necessary. There are two main types of specialised housing provision for disabled people. These are:

1   Wheelchair housing designed according to standards set out in HDD Occasional Paper 2/75 with features including entrances accessible

for wheelchair users and wheelchair access to a bedroom, bathroom and lavatory.

2   Mobility housing, which includes all housing designed to conform to standards set out in HDD Occasional Paper 2/74 for people who can walk but with difficulty; this type of accommodation would have widened doorways and a lavatory on the ground floor.

Living Independently (DoE 1994: 55) estimated that there was 'a slight shortfall in the availability of places in wheelchair housing of 0.6 units per 100 households containing non-elderly disabled adults' and a shortfall of 0.34 units per 100 households, requiring mobility housing. 'Slight' these shortfalls may be in units per 100 households but they conceal local variations in availability, and meeting the deficit of wheelchair accommodation would take many years at the 1990s rate of new construction. In addition a strong case has been made for ensuring that new homes are built so that they can be easily adapted to meet changing needs and offer the opportunity for disabled people to visit friends and relatives. The Joseph Rowntree Foundation has promoted the idea of 'lifetime homes'. A 'lifetime home' conforms to a checklist of 16 features including dropped kerbs, flat thresholds and provision for the installation of a lift if necessary.

Minor works grants up to a value of £1,080 per application are available to people claiming a means-tested benefit. These are discretionary and designed to help with such matters as thermal insulation and minor adaptations to enable elderly people to continue to live at home.

Financial support from central and local government has enabled various agencies to be established, such as 'Care and Repair' and 'Staying Put', to assist vulnerable people to make use of the grant system and other sources of finance for improvement, repair and adaptation. They also help to organise the appointment of a builder and to supervise the work. Unfortunately cutbacks in the finance available to local authorities for improvement grants has meant that the availability of grants – relative to the needs being discovered by the new community care procedures – has been severely restricted and, with the decline in house prices in the early 1990s, the scope for equity release (people borrowing money for improvements on the strength of the value of their homes) has diminished.

Sheltered housing for older people

Special housing for elderly people developed rapidly from the early 1960s. Sheltered housing schemes are officially divided into categories according to the level of support that is on offer. The official categories are:

- Category 1: accommodation designed specifically for fitter, more active elderly people, which may contain a common room, laundry or a guest room.

- Category 1.5: similar to Category 1 but must have warden support and an alarm system.
- Category 2: designed for less active elderly people and must have warden support, an alarm system and communal facilities.
- Category 2.5: designed for frail elderly people and can contain additional support facilities such as meals, extra wardens and sluice rooms.

In 1994 the average scheme in England was 'made up of 25% bedsitters, 66% one bedroomed and just 8% two bedroomed dwellings' and the median size of schemes 'was around 28 dwellings' (Elderly Accommodation Council 1994). Sheltered housing is normally administered by the housing department and in some authorities its costs are carried by the housing revenue account, thus some council tenants subsidise the welfare of elderly people. Following the Housing Act 1974 sheltered housing became a significant part of the development programme of housing associations who now own about 23 per cent of the total sheltered housing stock (DoE 1994). In the middle years of the 1980s a market in sheltered housing for sale developed, stimulated by leasehold schemes for the elderly administered by housing associations and the use of the equity that some elderly people had acquired through years of home ownership. In 1990 the National Federation of Housing Associations estimated that there were 6,000 leasehold units and 11,300 units developed by the private sector and managed by housing associations (NFHA 1991) but the slump in house prices and the high cost of service provision restricted the growth of sheltered housing for sale in the 1990s.

Surveys of the residents of sheltered housing have cast doubt on its role in the system of accommodation and care for elderly people. A study by the Department of the Environment (1994) confirmed the earlier findings of Butler, Oldman and Greve (1983) and Clapham and Munro (1990). The criteria used to allocate elderly people to sheltered accommodation were vague and varied between local authority areas. Although 59 per cent of the tenants of sheltered accommodation interviewed in the Clapham and Munro study gave poor health as the reason for moving, the researchers found no reason to suppose that the housing problems associated with poor health could not be solved without a move to sheltered accommodation. Clapham and Munro also noted that 'rarely was there a detailed assessment of different options of dealing with the difficulties older people may have faced. In general, sheltered housing was the only form of provision on offer, and the assessment process was not particularly discriminating between different types or levels of need or the factors creating them (for example, physical ability or housing circumstances)'.

The Department of the Environment study (1994) revealed that 40 per cent of residents of 'ordinary sheltered housing' had a 'dependency profile' rated zero and 24 per cent of the residents of 'very sheltered housing' also had a zero dependency rating. Such findings, together with the fact that many allocation procedures take into account not only assessed need but also the desire to maintain some balance between 'fit' and 'frail' tenants so that the 'fit' can help the 'frail' (Ministry of Housing and Local Government/Ministry of Health 1961) prompts a series of questions about sheltered housing. Is it being occupied by many elderly people simply because it exists and provides the only good quality, small and easily managed accommodation in the area? Is the system of allocation efficient if 24 per cent of the residents of *very* sheltered housing have a dependency profile of zero? Do the additional capital and revenue costs offer value for money in terms of other uses of the available finance such as additional home helps or lower rents? The Department of the Environment study came to the conclusion that:

... the majority of elderly and disabled people have no assessed need for any form of subsidised specialised housing or other housing with care support to remain at home. Of those that do have an assessed need, most wish to remain at home and can be enabled to do so through adaptations and domiciliary care support. This is also the most cost-effective solution to their housing needs. There is, however, a small but significant minority of elderly and disabled people who both need and want a move to specialised accommodation. Current provision meets most of this demand but there are some shortfalls in units for those with high levels of dependency and disability and extra-care requirements. There is also evidence of over-provision of some types of specialised accommodation and it may be that part of this stock can be converted to other uses more in line with current needs.

(Department of the Environment 1994: 180)

Many local authorities have experienced difficulty in letting their older sheltered housing – often bedsits with shared facilities – but the conclusion of the Department of the Environment that the need for sheltered accommodation has almost been met may be premature. The population over the age of 85 is expected to increase from 765,000 in 1991 to 1,220,000 in 2001 and the Department of the Environment study did not take into account the possible consequences of the new system of community care and the potential diversion of elderly people from residential care into sheltered housing.

Developing an appropriate pattern of accommodation for younger people with specific needs

The Housing Corporation has identified 11 categories of people (in addition to 'frail elderly') who have a 'special' housing need. These are:

- people with mental health problems;
- people with learning disabilities;
- people with physical disabilities, including wheelchair users and those with a sensory impairment;
- people with drug-related problems;
- young people at risk;

- ·people with alcohol-related problems;
- vulnerable single parents;
- people with HIV/AIDS;
- ex-offenders;
- refugees;
- women at risk of domestic violence.

The people who qualify for inclusion in one of these categories have diverse needs and wants for housing and often object to being classified into a 'special' need group (Ree and de Silva 1993). In an ideal world each individual would receive a pattern of service matched to his or her requirements as expressed in an individual programme plan (NFHA 1990). However, resource constraints and the need to link individual aspirations to an overall pattern of housing provision make this ideal difficult to achieve.

The existing range of accommodation is diverse and includes the remaining large institutions, many due for closure by the late 1990s; residential care homes; shared living schemes, where people with 'special' needs share a house with 'able people'; staffed hostels; clusters of flats and houses with a warden; cluster flats where people live independently but share some facilities; shared housing and self-contained houses; bedsitters and flats to which 'floating' support is delivered. As the movement in favour of community care gathered momentum the major 'interests' in community care – the voluntary sector, social services departments, health authorities and the private sector – all became involved in establishing 'community' provision using a variety of funding mechanisms. In the 1980s these funding mechanisms steered providers towards offering large dwellings shared by a number of residents. A report by the National Federation of Housing Associations and Mind (1990) commented:

> One of the most serious consequences of the unplanned growth of the board and lodging payments system has been the extent to which it has distorted the type of accommodation which has been provided for people with a mental health problem or a learning difficulty . . . Many agencies, in both the statutory and voluntary sectors, have opted for a shared housing solution just because some or all of the care and support costs are met automatically by the DSS. The structure of the board and lodgings payments system with its higher ceilings for registered homes than for other forms of shared housing has also encouraged the development of unnecessarily institutional forms of shared housing. There has been a strong temptation to deliberately set out to produce accommodation which meets the registered homes definition even when smaller shared schemes with less intensive support was more appropriate.
>
> (National Federation of Housing Associations 1990: 64)

The financial incentives for housing associations to build shared rather than independent accommodation were even stronger than for other agencies because hostel deficit grant was paid only for shared accommodation and, when the special needs management allowance was introduced to replace hostel deficit grant, it was set at a higher rate for shared accommodation than for self-contained schemes. Such shared accommodation – often in 'mini-institutions' – whilst appropriate in some cases, does not match the philosophy of 'normalisation' and the opportunity to experience an 'ordinary life' that is now part of the accepted wisdom of social services departments. The NFHA/Mind report (1990) summarised the results of consumer research on the things that people with a psychiatric problem or a learning disability believed were important to them:

● living independently but with the level of support they need;
● living in an area they like;
● being able to choose whether they live alone or with other people;
● being able to choose the other people they live with;
● not having to live with unnecessary rules and restrictions;
● being free to choose what and when they eat and when they get up and go to bed;
● having adequate privacy and peace, both within the house and in the neighbourhood in which they live.

In the 1980s the growth of accommodation for community care was unplanned, badly coordinated and insufficient, but following the concern expressed in the early 1990s about the marginalisation of housing from community care, improvements in strategic planning started to develop. In 1994 the Housing Corporation announced a review of existing 'special' needs accommodation and encouraged local authorities to produce a housing and community care strategy to complement the general housing strategy required by the Department of the Environment. Local authority community care plans and housing strategies produced in the middle 1990s demonstrate that closer liaison between social services and housing departments at the strategic level was developing. Forums have been established in some areas to facilitate discussion about the housing dimension of community care and several authorities are making a serious attempt to estimate the extent of unmet need in their areas and to plan new provision to meet this need.

Unfortunately, just as local authorities started to make progress in planning community care, the resources available to provide accommodation became subject to further curbs. The halt to new council building has meant that housing associations are the principal source of new accommodation. In 1995 the rental programme of the Housing Corporation was cut by 60 per cent and only 1,391 'special' needs units were approved for 1995–96 (NFHA 1995). Although some of this cutback may be met by additional resources for 'floating support', whereby help is provided to individuals according to their need for intensive housing support rather than as a result of residing in a particular unit of housing (SITRA 1994), there is a large deficiency in provision. In addition the reforms implemented in the early 1990s have not ensured that housing and care provision are sensitive to the needs of users and carers. Collins (1993: 29) maintains that some of the new National Health Service Trusts are providing finance for accommodation in the community linked to health service care which can result in a person 'merely receiving social care from the health service in a community setting thus perpetuating the exclusion of people with learning difficulties from the support services used by the rest of the population'.

Clapham, Munro and Kay (1994) have pointed out how the new system of revenue support for housing with care, although less likely to produce 'mini-institutions' than in the past, still encourages providers to offer 'packages' of housing and care that may not be tailored to individual needs. They have suggested that the existing system of state assistance for the running costs of housing with care schemes – a complex system involving special needs management allowance from the Housing Corporation to housing associations, housing benefit, contributions from voluntary organisations and assistance from local authorities – should be replaced by a direct payment to individuals based on a test of income. The benefit would be paid in cash 'which can be used to purchase care and support in an appropriate setting whether in residential care, supported accommodation or in mainstream housing' (Clapham, Munro and Kay 1994: 42). Such cash payments would enable care and support arrangements to be divorced from 'special' accommodation and allow 'ordinary' housing with 'floating' support to become the cornerstone of community care. The 'exit' politics involved in the use of cash has potent appeal to the New Right and, provided that there are suitable advisory arrangements and a strong 'voice' element in determining the types of accommodation available, the idea has potential in the empowerment of people with specific needs. However such 'open-ended' cash payments present difficulties of cost limitation and are inappropriate for those whose 'support and care' is a form of benign control. Thus it is more likely that the government will continue to move towards using local authority social services departments (which are cash-limited by central government) as rationers of care, and housing departments, controlled by the Department of the Environment, will ration 'bricks and mortar' through the mechanisms of local housing strategies.

Conclusion

Professional social work opinion has moved from supporting accommodation for people with 'special' needs in 'mini-institutions' and now favours 'floating support' brought to 'ordinary houses in ordinary streets'. Although some people in the professions related to medicine have resisted this change (Collins 1993) and progress even towards the establishment of 'mini-institutions' as a substitute for the larger institutions has been uneven (Audit Commission 1994), the dominant professional view of the pattern of 'special' needs accommodation has been established. This view has been endorsed by the pressure groups representing disabled people who are demanding independent living (Watson and Conway 1995). The danger is that 'floating' support in *existing* social sector accommodation might reinforce the tendency for those with specific needs to be concentrated in the most deprived areas. If appropriate patterns of accommodation with care and support are to develop then a sustained programme of additional accommodation is necessary. The Office of Public Management (1992) has estimated that there is a requirement for a minimum of 13,200 homes with support per year excluding provision for homeless mentally ill people and ex-prisoners.

References

Arnold, P. and Page, D. (1992) *Bricks and Mortar or Foundation for Action?*, School of Social and Professional Studies, Hull Polytechnic, Hull.

Audit Commission (1985) *Managing Social Services For The Elderly More Effectively*, HMSO, London.

Audit Commission (1986) *Making A Reality of Community Care*, HMSO, London.

Audit Commission (1994) *Finding A Place: a review of mental health services for adults*, HMSO, London.

BASW (1985) *Housing and Social* Work, British Association of Social Workers, Birmingham.

Butler, A., Oldman, C. and Greve, J. (1983) *Sheltered Housing For The Elderly*, George Allen and Unwin, London.

Checkland, S. G., and Checkland, E. A. (1973) *The Poor Law Report of 1834*, Penguin, London.

Clapham, D., Kemp, P. and Smith, S. J. (1990) *Housing and Social Policy*, Macmillan, London.

Clapham, D. and Munro, M. (1990) 'Ambiguities and Contradictions in the Provision of Sheltered Housing for Older People', *Journal of Social Policy*, 19 (1), pp. 27–45.

Clapham, D., Munro, M. and Kay, H. (1994) *A Wider Choice, revenue funding mechanisms for housing and community care*, Joseph Rowntree Foundation, London.

Collins, J. (1993) *The Resettlement Game – policy and procrastination in the closure of mental handicap hospitals*, Values into Action, London.

Darton, R. A. and Wright, K. G. (1993) 'Changes in the Provision of Long-stay Care, 1970–1990', *Health and Social Care*, 1, pp. 11–25.

Department of the Environment (1993) *English House Conditions Survey*, HMSO, London.

Department of the Environment (1994) *Living Independently: a study of the housing needs of elderly and disabled people*, HMSO, London.

Department of the Environment (1995) *The Future of Private Housing Renewal Programmes*, Department of the Environment, London.

Department of Health (1994) *Implementing Caring For People: Housing and Homelessness*, Department of Health, London.

Department of Health and Social Security, Scottish Office, Welsh Office and Northern Ireland Office (1981) *Growing Older*, Cmnd 8173, HMSO, London.

Elderly Accommodation Council (1994) *Sheltered Housing in England*, Elderly Accommodation Council, London.

Griffiths Report (1988) *Community Care: Agenda For Action*, HMSO, London.

House of Commons Health Committee: First Special Report (1994) *Memorandum From The Department of Health On Public Expenditure On Health and Social Services*, HMSO, London.

Housing Corporation (1994) *New Funding Framework For Special Needs Housing*, Housing Corporation, London.

Jones, K. (1994) *Asylums and After*, Athlone Press, London.

Lloyd, P. (1991) 'The Empowerment of Elderly People', *Journal of Ageing Studies* 5, pp. 125–35.

Mandelstam, M. and Schwehr, B. (1995) *Community Care Practice and the Law*, Jessica Kingsley Publishers, London.

Ministry of Housing and Local Government/Ministry of Health (1961) *Services for Old People*, HMSO, London.

Morris, J. (1990) *Our Homes, Our Rights: housing, independent living and physically disabled people*, Shelter, London.

National Federation of Housing Associations (1991) *The Future of Sheltered Accommodation – Who Cares?*, National Federation of Housing Associations, London.

National Federation of Housing Associations (1990) *Housing People With Special Needs*, Research Report 13, National Federation of Housing Associations, London.

National Federation of Housing Associations (1995) 'Approved Development Programme 1995/6', *Housing Association Weekly*, 21 April.

National Federation of Housing Associations/Mind (1990) *Housing: the Foundation of Community Care*, 2nd edn, National Federation of Housing Associations, London.

Office of Public Management (1992) *Assessment of the Housing Requirements of People With Special Needs over the Next Decade*, Office of Public Management, London.

Ree, S. and de Silva, R. (1993) *General Needs Housing Associations and Disabled People*, Joseph Rowntree Foundation, York

Secretaries of State for Health, Social Security, Wales and Scotland (1989) *Caring For People: Community Care in the Next Decade and Beyond*, Cm 849, HMSO, London.

Seebohm Committee (1968) *Report of The Committee on Local Authority and Allied Personal Social Services*, Cmnd 3703, HMSO, London.

SITRA (1994) *Floating Support Information Pack*, SITRA, London.

Wagner, G. (1988) *Residential Care: a positive choice*, HMSO, London.

Watson, L. and Conway, T. (1995) *Homes for Independent Living*, Chartered Institute of Housing, London.

Wistow, G., Knapp, M., Hardy, B. and Allen, C. (1994) *Social Care in a Mixed Economy*, Open University Press, Milton Keynes.

PART THREE

Assessment

Housing policy: The market or welfare pluralism?

Towards a free market in housing

State intervention in the housing market reached its peak in the middle years of the 1970s but subsequently the state has been 'rolled back', allowing the 'neutral judge' of the market a more important role in determining the pattern of housing provision. Local government has been assigned the task of 'enabling' other organisations to supply dwellings, the supervisory functions of the local and central state have been curtailed and general consumer and producer subsidies have been reduced.

A quasi or a full market?

The notion of a quasi-market was developed by the School of Advanced Studies at the University of Bristol as a way of understanding the policies adopted by the Conservatives in the late 1980s. Le Grand and Bartlett (1993: 10) maintain that quasi-markets are 'markets because they replace monopolistic state providers with competitive independent ones' but 'quasi' because they differ from conventional markets in that not all the organisations involved are interested in maximising profits or are in private ownership. In addition, consumer demand is not expressed in money terms but in an earmarked budget spent on behalf of the consumer by an agent, or is channelled to the consumer through a 'voucher' which can be spent only on a designated service. Advocates of quasi-markets assert that they promote greater efficiency but preserve specified social objectives. Bramley (1993: 154), whilst aware of the limitations of the concept when applied to housing, contends that the 'general concept of a quasi-market fits quite well as a description of the emerging pattern of social housing provision in Britain'.

There are a number of features of the pattern of housing in Britain that dovetail into the notion of a quasi-market.

● Housing benefit can be regarded as a form of income-related voucher for rented accommodation that is transferable between homes. A former housing minister endorsed this view of housing benefit when he said that 'there are attractions in a market where tenants can shop around – with their housing benefit cheques where available – and compare what is on offer from local authorities, housing associations, private landlords and in the owner-occupied sector.

People should have choice, and not be held back by the subsidy which traps them, actually or psychologically, in low rent, low-quality housing' (Sir George Young 1993).

- The housing management function of local government will be subject to competitive tendering by the late 1990s but the purchaser of management services (the local authority) will set the rules within which the provider has to operate.
- Bids by local authorities to central government for borrowing approvals are now evaluated in terms of efficiency in performance (according to norms defined by the government) rather than in accordance with the full extent of local need.
- Providers of 'social' housing make bids for grant assistance to the Housing Corporation and are successful to the extent that they meet designated objectives at the lowest cost.
- The structure of local authority rents must mimic the market.

However, although it is possible to identify features of a quasi-market in the operation of the housing system, the nature of the housing quasi-market differs from the systems working in other domains of social welfare. As Harloe (1995: 527) has pointed out: 'housing, like food production, has provided large-scale and profitable opportunities for capitalism in ways that have not been nearly so evident (or took a long time to develop) in the other spheres of provision for human needs'. The free market in housing was established in the nineteenth century and public housing never acquired a dominant 'institutional' position in welfare provision. 'Social' housing has always been a service for a minority of the population and is now 'residual', whereas the National Health Service, education and the personal social services are more universal, covering the majority of the population with a need for the service. Britain is far closer to a free market in housing than in health, education and the provision of personal social care but market economists maintain that further steps towards market principles remain to be taken.

A free market – the necessary steps?

In a free market, the state does not attempt to influence consumer preferences by special subsidies, there are no intermediaries between consumer and producers, expenditure is not earmarked through vouchers, there is little state regulation, supply and demand determine the price of a good and the state subsidises the poor only to the level that is necessary for minimal consumption (Hayek 1960). Five main obstacles have to be overcome if a market in housing is to be attained. The residual tax relief on mortgage interest has to be withdrawn, the 'social' nature of housing associations requires attention, local authority involvement in the provision of houses has to be ended, housing benefit has to be abolished and the state must withdraw from involvement in land use planning.

Tax relief on mortgage interest: Tax relief on mortgage interest can be allowed to 'wither on the vine' by keeping the limit on relief at £30,000 and allowing inflation to reduce its real value or, in the absence of an increase in house prices, the rate at which the relief is applied can be progressively reduced. This, of course, is a high risk political strategy, especially in the context of a depressed housing market.

Housing associations: Housing associations present a minor obstacle to the creation of a free market. Real rents in the housing association sector have increased since the late 1970s (see Table 10.1) and in the early 1990s the rate of increase was faster than in the private rented sector (Chaplin *et al.* 1995). Rents on some new properties reached the market level in the 1990s (Wilcox 1995). The distinction between associations and private developers can be eroded by allowing developers to claim grants equivalent to HAG. The White Paper *Our Future Homes* (DoE, Welsh Office 1995) announced that commercial organisations will be able to apply for grant assistance and will be regulated by the Housing Corporation according to rules similar to those applied to housing associations.

Local authority housing: Local authority housing presents more serious difficulties for the liberal economist and New Right politician. The strategy behind the 1988 Housing Act and the 1989 Local Government and Housing Act was to use the prospect of new capital investment to woo tenants from their local authority: the terms of transfer under tenants'choice were aimed at providing funds to the new landlord to improve the acquired dwellings, and Housing Action Trusts offered new capital investment as a prelude to sale to an

Table 10.1 **Rents and earnings in England: housing associations: 1980–94**

Year	Fair rent £	Assured rent £	Rent as % of average male earnings	
			Fair	Assured
1980	12.52		11.2	
1981	13.98		11.5	
1982	15.63		11.7	
1983	17.19		12.0	
1984	18.65		12.2	
1985	19.75		12.1	
1986	21.44		12.3	
1987	22.68		12.3	
1988	25.00		12.4	
1989	26.83	24.50	12.2	11.2
1990	29.94	29.97	12.5	12.1
1991	32.72	33.93	12.9	13.3
1992	36.48	39.03	13.6	14.5
1993	38.42	44.87	14.0	16.3
1994	41.38	45.90	14.6	16.2

Source: Wilcox (1995)

assortment of new owners. These measures failed to convince tenants that transfer was in their best interests and Mrs Thatcher declared
that she 'had expected more from "tenants' choice" and from HATs'
(Thatcher 1993: 601).

As a substitute for the failed policy of "tenants' choice", the Department of the Environment used its control over local authority rents and
the housing investment process to maintain the momentum towards a
pure market. Central government took firmer control over local authority rents and the housing investment process became dominated by
'performance'. It was made clear that a declared intention to build new
local authority homes and a reluctance to sell dwellings was an indica-
tor of poor 'performance'. These measures will take time to reduce
state housing to the residual role it performs in the United States, and
the contribution of the right to buy will be smaller than in the 1980s
unless there is a dramatic recovery of confidence in the housing market.
'Rent into mortgage' offers an alternative route to promoting home
ownership but its impact will be limited because tenants claiming housing benefit are not eligible to join. By 1995 only 11 tenants had used
the scheme.

The most productive option for believers in a free market would be
to increase council house rents to market levels by further reductions in

Table 10.2 **Average weekly unrebated local authority rent 1978–95/6**

	At current prices	At constant (April 1993 prices)
	£ per week	£ per week
1978	5.83	16.89
1979	6.41	16.87
1980	7.70	16.65
1981	11.42	22.03
1982	13.48	23.77
1983	13.97	23.69
1984	14.66	23.64
1985	15.54	23.43
1986	16.36	23.94
1987	17.70	24.85
1988	18.82	25.42
1989	20.70	25.88
1990	23.76	27.14
1991	27.28	29.29
1992	30.57	31.47
1993	33.52	33.52
1994/5	35.90	n.a.
1995/6	38.28[1]	n.a.

Note: [1] budgeted increase
Sources: *Hansard*, Jan. 1994 Col. 900–901,
ADC/AMA Housing Finance Survey 1994–95,
1995–96

the housing benefit 'subsidy' paid to local authorities. A push towards market rents in the local authority sector has been in operation since the late 1970s (see Table 10.2). Local authorities are required to ensure that their rent structures mimic the market, and the annual rent increases imposed by the Department of the Environment have reflected market conditions in different parts of the country. The continuation of this policy for a few more years would ensure that local authority rents reached market level. Local authorities would then be full participants in a free housing market and a substantial surplus would be generated from the Treasury from local authority housing revenue accounts – even at 1995–96 rent levels, council tenants in England paid £226 million more than was necessary to meet the real cost of their homes (Wilcox 1995). However, this strategy would increase the cost of housing benefit and deepen the 'poverty trap'.

Physical planning: The planning system presents the highest barrier to a pure market in housing because it is popular especially with those who have much to gain by the preservation of their rural havens from residential development. In the 1930s, when planning restrictions on land use were negligible, housing production was sustained, substantial and generally of a good quality but the planning controls of the post-war period have placed limits on the supply of land. Coleman, one of the leading advocates of markets in housing, has commented:

There is little sense in pointing to the merits of rented housing in helping labour migration and reducing unemployment when it is impossible to build houses – for rent or for sale – in some of the places where families and newly married couples want to live and where migrants want to go. Shortage of land in areas of high demand is the key to many problems in housing and to some extent in employment. A land price component of 40 per cent on average in Britain and much more in the southeast contributes to the house price problem.

(Coleman 1992: 135)

Housing benefit: The abolition of housing benefit would be the final step in the creation of a free market in housing. Housing benefit is related both to the income of the recipient *and* to the rent that must be paid. A social security system based only on income would cause considerable hardship to those living in high rent areas but the logic of a free market dictates that people with low incomes should not be living in such areas. Moreover, according to economic liberalism, the payment of a subsidy to enable them to live in 'high cost' areas creates a 'perverse incentive' to others to move to expensive locations (Hayek 1960).

The consequences of free markets

There are benefits in a free housing market. Consumers can determine the proportion of their budget they wish to spend on housing, and competition between the suppliers of new housing and the owners of existing dwellings ensures that the price of a dwelling reflects consumer preferences and the marginal cost of production. A free market also allows an objective choice between renting and home ownership. Information systems, essential to an efficient market, although inadequate at the moment, could be improved by a subsidised information service (perhaps on the model of home improvement agencies) and by firmer regulation of the housing exchange professionals. However, there are persuasive arguments against the use of pure market principles even if underpinned by targeted subsidies to the poor.

Market failure

Real world markets can fail for a number of reasons. People may become attached to a dwelling as a 'home' and if the dwelling is owned by a landlord then the landlord can exploit the tenant by raising the rent above the market rate. Financial institutions can acquire the power to make decisions about the future of entire neighbourhoods. Building societies 'redlined' some areas in the 1970s and, in the 1990s, they have refused to offer mortgages on the systems-built flats bought under the right to buy, thus making some of these homes virtually unsaleable. There may be 'missing markets' with no mechanism available to bring complementary products together; it was, for instance, the state policy of subsidised 'workmen's fares' that connected inner-city work and cheap suburban building sites (Barlow and Duncan 1994). And more recently it has been the state that has linked derelict land to new housing developments. As Maclennan and Gibb (1993) comment:

> In reality there are many cases where large-scale public coordination is required. Take the example of land redevelopment such as the London Docklands Development Corporation – if markets were complete then the prices themselves would perform this coordinating role.
>
> (Maclennan and Gibb 1993: 221)

Externalities

An externality occurs when the consumption of a good by one person affects the welfare of others in ways that are not reflected in the market price. In the nineteenth century housing consumption produced massive externalities (cholera, typhoid, tuberculosis). Public health measures have improved housing conditions but important negative externalities remain. An individual terraced house in poor repair affects the value of the house next door, and large areas of poor housing can influence the reputation of an entire city. The most significant externalities relate to the protection of rural areas from residential development and are controlled by the planning system. Unless such controls are abandoned then it cannot be said that a 'pure' market is operating. The planning controls of the post-war years have created winners and losers and the greatest losers have been those residing in tower blocks located in the inner city. These blocks were erected – at least in part – in response to the scarcity of land to house the 'overspill' from clearance areas, and this land shortage was caused by the application of building control in green belts. The residents of these tower blocks had no choice in their location and deserve compensation for their loss of welfare; the market offers no method of providing such compensation. In addition, good housing produces positive externalities:

Warm homes reduce ill health, available homes reduce ethnic and other social tensions, energy-efficient homes promote environmental well-being. Secure, adequate homes provide space for family life and personal development. They facilitate the development of the next generation capable of supplying labour

(Maclennan and More 1995: 225)

Social polarisation

Markets allocate dwellings according to ability to pay and, because location is by far the most important determinant of house prices, then markets generate spatial polarisation. This process has been fostered by government policies based on 'filtering' theory. 'Filtering' theory suggests that if someone can be encouraged to use a part of their own resources to move out of a local authority or housing association dwelling, then this dwelling will be available for a homeless family. Cash inducements and indirect subsidies have been made available to persuade people to move house in order to release dwellings for homeless people. Although such initiatives provide homes for those in dire need, they have intensified the trend towards geographical segregation according to income. Hedges and Clemens (1994) found that 76 per cent of council tenants think that being in a good area is just as important as having a good house or flat, and a study of cash incentive schemes offered by local authorities revealed that tenants made use of the scheme because they disliked their existing home or 'the area in which it was situated' (Turtle and Burgoyne 1994: ix). As Field (1995: 18) has observed, 'the poor are being as successfully segregated geographically as they were in Victorian times'. Such social polarisation has significant implications for equality of educational opportunity, racial equality, law and order and social integration. It also helps to extinguish markets because in areas where large numbers of people have to claim housing benefit it is difficult to decide whether rents are at 'market' level or are determined by the availability of state assistance.

The quality of 'social' housing

Market theory gives 'social' housing a 'residual' role in housing provision: the service should be confined to people with a very low income.

Universalists (those who believe in comprehensive services available to all without a test of means) maintain that services for the poor tend to be poor services. There is a body of evidence to support this view. The idea of targeting resources on those with low incomes so that they can receive a better service may seem persuasive but experience has demonstrated that a 'residual' service is unlikely to be well financed or appealing. How would people be attracted to the market if the residual provision was of a high quality? Four examples help to demonstrate the point.

- In the 1930s, 1950s and 1960s, when subsidies were switched from general needs to needs arising from slum clearance, the quality of the dwellings erected declined significantly.
- In the late 1980s, when improvement grants became means-tested, the funding for such grants was severely restricted and a rigid upper limit on the grant was imposed.
- Following the direction of housing associations towards provision for the homeless in the late 1980s, the quality of life on large estates built by housing associations has deteriorated (Page 1993).
- The increased cost to the Treasury of housing benefit has been more than matched by the reduction in general subsidies (Kemp 1994) and, more recently, by the real surplus produced in some local authority housing revenue accounts. Nonetheless the political visibility of the mounting cost of housing benefit has made it vulnerable to cuts. The 'targeting' of housing benefit in the 1980s was followed by subsequent reductions in its value and availability. In the middle 1990s regional ceilings were imposed on the rent that can be included in a claim for housing benefit, thus pushing people with low incomes into the poorer quality accommodation.

The persistence of historical injustices

There have been numerous historical injustices in the acquisition of land and homes and these require reparation before allocation by markets can be regarded as fair. Large tracts of land were initially acquired by force, and the state has played a major role in determining the price of houses through the tax advantages that have now been capitalised into the value of homes. In order for the outcomes of a current free market to be just, the rectification of historical injustice is necessary.

Work incentives and the poverty trap

One of the dilemmas of selectivity is that the more a benefit is restricted to those in dire need of assistance, the greater are the disincentives to work and save for the 'targeted' group. Income support pays mortgage interest for people without work but there is no system to relate low earned income to mortgage repayments for home owners, and some owner occupiers with mortgages can become significantly worse off by taking a job. Hills (1993) has calculated that with a £40,000 mortgage, a couple with one earner and two children aged 6 and 13 would need weekly earnings of £177 in 1993–94 for net income in work to be higher than claiming income support.

Between 1983 and 1988, the rate at which housing benefit was withdrawn from those with income above the basic threshold was 33 per cent of gross income. This taper – as it is now called – was set at 65 per cent of net income in April 1988. The impact of the 1988 taper on the real incomes of those claiming the benefit was dramatic. In 1994, over a range of gross earnings from £1 to £230, a couple with two children paying a rent of £50 each week would have the same real net income of about £195 per week (Wilcox 1995). Because family credit is taken into account in assessing eligibility for housing benefit, the importance of the contribution to the poverty trap made by housing benefit increases with the amount of rent that has to be paid. With a rent of £50, housing benefit stops at a gross income of £248 per week (couple with two children, 1994) but with a rent of £70, entitlement to housing benefit is extinguished at £295 per week (Wilcox 1995). The small gains made by those increasing their income over the range outlined above indicates that there is a powerful disincentive to work built into the system. The alignment of housing benefit for those in work with the entitlements of those out of work means that few renters actually become worse off by taking a job but for many people out of the labour force there is little to be gained financially by finding a job or, having joined the workforce, by working harder and longer.

In the absence of a sustained economic recovery that increases the wages of the lowest paid, the liberal economist has only one course of action. The state has to abandon the idea of using positive incentives to encourage work and substitute the 'stick' of hardship for the 'carrot' of reward. Pure markets with high levels of selectivity in social benefits must incorporate punitive rules relating to disqualification from benefit, otherwise the overall system of market incentives starts to crack. As market forces have been introduced, greater sanctions have been applied to those receiving state benefits. The rules, introduced in 1987, that disqualify young people from the receipt of housing benefit are an example of this, as is the new jobseeker's allowance, planned to replace unemployment benefit and income support in 1996. Jobseeker's *allowance* replaces unemployment *benefit*, it is means-tested after six months and is subject to new penalties; failure to comply with a jobseeker's direction issued by an employment advisor disqualifies a person from benefit. (Secretary of State for Social Security, Secretary of State for Employment 1994.)

Welfare pluralism

The deficiencies of the market as an allocative mechanism need to be corrected by a role for the state as both provider and regulator. As demonstrated in earlier chapters, the development of the provider role by the state through local government was profoundly influenced by Fabian socialism. Whereas it would be wrong to attribute all the deficiencies of local authority housing to Fabianism and its offshoots (the demand for quantity rather than quality in the 1960s and the dominance of 'modernism' in architecture played a major role), the Fabians did have an arrogant view of the capabilities of the ordinary person and did not promote consultation with tenants in either design or management. Today, academics and politicians working within the egalitarian tradition of Fabianism have abandoned such attitudes, and see the virtue of a more pluralist system of housing provision with the state acting as a regulator intervening to ensure both procedural fairness and greater equality of outcome. Hambleton and Hogget (1990) have named this approach 'pluralist collectivism' and have distinguished it from the 'old solutions' of bureaucratic paternalism and the newer pattern of privatisation. There are many variations on the theme of pluralist collectivism and the framework presented here is offered as an example to promote discussion on the available options.

A pluralist system of housing provision requires many different agencies operating in the supply of homes, with the state regulating these agencies and providing production and consumption subsidies to guarantee that the overall operation of the system fulfils collectively determined purposes. The first question that needs to be asked of a pluralist housing system relates to the nature of the providers of homes and, in particular, to the roles of housing associations, private landlords and local authorities. Home ownership chosen without the 'perverse incentive' of generous tax relief on mortgage interest, or because of the lack of an alternative, is not in dispute.

Housing associations

Housing associations have an assured place in a pluralist system of housing provision, but reform is necessary in order to reverse some of the trends apparent since the new financial regime for housing associations was introduced in 1988. The larger national associations – without roots in a value system that comes from identification with specific local areas, ethnicity, religion or social movements – are taking a larger share of the development programme and are rapidly assuming the nature of private landlords; a consultation paper issued by the Department of the Environment described housing associations as 'private sector bodies' (DoE 1995b). This trend needs to be halted by ensuring that, in the future, development resources go to associations with missions other than the market, and that positive steps are taken to encourage the participation of organisations under-represented in the voluntary housing movement: trade unions are an example. In addition it is important to the welfare pluralist project that a specific legal tenure is created for the tenants of housing associations. During the passage of the 1988 Housing Act the NFHA argued that a special housing association tenure should be legally established with provisions to restrict rents to affordable levels. This was firmly rejected by the government. The present 'tenant's guarantee' supervised by the Housing Corporation is rightly placed in inverted commas, for it provides no independent rights that are enforceable by tenants through the courts and has not prevented the large rent increases imposed on tenants since 1989. The membership of housing association management committees also requires regulation to ensure that tenants, local authorities and ethnic minorities are represented.

Private landlords

By tradition, egalitarians have been suspicious of private landlords but in 1992 the Joseph Rowntree Foundation 'brought together academics, housing pressure groups, practitioners and financiers, together with advisors from different parties' to discuss the future of private landlordism. From these discussions the Foundation concluded that 'a body of informed opinion had reached agreement in relation to the future supply of the private sector (for profit) rented housing' (Best *et al.* 1992: 3). The participants agreed that there was an urgent requirement for more homes to rent; moving in the rented sector costs little and hence private landlordism assists new households: young single people, job movers and those splitting up through divorce and separation.

According to the panel, subsidies to private landlords – if adequately regulated – are justified. Methods of providing such subsidies were offered by the management consultants Cooper and Lybrand (1993) who suggest that authorised investment trusts should be set up to channel resources into private landlordism, and that these trusts should be coupled with limited grant incentives offered on a competitive basis to those landlords who produced the most dwellings for a given sum. The Association of Residential Letting Agents (1995) also recommended the creation of authorised investment trusts and suggested that landlords should be able to offset the cost of purchase against the taxation of rental income. The White Paper *Our Future Homes: Opportunity, Choice, Responsibility* (DoE, Welsh Office 1995: 21) noted that 'only 8% of privately rented properties are owned by residential property companies' and adopted the notion of authorised investment trusts which would be offered the stimulus of exemption from capital gains tax and a reduced rate of corporation tax.

There is little doubt that private renting offers a flexibility to some people that is difficult to obtain in either the owner-occupied sector or through 'social', housing but rent regulation has to accompany state subsidy. A proposal contained in a consultation paper (DoE 1995b) linked to *Our Future Homes*, suggests a means to achieve this objective: the rents that a commercial landlord intended to charge would be a factor taken into account by the Housing Corporation when allocating grant assistance, and future rent increases would be limited to inflation plus or minus a given factor.

Local authorities as providers

The middle 1980s were a period of crisis for local authorities as suppliers of houses. They were attacked by the New Right as being bureaucratic and inefficient, to which the New Left added the charges of paternalism and arrogance. Some of this criticism was justified. It is doubtful that tower blocks and deck-access flats would have continued for so long had there been more tenant involvement or a greater element of consumerism in local authority processes, and many councils took too long to recognise and adapt to the changes in the socio-economic composition of their tenants. However, local authority housing departments changed in the late 1980s. Prompted by the New Left, the inducements of the Estate Action programme and the emphasis on performance in resource allocation, housing departments have decentralised their management, shown far greater willingness to involve tenants in decisions and have obtained more efficiency from the other local authority departments that supply services to housing. Although some devolution of stock to smaller local government units or housing associations may be desirable – the larger metropolitan districts have too many dwellings for sensitive management to be sustained – local authorities still have considerable potential as suppliers of rented housing. They have a substantial asset base in their existing stock which could be used to finance both improvement and, where necessary, new build and they are controlled by democratically accountable councillors who can use political authority when taking up the grievances of their tenants.

The creation of specific housing companies to which local authority housing stock could be transferred has received considerable support in recent years. John Smith's Commission On Social Justice (1994: 343) suggested that 'local authorities should be given the power to establish local housing companies responsible for developing and managing social rented housing'. The rationale of such companies stems from the European and Treasury rules that are assumed to place a straitjacket on investment in local authority housing. It is argued that if local authorities were to transfer their stock to 'arms length' companies then borrowing for capital investment would not count as part of the Public Sector Borrowing Requirement and hence more resources would be available for investment in 'social' housing. *Our Future Homes* (1995: 29) endorsed the idea of local housing companies in which local authorities have a stake but stated 'they would need to be clearly in the private sector;

local authority nominees would need to be in the minority on the board'. Within existing Treasury rules this proposal has a pragmatism that is difficult to refute, but a rule that implies that all public sector investment is bad whereas all private sector investment is good seems perverse. Tenants have clearly demonstrated that they want local government to be responsible for their dwellings so why not change the rules and allow local authorities to raise capital on the strength of their assets whilst retaining local authority housing under democratic control? The Chartered Institute of Housing (1995) has suggested that if the Treasury changed its operational definition of the public sector deficit from the Public Sector Borrowing Requirement (borrowing for capital investment by public sector organisations) to the General Government Financial Deficit (which is used in many European Union countries and excludes borrowing for capital investment financed through charges), then local authorities could set up wholly owned 'local housing corporations' as a method of attracting private finance.

Housing cooperatives

Clapham (1989) has suggested that the role of local authorities as housing providers could be assumed by housing cooperatives. Document 22 (page 227) lists some of the advantages and limitations of cooperatives. They have a contribution to make to diversity in housing supply but their limited impact on the pattern of housing provision should not be attributed only to lack of concrete support from successive governments. Cooperatives take a great deal of time and effort to set up and, once established, the spirit of participation essential to the cooperative ideal can be difficult to sustain. Birchall quotes one member of the National Federation of Housing Associations as saying:

Co-ops are full of people who daren't admit publicly what they say privately, that co-ops are not actually full of people in control of their housing, but in fact have too many apathetic and uninvolved individuals who are housed from the sweat of the collective brow of a minority of hard-working co-op members.

(Birchall 1988: 164)

The strategic/enabling role of local government

The White Paper (1987) which announced the planned demise of local authorities as providers of homes, stated that, in future, local authorities should concentrate on their strategic/enabling role. The notion that local authorities should take a comprehensive view of the need and demand in their areas was not new; it was included in the 1919 Housing and Town Planning Act 1919, recommended by the Seebohm Report in 1968 and it informed the introduction of housing investment programmes in 1977. What was new in the post-war era was the concept of 'enabling'. Nicholas Ridley, as Secretary of State for the Environment, promoted the idea of 'enabling' – not just for housing but for all local services – in a pamphlet published in 1988. He argued that local authorities 'will need to operate in a more pluralist way than in the past, alongside a wide variety of public, private and voluntary agencies. It will be their task to stimulate and assist these other agencies to play their part instead of, or as well as, making provision themselves' (Ridley 1988: 25).

The 'enabling' role has promoted extensive discussion about the future of local government (Cochrane 1993, Brooke 1991, Stewart and Stoker 1989, Holliday 1991) but so far the debate has concentrated on the mechanisms of enabling rather than its purpose. Ridley was a fervent supporter of the free market; the objective of an 'enabling' authority was to liberate market forces: the state should not attempt to promote any 'patterned' principle of social justice. It is therefore surprising that the term 'strategic' was used in the White Paper on housing policy, because 'strategic' implies the specification of objectives whereas 'enabling' signifies that objectives are set elsewhere.

The dominance of the market model was reflected in the Department of the Environment's Annual Report for 1992:

The Government's overall aim is that a decent home should be within reach of every family. In the longer term, this might be achieved by relying on the market for supply, and on income-related assistance so poorer families can afford decent housing.

(quoted in Smith 1995: 2–3)

Subsequent advice from the Department of the Environment has concentrated on recommending local authorities to use their capital receipts and land banks to promote private sector developments and to stimulate the private landlord sector (DoE 1995a). Social objectives such as ensuring that housing is affordable without recourse to benefits, the promotion of social integration and the active promotion of equal opportunities for women and black people have not been on the agenda although in 1995 the government started to speak of 'mixed communities' and the 'limits of what can be achieved through higher rents' (DoE 1995: 35, 27).

In order to make their strategic role meaningful, local authorities require greater freedom to determine their objectives, and a range of additional powers to enable these objectives to be achieved. This issue can be illustrated by reference to the planning system.

In the 1970s a few local authorities used planning agreements to promote the supply of affordable houses. This practice was reintroduced in the middle 1980s but was related to securing housing to meet local needs in rural areas on sites that would not normally have received planning permission and to agreements on large private sector sites concerning the provision of a proportion of 'affordable' homes (Barlow, Cocks and Parker 1994). The legality of affordability conditions attached to planning consents, and their acceptability to central government, was in doubt but circulars issued under the Planning and Compensation Act 1991 appeared to give government approval to such conditions provided that decisions on individual sites were related to a local plan. The term 'appeared' has been used because the Department of the Environment remained vague about the degree of permissible intervention. Planning policy guidance note no. 3 (1992) stated that planning obligations 'cannot normally be used to impose restrictions on tenure, price or ownership' and the legal basis of affordability conditions remains insecure. Barlow, Cocks and Parker (1994) comment:

. . . challenges to the use of planning powers to secure affordable housing could arise in a number of ways. Most fundamentally, it may be asked whether affordable housing is a legitimate planning purpose. In addition, the use of provisions relating to density, restrictions on phasing, or even definitions of 'affordability' could be questioned. Any such challenges could indirectly lead to an examination of the status of affordable housing. Problems are also likely to arise in respect of the maintenance of affordable housing in perpetuity

(Barlow, Cocks and Parker 1994: 58)

Although the recession in house prices in the early 1990s has meant that the use of planning gain as an instrument for securing 'social' housing has produced disappointing results (Goodlad 1993), there is much to be gained from the refinement of the planning dimension of the strategic role of local government. Local authorities could be given a clear legal power to specify the tenure (renting is the most 'targeted' method of securing affordable housing) and to set out the type of homes to be built on specific sites identified in the local plan, thus returning some of the development gain to the community and taking a step towards the creation of more balanced local communities.

A new system of housing finance

In the 1980s important changes were made to the system of housing finance. In 1979–80 68 per cent of government help towards housing costs was spent on 'bricks and mortar' producer subsidies and 10 per cent on housing benefit. In 1994–95 49 per cent of state expenditure was on 'bricks and mortar' subsidies and 27 per cent on housing benefit (DoE, Welsh Office 1995). The withdrawal of 'bricks and mortar' producer subsidies to 'social' housing and the reliance on 'selective' housing benefit has pushed low income groups into renting, encouraged those with higher incomes into home ownership where tax reliefs are available, and has created a 'poverty trap' for those on low incomes.

The abolition of tax relief on mortgage interest, the taxation of the capital gains arising from owner-occupation and land ownership, and permitting local government to use the maturity value of the council stock through a mechanism that redistributes from the asset-rich to the asset-poor authorities would release sufficient resources to:

- modify the impact of the poverty trap by reducing the taper on housing benefit from its present level of 65 per cent to a more reasonable 50 per cent, extend the threshold of eligibility to housing benefit for single people and create a 'level playing field' in housing subsidies by including owner-occupiers with low incomes in either a reformed housing benefit scheme or in a specific mortgage benefit scheme, as suggested by Webb and Wilcox (1991);
- provide producer subsidies to community-based housing associations at a level sufficient to enable them to let homes at affordable rents;
- boost the resources available for urban renewal.

Housing policy: the past and the future

In the twentieth century considerable progress has been made in improving housing conditions. Despite the loss of ten years of house building in two wars, the majority of citizens have experienced a transformation in their housing conditions to the extent that the absence of central heating is now seen as a housing deprivation (see Table 10.3). Nonetheless, in the context of the resources devoted to 'the housing issue' in terms of taxes forgone and direct state expenditure, the extent of homelessness, insecurity, unfitness and overcrowding and the degree of social segregation is disturbing.

The large-scale, paternalist solutions of the 'Fabian era' produced too many badly designed housing estates which the market-orientated policies of the 1980s have helped to fill with people on low incomes and a disproportionate share of the most difficult tenants. The renewal of the private housing stock has not been targeted on those with low incomes, with the result that, in addition to trying to survive on a meagre income, many people have to cope in an unfit house that injures their health and compounds their financial difficulties. The neglect of overcrowding in the 1980s has blighted the lives of many young people

Table 10.3 **Households lacking basic amenities: Great Britain 1951–91 (percentages)**

Amenity	1951	1961	1971	1981	1991
Bath or shower[1]	37.6	22.4	9.1	1.9	0.3
Flush toilet					
Internal or external	7.7	6.5	1.2	..	..
Internal	..	..	11.5	2.7	0.5
Hot water tap	..	21.8	6.4	..	..
Central heating	..	..	..	..	18.9

Note: [1] Prior to 1991 data relate to fixed bath only.
Source: *Social Trends* (1995)

and has unfairly prejudiced their opportunities for success in a market economy. The tax concessions granted to owner-occupation have been capitalised in house prices which – despite the housing recession in the early 1990s – have made secure access to this sector difficult for people with limited incomes and have compounded unjustifiable disparities in wealth. The polarisation of housing standards between areas has made it easier for the privileged, the 'just over 40 per cent whose market power has increased since 1979', to ignore the difficulties of the 'absolutely disadvantaged', the 30 per cent whose children are 'poorly fed, their families under stress and without access to amenities' (Hutton 1995: 106–8). A more pluralistic network of housing provision, underpinned by a redistributive taxation/subsidy system and planning policies aimed at promoting integration on a geographical basis, are required in the future.

References

Association of Residential Letting Agents (1995) *Before It's Too Late*, ARLA, London.

Barlow, J., Cocks, R., and Parker, M. (1994) *Planning For Affordable Housing*, Department of the Environment, HMSO, London.

Barlow, J. and Duncan, S. (1994) *Success and Failure in Housing Provision*, Pergamon, Oxford.

Best, R., Kemp, P., Coleman, D., Merrett, S. and Crook, T. (1992) *The Future of Private Renting: consensus and action*, Joseph Rowntree Foundation, York.

Birchall, J. (1988) *Building Communities: the co-operative way*, Routledge and Kegan Paul, London.

Bramley, G (1992) 'The enabling role for local housing authorities: a preliminary evaluation', in Malpass, P. and Means, R. (eds) *Implementing Housing Policy*, Open University Press, Milton Keynes.

Bramley, G. (1993) Quasi-Markets and Social Housing, in Le Grand, J. and Bartlett, W. *Quasi-Markets and Social Policy*, Macmillan, London.

Brooke, R. (1991) *Managing the Enabling Authority*, Longman, London.

Central Statistical Office (1995) *Social Trends*, HMSO, London.

Chaplin, R. *et al.* (1995) *Rents and risks – investing in housing associations*, Joseph Rowntree Foundation, York.

Chartered Institute of Housing (1995) *Challenging the Conventions – public borrowing rules and housing investment*, Chartered Institute of Housing, London.

Clapham, D. (1989) *Goodbye Council Housing*, Unwin Paperbacks, London.

Cochrane, A. (1993) *Whatever Happened to Local Government?* Open University Press, Buckingham.

Coleman, D. A. (1992) 'The 1987 Housing Policy: an enduring reform', in Birchall, J. (ed.) *Housing Policy in the 1990s*, Routledge, London.

Commission on Social Justice (1994) *Social Justice, strategies for national renewal*, Vintage, London.

Cooper and Lybrand (1993) *Rented Housing After the BES*, Cooper and Lybrand, London.

Department of the Environment (1992) *Planning Policy Guidance: Housing*, PPG3 (revised), HMSO, London.

Department of the Environment (1995a) *Housing Strategies*, HMSO, London.
Department of the Environment (1995b) *More Choice in the Social Rented Sector*, Department of the Environment, London.
Department of the Environment, Welsh Office (1995) *Our Future Homes: opportunity, choice, responsibility*, Cm 2901, HMSO, London.
Field, F. (1995) *Making Welfare Work*, Institute of Community Studies, London.
Goodlad, R. (1993) *The Housing Authority as Enabler*, Longman, London.
Hambleton, R. and Hogget, P. (1990) *Beyond Excellence – quality local government in the 1980s*, Working Paper 85, SAUS, Bristol.
Harloe, M. (1995) *The People's Home?*, Blackwell, Oxford.
Hayek, F. A. (1960) *The Constitution of Liberty*, Routledge, London.
Hedges, B. and Clemens, S. (1994) *Housing Attitudes Survey*, HMSO, London.
Hills, J. (1993) *The Future of Welfare: a guide to the debate*, Joseph Rowntree Foundation, York.
Holliday, I. (1991) 'The New Suburban Right in British Local Government – Conservative views of the local', *Local Government Studies*, 16 (6), pp. 45–62.
Hutton, W. (1995) *The State We're In*, Jonathan Cape, London.
Kemp, P. (1994) 'Housing Allowances and the Fiscal Crisis of the Welfare State', *Housing Studies*, 9 (4), pp. 331–45.
Le Grand, J. and Bartlett, W. (1993) *Quasi-Markets and Social Policy*, Macmillan, London.
Maclennan, D. and Gibb, K. (1993) 'Political Economy, Applied Welfare Economics and Housing in the UK', in Barr, N. and Whynes, D. (eds) *Current Issues in the Economics of Welfare*, Macmillan, London.
Maclennan, D. and More, A. (1995) 'Housing' in Jackson, P. and Lavender, M. *The Public Services Yearbook 1995/6*, Chapman and Hall, London.
Page, D. (1993) *Building for Communities: a study of new housing association estates*, Joseph Rowntree Foundation, York.
Ridley, N. (1988) *The Local Right: enabling not providing*, Centre For Policy Studies, London.
Secretary of State for Social Security, Secretary of State for Employment (1994) *Jobseeker's Allowance*, Cm 2687, HMSO, London.
Smith, M. E. H. (1993) *Housing – Today and Tomorrow*, 2nd Supplement to the *Guide to Housing*, Housing Centre Trust, London.
Stewart, J. and Stoker, G. (1989) *The Future of Local Government*, Macmillan, London.
Thatcher, M. (1993) *The Downing Street Years*, HarperCollins, London.
Turtle, J. and Burgoyne, L. (1994) *Cash Incentives to Council Tenants*, DoE, London.
Webb, S. and Wilcox, S. (1991) *Time for Mortgage Benefits*, Joseph Rowntree Foundation, York.
Wilcox, S. (1994) *Housing Finance Review, 1994/5*, Joseph Rowntree Foundation, York.
Wilcox, S. (1995) *Housing Finance Review, 1995/6*, Joseph Rowntree Foundation, York.
Young, G. (1993) 'Speech at LSE Housing Conference', 4 March, Department of the Environment, London.

Documents

List of Documents

Document 1
A SOCIAL REFORMIST APPROACH TO THE HOUSING ISSUE

1   A large minority of poorer and disadvantaged people have not benefited from generally improved housing conditions over the last forty years. Creating fairness and more equality in housing is as important as other social policy reforms, and the objectives of greater equality and improved life chances cannot be attained without reforming housing policy.

2   Meaningful rights and effective remedies for consumers in all tenures must be enshrined in statute, backed up with support and advice. Tenant involvement at the neighbourhood level in the social rented sector must not be seen as an optional extra, but equally its exact form should not be imposed. Owner-occupiers need to be assisted to ensure a better deal at the point of purchase and with maintenance. Public education is needed to develop an appreciation of the obligations as well as privileges of different tenures.

3   Homelessness has affected more than three million people in the last ten years. The rights of homeless people must be enhanced, rather than diminished, as current proposals suggest. Reforms to social security should remove age-related discrimination and restore Income Support entitlement to 16 and 17 year olds. Better coordination between health, housing and social services are required.

4   The crucial links between housing and community care needs must be recognised through increased supply and conversion of housing, and through financial reforms to enable community care to be a reality in housing projects.

5   The supply of accessible and decent quality rented housing must be increased. This will assist disadvantaged groups and homeless people, providing equal opportunities principles are applied in the allocation and management, and care is taken in the design of new developments. The strengths of council housing when it works well – including tenant loyalty, electoral accountability, and fair allocation – should not be lost. Housing associations can bring pluralism and diversity to the provision of social housing, but this role comes under strain when housing associations are expected to become the major providers of social housing in an area.

6   Housing management must be improved through a programme of measures including education and management development, tenant involvement, and small scale management; housing construction on its own does not make a housing policy.

7   In design terms, much housing built in the 1950s, 1960s and 1970s is a disaster. Housing design must be small scale, and reflect people's needs. The problematic council housing estates of the 1960s and 1970s are a major priority, not least because of their concentrations of disadvantaged and stigmatised people.

8   There are 1.5 million unfit dwellings in England alone. Renewal programmes for older housing are insufficient to ensure the adequate upkeep, let alone the improvement, of existing housing. Additional private and public resources must be invested, and the implications of high levels of owner-occupation accepted by government and consumers.

9   Local and national government are key strategic planners, and need to reassert their commitment to achieving decent quality housing for all. The autonomy and capacity of local authorities to play this role must be enhanced if the 'enabling network' is to have any meaning. Other agencies and individuals in the private, public and voluntary sectors have an important role, but the democratic deficit in the development of quangos must be overcome.

10   The reduction of segregation, stigma and discrimination in housing is as important as the absolute improvements in physical standards that are required.

From: Goodlad, R. and Gibb, K., *Housing and Social Justice*, IPPR, London (1994)

Document 2
HAYEK ON STATE HOUSING

The first point to note is that any group of people whom the government attempts to assist through a public supply of housing will benefit only if the government undertakes to supply all the new housing they will get. Provision of only part of the supply of dwellings by authority will in effect be not an addition to, but merely a replacement of, what has been provided by private building activity. Second, cheaper housing provided by government will have to be strictly limited to the class it is intended to help, and, merely to satisfy the demand at the lower rents, government will have to supply considerably more housing than that class would otherwise occupy. Third, such limitation of public housing to the poorest families will generally be practicable only if the government does not attempt to supply dwellings which are both cheaper and substantially better than they had before; otherwise the people thus assisted would be better housed than those immediately above them on the economic ladder; and pressure from the latter to be included in the scheme would become irresistible, a process which would repeat itself and progressively bring in more and more people. A consequence of this is that, as has again and again been emphasised by the housing reformers, any far-reaching change in housing conditions by public action will be achieved only if practically the whole of the housing of a city is regarded as a public service and paid for out of public funds. This means, however, not only that people in general will be forced to spend more on housing than they are willing to do, but that their personal liberty will be gravely threatened. Unless the authority succeeds in supplying as much of this better and cheaper housing as will be demanded at the rents charged, a permanent system of allocating the available facilities by authority will be necessary – that is, a system whereby authority determines how much people should spend on housing, and what sort of accommodation each family or individual should get. It is easy to see what powers over individual life authority would possess if the obtaining of an apartment or house were generally dependent on its decision.

It should also be realised that the endeavour to make housing a public service has already in many instances become the chief obstacle to the general improvement of housing conditions by counteracting those forces which produce a gradual lowering of the cost of building. All monopolists are notoriously uneconomical, and the bureaucratic machinery of government even more so; and the suspension of the mechanism of competition and the tendency of any centrally directed development to ossify are bound to obstruct the attainment of the desirable and technically not impossible goal – a substantial and progressive reduction of the costs at which all the housing needs can be met.

Public housing (and subsidised housing) can thus, at best, be an instrument of assisting the poor, with the inevitable consequence that it will make those who take advantage of it dependent on authority to a degree that would be politically very serious if they constituted a large part of the population.

From: Hayek, F. A., *The Constitution of Liberty*, Routledge and Kegan Paul, London (1960), pp. 345–46

Document 3
KARL MARX ON THE STATE

No government in the world has been able to make *regulations* concerning pauperism *immediately*, without first consulting its officials. The English Parliament, indeed, sent commissioners to all the European countries to gather information about the different administrative measures for the relief of pauperism. In so far as States have concerned themselves at all with pauperism, they have remained at the level of *administrative and charitable measures*, or have sunk below this level. Can the *State* act in any other way? The State will never look for the cause of *social imperfections in the State and social institutions themselves*, as 'A Prussian' demands of his King. Where there are political parties, each party finds the source of such evils in the fact that the opposing party, instead of itself, is at the *helm of State*. Even the radical and revolutionary politicians look for the source of the evil, not in the nature of the State, but in a particular *form of the State*, which they want to replace by another form. The *State* and the. *structure of society* are not, from the standpoint of *politics*, two different things. The State is the structure of society. In so far as the State admits the existence of *social evils*, it attributes them to *natural laws* against which no human power can prevail, or to *private life* which is independent of the State, or to the *inadequacies of the administration* which is subordinate to it. Thus in England poverty is explained by the *natural law* according to which population always increases beyond the means of subsistence. From another aspect, England explains pauperism as the consequence of the *evil* dispositions of the poor, just as the King of Prussia explains it by the *unchristian disposition of the rich*, and as the Convention explains it by the *sceptical, counter-revolutionary outlook of the property owners*. Accordingly, England inflicts penalties on the poor, the king of Prussia admonishes the rich, and the Convention beheads property owners.

In the last resort, every State seeks the cause in *adventitious or intentional defects in the administration*, and therefore looks to a *reform* of the administration for a redress of these evils. Why? Simply because the administration is the organising activity of the State itself.

The *contradiction* between the aims and good intentions of the administration on the one hand, and its means and resources on the other, cannot be removed by the State without abolishing itself, for it rests upon this contradiction. The State is founded upon the contradiction between *public* and *private life*, between *general* and *particular* interests.

From: Bottomore, T. and Rubel, M., *Karl Marx: Selected Writings in Sociology and Social Philosophy*, Penguin Books, London (1961) pp. 211–13

Document 4
PUBLIC HEALTH, LOCAL AUTONOMY AND THE CENTRAL STATE

... a few doctrinaires nursed in the narrow conceits of bureaucracy, scornful alike of popular knowledge and of popular government, seized upon the sanitary theory as a means of exercising central power of domiciliary inspection and irresponsible interference with the conduct and property of Englishmen. The ready plea, of course, was the inherent right of every man to the enjoyment of the means necessary to health; and hence the duty incumbent on the Government of making every man healthy. Well, could it be shown that half a dozen men, constituting a board and sitting in a Government office, could so regulate the social and domestic conduct of the inhabitants of this country to ensure to them the safe removal of all those causes which naturally impair their health and shorten their lives, it might admit of an argument, whether, for the sake of the inestimable boon of health, it would not be desirable to surrender to such a board our most cherished political institutions. But this has not been proved. The contrary has been proved. For several years a Central Board of Health ruled with considerable activity and vigour, but with slender success. It is doubtful whether the notable Whig scheme of despatching those favourite Whig animals, briefless barristers of seven years' standing and crotchety engineers, to scour the country as sanitary inspectors, has not resulted in causing more disease than it has cured. At any rate, no doubt can exist as to the unpopularity of this scheme. And no doubt can exist that any scheme which is unpopular in this country must fail. ... The truth is we do not like paternal governments. ...This is another reason why the CHADWICKIAN sanitary regime so signally failed ...

From: *The Lancet*, 12 February 1858

Document 5
REVOLT ON THE CLYDE

During the whole period of the strike, the campaign against increased rents had been growing in volume. Following the strike, greater forces than ever were thrown into it. In Govan, Mrs Barbour, a typical working-class housewife, became the leader of a movement such as had never been seen before, or since for that matter. Street meetings, back-court meetings, drums, bells, trumpets – every method was used to bring the women out and organise them for the struggle. Notices were printed by the thousand and put up in the windows: wherever you went you could see them. In street after street, scarcely a window without one: 'WE ARE NOT PAYING INCREASED RENT'. These notices represented a spirit amongst the women that could not be overcome. The factors (agents for the property owners) could not collect the rents. They applied to the courts for eviction warrants. Having obtained these, sheriff's officers were sent to serve them and evict the tenants. But Mrs Barbour had a team of women who were wonderful. They could smell a sheriff's officer a mile away. At their summons women left their cooking, washing or whatever they were doing. Before they got anywhere near their destination, the officer and his men would be met by an army of furious women who drove them back in a hurried scramble for safety. . . .

Attempt after attempt was made to secure evictions, all of which ended in futility. It was obvious to the sheriff that the situation was too desperate to play with. He telephoned to London and got put through to the Minister of Munitions, Mr Lloyd George. 'The workers have left the factories,' he said, after explaining the character of the case. 'They are threatening to pull down Glasgow. What am I to do?' 'Stop the case,' he was told, 'a Rent Restriction Act will be introduced immediately.'

From: Gallacher, W., *Revolt on the Clyde*, Lawrence and Wishart, London (1963), pp. 52–57

Document 6
ANEURIN BEVAN ON THE HOUSING ISSUE

He protested against the whole pre-war system of building; it produced 'castrated communities'. The arrangement whereby the speculative builders built for one income group and the local authorities for another was a 'wholly evil thing from a civilised point of view, condemned by anyone who had paid the slightest attention to civics and eugenics; a monstrous infliction upon the essential psychological and biological oneness of the community'. Local authorities had been left to provide 'twilight villages' whereas the speculative builders were responsible for 'the fretful fronts stretching along the great roads out of London', belonging to what he understood was called 'the marzipan period'. The local authorities could never do worse and, given the chance of architectural diversification, they should do much better. Sound social needs, as much as aesthetics, should point in that direction. 'After all, you know, a man wants three houses in his lifetime: one when he gets married, one when the family is growing up, and one when he is old; but very few of us can afford one.' A much wider embrace of municipal ownership could offer a tentative solution to these complexities. By the same reasoning, local authorities should strive to find hospitality for all age groups on their estates. 'I hope that the old people will not be asked to live in colonies of their own – they do not want to look out of their windows on endless processions of the funerals of their friends; they also want to look at processions of perambulators ... The full life should see the unfolding of a multi-coloured panorama before the eyes of every citizen every day.'

From: Foot, M., *Aneurin Bevan 1945–1960*, Davis-Poynter, London (1973), pp. 75–76

Document 7
THE IMPORTANCE OF PRODUCTION

Housing is the Ministry's major pre-occupation; and for successive Ministers the number of houses built each year (calendar year) has been a critical test. Between the end of the war in 1945 and December 31, 1968, about five and a half million new houses were built, more than half of them by local and other public authorities including housing associations. That means that over a third of all the houses in England have been built in the last twenty-three years. During the same years over three-quarters of a million slum houses were demolished or closed, although slum clearance was not re-started on any scale until 1954; and over a million sub-standard houses were improved, with the aid of grants, by the provision of water closets, hot water, baths, etc. Twenty new towns were started, and seven of them are now almost fully grown. The standard of local authority housing rose (though with a check when the emphasis was on a sharp increase in numbers) and most of those now being built by local authorities and new town corporations are very good indeed, if not always a pleasure to look at. It has been a big achievement.

But it is impossible to be complacent about housing. In terms of numbers the British achievement in the post-war years does not compare well with that of some European countries. Even in terms of quality it lags behind one or two. Still, despite all the new building, many thousands of families are abominably housed; overcrowded and/or living in houses admittedly not fit for human occupation. Still in the older industrial areas life for many more is intolerably drab. In London and one or two other of the great cities homelessness is, for some, a terrifying possibility. Of all the subjects with which the Ministry deals housing is the most intractable.

From: Sharp, E., *The Ministry of Housing and Local Government*, George Allen and Unwin, London (1969), p. 69

Document 8
MODERN LIVING

On each floor there were covered walkways, in keeping with Corbu's idea of 'streets in the air'. Since there was no other place in the project in which to sin in public, whatever might ordinarily have taken place in bars, brothels, social clubs, pool halls, amusement arcades, general stores, corncribs, rutabaga patches, hayricks, barn stalls, now took place in the streets in the air. Corbu's boulevards made Hogarth's Gin Lane look like the oceanside street of dreams in Southampton, New York. Respectable folk pulled out, even if it meant living in cracks in the sidewalks. Millions of dollars and scores of commission meetings and task-force projects were expended in a last-ditch attempt to make Pruitt-Igoe habitable. In 1971, the final task force called a general meeting of everyone still living in the project. They asked the residents for their suggestions. It was a historic moment for two reasons. One, for the first time in the fifty-year history of worker housing, someone had finally asked the client for his two cents' worth. Two, the chant. The chant began immediately: 'Blow it . . . *up!* Blow it . . . *up!* Blow it . . . *up!* Blow it . . . *up!* Blow it . . . *up!*' The next day the task force thought it over. The poor buggers were right. It was the only solution. In July of 1972, the city blew up the three central blocks of Pruitt-Igoe with dynamite.

From: Wolfe, T., *From Bauhaus to Our House*, Jonathan Cape Ltd, London (1981), p. 82

Document 9
THE CONSERVATIVES ON COUNCIL HOUSING (1987)

1.9   Local authority housing now dominates the rented sector. The growth of municipal housing since the War has certainly been effective in increasing the total housing stock, and in clearing slums. But the system of ownership and management brought with it has often not been in the tenant's best long-term interest. In some areas the system has provided good quality housing and management. But in many big cities local authority housing operations are so large that they inevitably risk becoming distant and bureaucratic. Intensive design and bad management have alienated tenants and left housing badly maintained. As the quality of the housing and of its environment has declined, so a wide range of social problems has emerged; crime and violence have increased; many people have left for better opportunities elsewhere; local enterprise and employment have disappeared; and whole communities have slipped into a permanent dependence on the welfare system from which it is extremely difficult for people to escape.

1.10   These problems have often been compounded by indiscriminate subsidies from the rates to hold down rents, which have meant that people who do not need subsidy have become accustomed to it alongside those whose needs are real. Not only are resources wasted as a result, but the independence and self-motivation of communities can in the long term be damaged. The Government's objective is to begin to reverse this process in the worst areas, and to support the independence of local communities where that spirit already exists, by giving more opportunity for tenants to control their own destinies, and by targeting the help that will very often be needed on those who genuinely require it.

1.11   There are other reasons too why it is not healthy for the public sector to dominate provision of rented housing. At the national level, investment in housing has to compete with other public sector spending programmes; and private investment has not been available to supplement limited public sector resources in order to provide alternative forms of renting on a sufficient scale. At the local level, short term political factors can override efficient and economic management of housing in the long term, leading to unrealistically low rents and wholly inadequate standards of maintenance. Local authority housing allocation methods can all too easily result in inefficiencies and bureaucracy, producing queuing and lack of choice for the tenant. A more pluralist and more market-oriented system will ensure that housing supply can respond more flexibly to demand, will give the tenant wider choice over his housing and will allow greater scope for private investment and more effective use of public sector money.

1.12   The housing association movement has shown that a bridge can be provided between the public and private sectors. The movement offers good quality rented accommodation for those with special needs or on low incomes. New techniques are being developed which allow private sector resources to supplement public investment, and these will be encouraged and expanded since they open the possibility of more homes being provided for a given amount of public money.

From: Department of the Environment, *Housing: The Government's Proposals*, Cm 214, HMSO, London (1987), pp. 2–3

Document 10
THE WORKHOUSE IN THE 1960s

It is not only the workhouse buildings and stark interiors that draw one back into Dickens, but the faces of both warders and inmates. Behind the great iron gate is a little office where on entering one is interrogated. I delivered my set of facts mechanically, having related them so many times to officials and friends and accommodation agencies. Harrowing though it was to me and my children, I now knew it meant nothing to anyone else. Between appointments we had tramped the streets, two in the pram and one dragging behind, but where furnished rooms are concerned, the No Coloured bar is equalled by the No Children one. We had been occupying an exquisite drawing-room for ten days, and its owners could stand the sacrilege no longer. . . .

My story having been taken down laboriously, we were directed to what are called the family quarters, though no husbands are allowed there. A nurse issued us with a knife, fork, spoon and teaspoon apiece, and the warning: 'If you lose 'em you don't get no more.'

By the end of our week we were managing with one fork and two teaspoons between us, though how and when the rest were nicked I have no idea.

Then we were taken to a cubicle – you couldn't call it a room – connected by an opening to a similar space occupied by another family. Apart from two narrow beds and my own cot, the only article of furniture was a battered chest-of-drawers. The inch-deep mattresses and the pillows might have been filled with sand. Boarding school and hospital beds are Dunlopillo by comparison. My seven-year-old girl lay sobbing, the four-year-old boy lay sucking his thumb. His eyes seldom left my face these days. A nurse looked in to tell the girl off for making a noise, so I read them a Beatrix Potter and heard their prayers. In the morning I would hear their nightmares. There is no ruder awakening than one's first morning here. A bell clangs, nurses bang on doors and shout, and from a low rumbling and whining there mounts a steady crescendo of sub-human sounds reaching deafening proportions in the dining hall. The mingled smells of food and bodies is loud, too. The children again wept and recoiled from the sheer impact of it all. They would not sit at a table but queued with me, the boy removing his thumb to say quietly 'I am going everywhere you go,' which had been almost his sole utterance for weeks.

We took grey porridge and greasy kippers to a table, but were not hungry. I hesitate to condemn the food, since it may well have been the conditions under which it was eaten that made it so revolting. There was certainly plenty of it, and plenty left on plates which we carried to the sink in which we washed ourselves, the debris first being slung into great bins in the same room. After two or more meals they were brimming with an indescribable glutinous mess. We rinsed dishes and our precious cutlery in running hot water without soap powder. A lot of food was slopped on the way down the stone passage, on either side of which were the sleeping quarters. Volunteers swept up, but even cleaning operations here induced nausea, whether caused by the dirty brooms, the type of filth they were sweeping, the straggle-haired women behind them or simply the bare battered, bleak background.

After breakfast we cowered in our cubicle until a nurse put her head in and said sharply: 'Get this room cleaned. Clear all that stuff off of the dressing-table and window-sill.'

The children were making brave attempts at home-making by arranging their empty packets and cotton reels along ledges.

'What's that cup doing in here?'

I explained I must drink water, for the baby's feeds.

'I'll have to ask Matron about that. Now look lively. Once your room's tidy you have to stay out of it during the day. Everything must be in the drawers or in cases under the beds.'

There was neither playroom nor playground for the swarms of children and it was not safe to put a baby outside in its pram in case its eyes were attacked by an older child. The small common room at the end of the corridor was therefore crammed with seedy prams and push-chairs, as well as women and children. This room was as desolate as everywhere else; some broken and bashed-about chairs, a rickety table, no radio, telly or tinny piano, not even a proper window. It was like a communal cell, a painting by Hogarth . . .

From: Cecil, M., 'In the Workhouse', *New Statesman*, 12 January 1962, pp. 38–39

Document 11
DEFINING HOMELESSNESS

When does someone have no accommodation?

5.5 Under s.58(2) of the Act someone is treated as having no accommodation – and is therefore homeless – unless there is some accommodation which s/he (together with any other person mentioned in para 5.3) is entitled or permitted to occupy in one of the following ways:

(a) by virtue of an interest in it (e.g. as an owner, lessee or tenant) or by virtue of an order from a court;

(b) by virtue of an express or implied licence to occupy it, (e.g. as a lodger, as an employee with a service occupancy, or where s/he is living with relatives);

(c) by virtue of some protection given him/her by law, (e.g. someone retaining possession as a statutory tenant under the Rent Acts after his/her contractual rights to occupy have expired or been terminated).

This means that if someone has been occupying property as a licensee and the licence has been terminated they are homeless. This would include, for example: people who have been asked to leave by friends or relatives; those required to leave hostels, hospitals or refuges: former employees occupying premises under a service occupancy which is dependent upon a contract of employment which has ended. Authorities should be alert to the possibility of collusion between parents and children where the child has been asked to leave the family home. In all these circumstances authorities should not ask applicants to obtain a court order, sufficient evidence of homelessness is provided by confirmation of the termination of the applicant's licence.

5.6   Homeless applicants include those who are no longer entitled to occupy accommodation because their landlord has defaulted on the mortgage on the property in which they are tenants. The Council of Mortgage Lenders' Statement of Practice on the Handling of Mortgage Arrears, notes that before taking possession a lender will try to liaise with the relevant local authority departments to ensure that alternative accommodation is available where appropriate. The Council of Mortgage Lenders' Statement of Practice on the Handling of Possession Procedures provides a useful overview of mortgage lenders' practice when dealing with possession cases and notes that in such cases a number of lenders send a letter addressed to 'the occupier' of a property advising them of the impending proceedings in a bid to inform any possible undisclosed tenants. The Statement also notes that lenders may consult the electoral roll before commencing possession proceedings in order to confirm whether there are any undisclosed tenants living in the property who need to be notified of the proceedings.

From: Department of the Environment, *Homelessness Code of Guidance* (revised third edition), HMSO, London (1991), pp. 20–21

Document 12
ACCESS TO LOCAL AUTHORITY AND HOUSING ASSOCIATION TENANCIES

... While the total number of new lettings of local authority property has remained relatively steady over the last ten years (in the range 230,000 to 240,000) the proportion of these going to households accepted by local authorities as statutorily homeless has more than doubled, from less than 20% in 1983/84 to over 45% in 1992/93. Moreover, the number of households accepted as homeless has more than doubled since 1978 when the present legislation took effect, and in some parts of London virtually all housing within the local authority's gift now goes to statutorily homeless households, although this may well say more about demand than about need. While the number of statutorily homeless households has shown a welcome decline over the last year, the underlying trend could continue upward unless steps are taken to alter the current legislation.

Recent research conducted for the Department shows that people rehoused from the waiting list are in many important respects (such as income, employment status and previous tenure) similar to households re-housed through the homelessness route. The housing needs of the two groups may have much in common. But statutorily homeless households receive automatic priority over others on the waiting list in the allocation of tenancies. As a result, in some areas – particularly in parts of London – it is almost impossible for any applicant ever to be re-housed from the waiting list. In most parts of the country the problem is not so great, and waiting list applicants stand a better chance of being re-housed. Nevertheless, it appears from the research that, of those who did manage to get re-housed, people using the waiting list route had to wait nearly twice as long (on average 1.2 years as against 0.7 years) as people re-housed under the homelessness legislation (who would be temporarily accommodated elsewhere by the local authority in the intervening period). Inevitably, this makes the homelessness route seem the more attractive way into subsidised housing for those wishing to be re-housed. Someone who faces the possibility of homelessness will realise that anyone meeting the necessary criteria and taking no other action to find alternative accommodation will be accepted by the authority as statutorily homeless, and that the authority will be obliged to offer that individual and other members of that household permanent re-housing as soon as practicable and provide temporary accommodation in the interim. If, on the other hand, the person in question takes the initiative in finding alternative accommodation (which may be no different in character from the 'temporary' accommodation which the local authority would otherwise provide), the only route into a local authority or housing association tenancy is through the slower and less certain avenue of the waiting list.

From: Department of the Environment, *Access to Local Authority and Housing Association Tenancies: A Consultation Paper*, Department of the Environment, London, pp. 3–4

Document 13
THE IMPACT OF CLEARANCE IN THE NINETEENTH
CENTURY

Overcrowding was in part the result of sanitary clearance, which left the dispos-
sessed nowhere to go. The pulling down of buildings inhabited by the very
poor, whether undertaken for philanthropic, sanitary or commercial purposes,
does cause overcrowding into the neighbouring slums, with the further consequence
of keeping up the high rents. Even if the classes so disturbed could afford to
pay for better accommodation, they have not the faculty to seek it. When
notice is given they never seem to appreciate the fact that their homes are
about to be destroyed until the workmen come to pull the roof from over their
heads. Lord Shaftesbury described how the inhabitants had been seen like
people in a besieged town, running to and fro, and not knowing where to turn.
The evidence of the inability of the poor to protect themselves in this and in
other particulars is conclusive.

Railway construction had also added seriously to the difficulties and railway
companies had shown complete disregard for the people they had turned out to
build stations, etc. The building of St Pancras Station in the 1860s, for instance,
had led to the destruction of five hundred homes. Parts of St Pancras, therefore
had not become more overcrowded simply because they were already so full
that they could not crowd in more. A case of eleven families in eleven rooms
was noted, and another, from Newcastle, of 140 families in thirty-four houses.
Old houses were divided into tenements and as the doors were never closed
many people (known in Southwark as ''appy dossers') regularly slept on the
stairs and in the passages.

The Peabody Trust and other organisations had done valuable work, but their
tenements were in the main too expensive: 'model dwellings do not reach the
class whose need is greatest'.

The failure to achieve more improvement was administrative however, rather
than legislative. Far too many Medical Officers of Health were non-resident,
and inspectors of nuisances were both unskilled and uncommon. The Commission recommended that inspectors should be properly trained and that authorities should be advised to appoint full-time medical officers, who should be
compelled to live in the area for which they were responsible.

In a special section the Commission also recommended that the population
should be encouraged to spread itself. Many people had to live near their work,
but might be encouraged to move into areas of lower rent if there were cheap
fares on the railways. Already 'the State has interfered in this matter in the
public interest rather with reference to what the working classes can afford than
to what will pay the railway companies', and the Board of Trade should make
more use of its powers to compel the railways to offer cheap fares. One comfort-
ing conclusion that the commission did reach was that the standard of morality
in the overcrowded areas was 'higher than might have been expected', and
Mearns when giving evidence was forced to modify the charges of immorality
which he had made in his *Bitter Cry.*

From: Bruce, M., *The Rise of the Welfare State*, Weidenfeld and Nicolson,
London (1973), pp. 97–98

Document 14
CLEARANCE IN THE 1960s

1 Most Local Authorities have been over-ambitious and totally unrealistic when drawing up clearance plans; the plans seem to have been drawn up without any reference to the ability of the authority to carry them through within the time period originally envisaged. Limited, achievable programmes would have been far more appropriate and would have enabled authorities to concentrate their resources and refine their techniques in dealing with smaller and more manageable areas.

2 Residents of clearance areas are very often 'written off' as far as welfare agencies, educational authorities and town hall staff generally are concerned. It is considered not worth attempting to keep the area clean, free of rubbish, rubble and rodents; short life houses are deemed unsuitable for maintenance and repair. An area of generally unfit housing, once designated a clearance area, becomes an area of appalling and disgusting dereliction, whose residents suffer every kind of the most distressing social deprivation and physical discomfort.

3 Some delays have occurred because of insuperable problems faced by local government for which responsibility must be borne by central government. The strictures of the housing cost yardstick, the shortage of building labour and materials have together had a severe effect on local authority housebuilding over the past few years and this has inevitably restricted the rehousing of people from clearance areas.

4 Much of the distress caused to residents of clearance areas stems from the high-handed attitude of local authority departments who show contempt for the feelings and fears of those whose lives are completely overshadowed by uncertainty about the future and depression over their present living conditions. There is a patent lack of honesty in local authorities' dealings with these people and in many cases no information at all is forthcoming from the departments involved in decisions affecting these areas.

5 Life in a clearance area is indescribably appalling; conditions there would revolt and disgust anyone who spent a few hours walking through the streets and talking to the residents. It is abhorrent that such conditions should be allowed to exist at all; the fact that they should be allowed to persist for years is one of our society's greatest crimes.

From: Shelter, *Slum Clearance*, Shelter, London (1973), p. 29

Document 15
THE FITNESS STANDARD

STATUTORY STANDARD – Housing Act 1985 as amended by Local Government and Housing Act 1989

Fitness for human habitation

604. – (1) Subject to subsection (2) below, a dwelling-house is fit for human habitation for the purposes of this Act unless, in the opinion of the local housing authority, it fails to meet one or more of the requirements in paragraphs (a) to (i) below and, by reason of that failure, is not reasonably suitable for occupation, –

(a)   it is structurally stable;
(b)   it is free from serious disrepair;
(c)   it is free from dampness prejudicial to the health of the occupants (if any);
(d)   it has adequate provision for lighting, heating and ventilation;
(e)   it has adequate piped supply of wholesome water;
(f)   there are satisfactory facilities in the dwelling-house for the preparation and cooking of food, including a sink with a satisfactory supply of hot and cold water;
(g)   it has a suitably located water-closet for the exclusive use of the occupants (if any);
(h)   it has, for the exclusive use of the occupants (if any), a suitably located fixed bath or shower and wash-hand basin each of which is provided with a satisfactory supply of hot and cold water; and
(i)   it has an effective system for the draining of foul, waste and surface water.

From: Department of the Environment, *Local Government and Housing Act 1989: Area Renewal, Unfitness and Enforcement Action*, circular 6/90, March 1990, Department of the Environment, London

Document 16
OVERCROWDING IN THE NINETEENTH CENTURY

As another exemplification of this state of things, I may mention the following instance rather extraordinary in its facts, but an example of the overcrowding of some of these places.

In the course of the first months that I was attached to the dispensary, an aged Irish woman applied to me with a broken rib; she declined going into a hospital; the dispensary therefore supplied her with a flannel roller, and I promised to visit her and apply it.

On reaching her home, I found that it consisted of one corner of a room on the first floor of a house in Peter Street.

The landlady of this room, who herself occupied the central part, near the fireplace, had tenants in the other three corners, in one of which was a widow with three or four children.

I applied the bandage to my patient, who went on, to use her own words, very comfortably for four or five days, at the end of which time I found her in considerable pain from the following cause:

Not being able to go out as usual with her basket to sell fruit and vegetables, she could not pay her daily rent, and therefore, on the suggestion of the landlady, consented to under-let half of her bed ; but it happened unfortunately, that the new tenant being bulky in person, occupied more than her fair proportion of the joint tenancy, so as to press against the broken rib of my poor invalid, and displace it, thus producing a recurrence of the pain and suffering from which she had but just been freed!!!

From: *Evidence submitted to the Commission of Inquiry into the State of Large Towns and Populous Districts*, 1844, reproduced in Barnes, H., *The Slum: its story and solution*, P. S. King and Son, London (1931), p. 63

Document 17
THE ESTATE OFFICE

Local management depends on a fully staffed estate office which holds all tenancy records and management information and opens daily to residents. The office should cover the following functions:

- repairs ordering, supervision and inspection;
- rent control, arrears prevention and action;
- control of empty dwellings;
- lettings to applicants;
- welfare advice and all tenancy matters such as enforcement of tenancy conditions;
- tenant consultation and involvement;
- maintenance of communal areas;
- estate cleaning;
- liaison with other services and voluntary bodies;
- coordination of major repair and improvement contracts;
- control of an estate budget.

These essential estate management tasks cannot be readily delivered from within a large, centrally organised housing department to a large, run-down estate.

A model local office should be open to the public, morning and afternoon, five days a week, and provide for late opening one day a week if there is demand.

The office will house all estate management staff and provide a base for caretakers.

The office should have a reception area for residents, and staff will either attend to the public on a rota basis or there will be a receptionist who might also help with clerical work. There should be an interview room for private or difficult discussions. Tenants and staff should be able to sit down in a quiet place for this.

Between 30 and 60 tenants a day will call into the office over myriad different issues. Staff doing reception should be able to handle often difficult problems politely and calmly. A friendly atmosphere is essential to defuse possible tension, and conflict over such things as transfers, neighbour disputes, repairs complaints and other mistakes or misunderstandings. Staff must feel confident to deal with the public and must also feel secure in their office.

From: Power, A., *The PEP Guide to Local Housing Management*, Department of the Environment, London (1987), p. 4

Document 18
BUILDING FOR COMMUNITIES?

Only a small proportion of new tenants are in full-time work (21%) and a further 4% work part-time: the average income of working households was found to be £158.27. But 7.5% of new tenants are not in either full-time or part-time work and 54% derived their incomes wholly from state benefits or pensions: the average income of those not in work was found to be only £72.38. It is clear from this that the explanation for the low average income of new housing association tenants is that only one in four is in any kind of work; the majority rely wholly or in part on state benefits and pensions; and those who are in work get very low pay.

Direct comparison between GHS and CORE shows the difference in economic status between existing and new tenants:

- only 45% of economically active new tenants are in work, 53% of them are unemployed and a further 2% are undergoing training; this compares to 87% of economically active existing tenants who are working and only 13% who are unemployed.
- a smaller number of new tenants (27%) are retired compared to 41% of existing tenants.
- more new tenants are economically active (55% as compared to 38% for existing tenants).

From these comparisons it is apparent that the characteristics of new housing association tenants are significantly different from those housed previously. New tenants are much more likely to be economically active but, if they are, they are more likely to be unemployed than in work. Conversely, fewer pensioners are now housed by associations.

Two general conclusions can be drawn from this analysis: first, the results are consistent with the post-1988 Act assumption by housing associations of the role of main provider of general needs housing; second, the new tenants are even more economically disadvantaged than those housed previously – although younger and more likely to be economically active, their incomes are lower and they are less likely to have a job, more likely to be unemployed and more likely to be wholly dependent on state benefits or pensions.

From: Page, D., *Building For Communities: A Study of Housing Association Estates*, Joseph Rowntree Foundation, York (1993), p. 30

Document 19
HOUSING AND ETHNICITY: SELECTED STATISTICS

Table 1: Population by ethnic group 1991: Thousands and percentages

	All ethnic minority groups	White	All minority groups as a % of total population	% of minority groups born in Great Britain
Great Britain	3,015	51,874	5.5%	46.8

Source: Office of Population Censuses and Surveys/General Register Office.

Table 2: Households in worst housing[1]: by ethnic group of head of household 1991

Ethnic group	%
Pakistani/Bangladeshi	20
Indian	11
White	9.5
West Indian	9

Note
[1] The ten per cent of dwellings with the highest urgent repair costs, and costs to make the dwelling fit for habitation. The cut-off point is £26 per square metre.

Source: Adapted from Central Statistical Office, *Social Trends*, HMSO, London (1994).

Table 3: Rooms per person: by ethnic group and head of household 1991, Percentages

	Under 1	1 to 2	Over 2
Indian	7	64	28
Pakistani/Bangladeshi	33	52	15
West Indian	2	58	41
Other or mixed	5	63	32
All ethnic minority groups	9	61	31
White	1	45	54
Not stated	2	47	51
All ethnic groups	1	46	53

Source: *Social Trends* 1994

Table 4: Tenure by ethnic group of household, 1991, Percentages

	Owned Outright	Buying	Rented Privately	Housing Association	Local Authority
Black	6.7	35.5	9.1	10.7	36.8
Indian	16.5	65.2	6.6	2.2	7.8
Pakistani	19.4	57.3	9.6	2.2	10.4
Bangladeshi	5.2	3.3	9.6	6.0	37.0
Born in Ireland	19.6	35.9	10.9	5.1	26.3
White	24.4	42.2	7.0	3.0	21.4
All	23.9	42.2	7.2	3.1	21.4

Source: Calculated from Census returns 1991

Table 5: Households with more than 1.5 persons per room: 1991

Ethnic group	%
All	0.49
White	0.36
Black[1]	2.44
Indian	2.68
Pakistani	7.91
Bangladeshi	19.09
Born in Ireland	0.85

[1] Black Caribbean, Black African and Black (other)

Source: Calculated from Census returns 1991

Document 20
RACE AND COUNCIL HOUSING IN HACKNEY

Table 9.1 The Recording of Housekeeping Standards Between Different Racial Groups (Transfers)

Housekeeping standards	Black		White		Total	
	%	No.	%	No.	%	No.
All good/excellent	66	31	70	89	68	120
Mixed tending to 'good'	30	14	20	23	23	40
Mixed tending to 'bad'	4	2	9	12	8	14
All 'bad'	0	0	1	1	1	1
	100	47	100	128	100	175

Table 9.2 The Recording of Housekeeping Standards Between Different Racial Groups (Waiting List)

Housekeeping standards	Black		White		Total	
	%	No.	%	No.	%	No.
All good/excellent	50	40	81	71	66	111
Mixed tending to 'good'	40	32	17	15	28	47
Mixed tending to 'bad'	10	8	2	2	6	10
All 'bad'	0	0	0	0	0	0
	100	80	100	88	100	168

Note: The difference between black and white applicants in the 'all good/excellent' category is significant at a one per cent level of confidence.

Table 9.3 The Recording of Housekeeping Standards Between Different Racial Groups (Decants)

Housekeeping standards	Black		White		Total	
	%	No.	%	No.	%	No.
All good/excellent	48	44	66	81	54	114
Mixed tending to 'good'	23	21	16	20	19	41
Mixed tending to 'bad'	22	20	15	18	18	38
All 'bad'	7	7	3	3	9	10
	100	92	100	122	100	214

Notes: (i) The difference between black and white applicants in the 'all good/excellent' category is significant at a one per cent level (ii) The difference between black and white applicants in the 'all bad' category is significant at a five per cent level.

9.8 Tables 9.1 to 9.3 show that in each of the three access channels the majority of applicants had some reference to housekeeping standards on their files. Generally, transfer applicants received the better 'grading', followed by the decant and waiting list channels. The main differences that occurred between black and white applicants were in these latter two channels. In the waiting list (Table 9.2), white applicants were more likely to have received all 'good/excellent' gradings (81 per cent) than black applicants (50 per cent). A similar pattern occurred in the decant channel (Table 9.3) where again, white tenants were more likely to have received all 'good/excellent' gradings (66 per cent) than black tenants (48 per cent). In the decant channel, black applicants were also more likely to have received the poorer-standard gradings with 29 per cent receiving this kind of assessment.

From: Commission for Racial Equality, *Race and Council Housing in Hackney: Report of a Formal Investigation*, CRE, London (1984), p. 71

Document 21
THE LAST REFUGE

Segregation

Six of the thirty-nine institutions which we visited were for men only or women only. In all but four of the other thirty-three there was a fairly strict segregation of the sexes. Men and women were housed in separate blocks or wards and rarely shared the same dining- or day-rooms. Those in charge were ambivalent in their attitudes. 'They are not encouraged in each other's day-rooms, though they are allowed to sit outside together in summer.' 'They separate naturally. Most stay in the day-rooms attached to the dormitories. We don't mind them visiting. When we have a concert most of the men sit together and most of the women.' Many claimed that the residents, and particularly the men, had little desire to mix with the opposite sex. Some felt it was improper to encourage mixing. But the lay-out and the amenities of the buildings and the division of duties among the staff depended on the principle of segregation. 'From an administrative point of view it's much easier to have them separated . . . If they weren't you would have problems with bathroom and toilets and staffing.'

One of the consequences was the separation of man and wife. There are not many married persons in institutions and the husbands or wives of some of these are at home or in hospital. But there were a number of husbands and wives in the thirty-nine we visited who were living in different wards or blocks: again, excuses were found for this practice. 'When we get married couples we try to put the woman on one floor and the man above. It's remarkable how often the woman says she's been looking forward to this all her life.' In one institution there were eight married couples who did not live or sleep together, in a few others five or six and in several two or three. In only six of the thirty-nine institutions was there accommodation for married couples and the largest of these had less of this accommodation than in 1894. Among the total of 225 new residents in our sample for interview 22 were married. In 13 instances the husband or wife was at home and in a further two in hospital. In the remaining 7 the husband or wife were in different blocks or wards of the same institution. All seven wanted to be together. As one wife put it, 'They said we could be together when we came here and that we'd only be parted at night, but it isn't so. They don't want him in the ladies' room and they say "No gentlemen allowed in here" when he comes along . . . We can't be together. We're separated.'

From: Townsend, P., *The Last Refuge*, Routledge and Kegan Paul, London (1962), p. 56

Document 22
THE ADVANTAGES AND LIMITATIONS OF
COOPERATIVES

Respondents to the Review were mainly from within the co-op movement. They claimed advantages of four main kinds for co-ops over 'traditional' local authority or housing association renting:

(i)   Co-ops were said to provide a source of rented housing for people not adequately housed by other agencies, particularly groups like the 'non-priority homeless' and ethnic minorities, and thus to offer an alternative or complement to the most common main provider, the local authority.
(ii) Co-ops were said to build and sustain local communities, even in unpromising circumstances (e.g. on run-down local authority estates). The community spirit generated was said to create feelings of security, belonging and involvement; and to lead to lower running costs through less vandalism and graffiti.
(iii) The co-op model involved consumer control over the design and refurbishment of housing and over its management and maintenance. Local control was said to lead to high tenant satisfaction, to avoid costly design mistakes, to give pride of ownership (in the local environment as well as individual homes), and to produce a more efficient management service. These effects in turn were said to protect the capital invested in the stock.
(iv) Co-ops discouraged dependence and encouraged self-reliance. The responsibilities which co-ops place on individual members were said to engender self-confidence and skills which could help unemployed members when seeking jobs elsewhere. It was pointed out that co-ops could also generate their own spin-off employment opportunities, e.g. local repairs teams, laundries, shops, etc.

A number of disadvantages were suggested:

(i)   Co-ops were said to take greater time and effort than other forms of management to set up, requiring substantial help with initial development and training.
(ii) It was said that participation could be a major problem once co-ops were up and running, given the important responsibilities and duties involved for tenants.
(iii) It was suggested generally that co-ops were 'expensive'.

The following was suggested as a limitation:

(iv) Co-ops were said to work well only when there was a strong impetus for their formation from tenants themselves. They could not be imposed on uncommitted tenants and could not provide a general model for the owner ship and management of rented housing.

From: Department of the Environment, *Tenants in the Lead*, HMSO, London (1989), p. 8

Select Bibliography

Audit Commission (1986) *Making A Reality of Community Care*, HMSO, London.
Audit Commission (1992) *Developing Local Authority Housing Strategies*, HMSO, London.
Balchin, P. N. (1995) *Housing Policy: an introduction*, 3rd edn, Routledge, London.
Barr, N. (1993) *The Economics of the Welfare State*, Weidenfeld and Nicolson, London.
Beevers, R. (1988) *The Garden City Utopia: a critical biography of Ebenezer Howard*, Macmillan, London.
Birchall, J. (1992) *Housing Policy in the 1990s*, Routledge, London.
Blackman, T. (1995) *Urban Policy in Practice*, Routledge, London.
Blake, J. and Dwelly, T. (1994) *Home Front*, Roof, London.
Boleat, M. and Taylor, B. (1993) *Housing in Britain*, Council of Mortgage Lenders, London.
Braham, P., Rattans, A. and Skellington R. (1992) *Racism and Antiracism*, Sage, London.
Burnett, J. (1986) *A Social History of Housing*, Routledge, London.
Cherry, G. E. (1993) *Cities and Plans*, Edward Arnold, London.
Clapham, D., (1989) *Goodbye Council Housing*, Unwin Paperbacks, London.
Clapham, D., Kemp, P. and Smith, S. J. (1990) *Housing and Social Policy*, Macmillan, London.
Cochrane, A. (1993) *Whatever Happened to Local Government?*, Open University Press, Buckingham.
Cole, T. and Furbey, R. (1994) *The Eclipse of Council Housing*, Routledge, London.
Coleman, A. (1985) *Utopia On Trial*, Hilary Shipman Limited, London.
Commission for Racial Equality (1984) *Race and Council Housing in Hackney: report of a formal investigation*, Commission for Racial Equality, London
Cope, H. (1990) *Housing Associations: Policy and practice*, Macmillan, London.
Crook, T., Hughes, J. and Kemp, P. (1995) *The Supply of Privately Rented Homes: Today and Tomorrow*, Joseph Rowntree Foundation, York.
Donnison, D. and Maclennan, D. (1991) *The Housing Service of the Future*, Longman, London.
Department of the Environment (1987) *Housing: The Government's Proposals*, Cm 214, HMSO, London.
Department of the Environment (1994) *Living Independently: a study of the housing needs of elderly and disabled people*, HMSO, London.
Department of the Environment (1994) *Access to Local Authority and Housing Association Tenancies: a consultation paper*, DoE, London.
Department of the Environment and the Welsh Office (1995) *Our Future Homes: opportunity, choice, responsibility*, Cm 2901, HMSO, London.

Duncan, S. and Evans, A. (1988) *Responding To Homelessness: local authority policy and practice*, HMSO, London.

Dunleavy, P. (1981) *The Politics of Mass Housing in Britain: a study of corporate power and professional influence in the Welfare State*, Clarendon Press, Oxford.

Dunleavy, P. (1987) *Public Housing in Urban Change and Conflict*, Unit 26, The Open University, Milton Keynes.

European Observatory On Homelessness (1993) *Abandoned: Profile of Europe's Homeless People*, FEANTSA.

Evans, A. (1988) *No Room! No Room!: the costs of the British town and country planning system*, Institute of Economic Affairs, London.

Field, F. (1995) *Making Welfare Work*, Institute of Community Studies, London.

Forrest, R. and Murie, A. (1991) *Selling The Welfare State*, Routledge, London.

Forrest, R., Murie, A. and Williams, P. (1990) *Home Ownership: differentiation and fragmentation*, Unwin Hyman, London.

Gauldie, E. (1974) *Cruel Habitations: a history of working-class housing 1780–1918*, Allen and Unwin, London.

George, V. and Wilding, P. (1994) *Welfare and Ideology*, Harvester Wheatsheaf, London.

Gilroy, R. and Woods, R. (eds) (1994) *Housing Women*, Routledge, London.

Glendinning, M. and Muthesius, S. (1994) *Tower Block: modern public housing in England, Scotland, Wales and Northern Ireland*, Yale University Press, New Haven, Connecticut.

Glennerster, H. and Turner, T. (1993) *Estate Based Housing Management: an evaluation*, Department of the Environment, HMSO, London.

Goodlad, R. (1993) *The Housing Authority as Enabler*, Longman, London.

Gough, I. (1979) *The Political Economy of the Welfare State*, Macmillan, London.

Government Statistical Office (1994) *Housing and Construction Statistics 1983–1993*, HMSO, London.

Grant, C. (ed.) (1992) *Built to Last*, Roof, London.

Greed, C. H. (1994) *Women and Planning*, Routledge, London.

Green, H. and Hansbro, J. (1995) *Housing in England 1993/4*, Office of Population Censuses and Surveys, HMSO, London.

Griffiths Report (1988) *Community Care: agenda for action*, HMSO, London.

Harloe, M. (1995) *The People's Home?*, Blackwell, London.

Harris, J. (1993) *Private Lives, Public Spirit: a social history of Britain 1870–1914*, Oxford University Press, Oxford.

Hayek, F. A. (1960) *The Constitution of Liberty*, Routledge, London.

Hayek, F. A. (1973) *Law, Legislation and Liberty*, vol. 1, Routledge and Kegan Paul, London.

Hayek, F. A. (1976) *Law, Legislation and Liberty*, vol. 2, Routledge and Kegan Paul, London.

Hayek, F. A. (1979) *Law, Legislation and Liberty*, vol. 3, Routledge and Kegan Paul, London.

Hedges, B. and Clemens, S. (1994) *Housing Attitudes Survey*, Department of the Environment, London.

Hennessy, P. (1992) *Never Again, Britain 1945–51*, Cape, London.

Heseltine, M. (1987) *Where There's a Will*, Hutchinson, London.

Hills, J. (ed.) (1990) *The State Of Welfare: the Welfare State in Britain since 1974*, Oxford University Press, Oxford.

Hills, J. (1991) *Unravelling Housing Finance*, Clarendon Press, Oxford.

Hills, J. (1995) *Joseph Rowntree Foundation Inquiry into Income and Wealth*, Vol. 2, Joseph Rowntree Foundation, York.

Hudson, S. and Liddiard, M. (1994) *Youth Homelessness: The Construction of a Social Issue*, Macmillan, London.

Hutton, W. (1995) *The State We're In*, Jonathan Cape, London.

Ineichen, B. (1993) *Homes and Health: how housing and health interact*, E and FN Spon, London.

Jencks, C. (1994) *The Homeless*, Harvard University Press, London.

Kemeny, J. (1994) *Understanding European Rental Systems*, SAUS, Bristol.

Kirby, D. (1979) *Slum Housing and Residential Renewal: the case of urban Britain*, Longman, London.

Leather, P., Mackintosh, S. and Rolfe, S. (1994) *Papering Over the Cracks*, National Housing Forum, London.

Le Grand, J. and Bartlett, W. (1993) *Quasi-Markets and Social Policy*, Macmillan, London.

Little, J. (1994) *Gender, Planning and the Policy Process*, Pergamon, London.

Malpass, P. (1990) *Reshaping Housing Policy*, Routledge, London.

Malpass, P. and Means, R. (eds) (1993) *Implementing Housing Policy*, Open University Press, Buckingham.

Malpass, P. and Murie, A. (1994) *Housing Policy and Practice*, Macmillan, London.

Mandelstam, M. and Schwehr, B. (1995) *Community Care Practice and the Law*, Jessica Kingsley Publishers, London.

Means, R. and Smith, R. (1994) *Community Care: policy and practice*, Macmillan, London.

Morris, J. (1990) *Our Homes, Our Rights: housing, independent living and physically disabled people*, Shelter, London.

Morris, J. and Winn, M. (1990) *Housing and Social Inequality*, Hilary Shipman, London.

Murray, C. (1984) *Losing Ground*, Basic Books, New York.

National Federation of Housing Associations (1991) *The Future of Sheltered Accommodation – who cares?*, National Federation of Housing Associations, London.

National Federation of Housing Associations/Mind (1989) *Housing: the Foundation of Community Care*, 2nd edn, National Federation of Housing Associations, London.

Newton, J. (1994) *All in One Place: The British Housing Story 1973–1993*, Catholic Housing Aid Society, London.

Page, D. (1993) *Building for Communities: a study of new housing association estates*, Joseph Rowntree Foundation, York.

Pinto, R. (1993) *The Estate Action Initiative*, Avebury, Aldershot.

Power, A. (1987) *Property Before People: the management of twentieth-century council housing*, Allen and Unwin, London.

Power, A. (1993) *Hovels to High Rise: state housing in Europe since 1850*, Routledge, London.

Power, A. and Tunstall, R. (1995) *Swimming Against the Tide: polarisation or progress on 20 unpopular council estates*, Joseph Rowntree Foundation, York.

Prescott-Clarke, P., Clements, S. and Park, A. (1994) *Routes into Local Authority Housing*, Department of the Environment, HMSO, London (1994).

Ridley, N. (1988) *The Local Right: enabling not providing*, Centre for Policy Studies, London.

Ridley, N. (1991) *My Style of Government: the Thatcher years*, Fontana, London.

Saunders, P. (1990) *A Nation of Home Owners*, Unwin Hyman, London.

Secretaries of State for Health, Social Security, Wales and Scotland (1989)

Caring For People: Community Care in the Next Decade and Beyond, Cm 849, HMSO, London.

Sim, D. (1993) *British Housing Design*, Longman, London.

Smith E. M. (1995) *Housing – Today and Tomorrow*, Housing Centre Trust, London.

Smith, S. (1989) *The Politics of 'Race' and Residence*, Polity Press, London.

Standing Conference on Public Health (1994) *Housing, Homelessness and Health*, The Nuffield Provincial Hospitals Trust, London.

Stevenson, J. (1984) *British Society 1914–45*, Penguin Books, Harmondsworth.

Swenerton, M. (1981) *Homes Fit For Heroes: the politics and architecture of early state housing in Britain*, Heinemann, London.

Teymour, M., Marcus, T. A. and Woolley, T. (1988) *Rehumanizing Housing*, Butterworths, London.

Thatcher, M. (1993) *The Downing Street Years*, HarperCollins, London.

Timmins, N. (1995) *The Five Giants*, HarperCollins, London.

Wagner, G. (1988) *Residential Care: a positive choice*, HMSO, London.

Watson, L. and Conway, T. (1995) *Homes for Independent Living*, Chartered Institute of Housing, London.

Whitehead, C. and Kleinman, M. (1992) *Housing The Nation: choice, access and priorities*, Department of Land Economy, University of Cambridge, Cambridge.

Wilcox, S. (1995) *Housing Finance Review, 1995/6*, Joseph Rowntree Foundation, York.

Willetts, D. (1992) *Modern Conservatism*, Penguin Books, London.

Wistow, G., Knapp, M., Hardy, B. and Allen, C. (1994) *Social Care in a Mixed Economy*, Open University Press. Milton Keynes.

Yelling, J. A. (1992) *Slums and Redevelopment, policy and practice in England with particular reference to London*, UCL Press, London.

INDEX